Praise

Ken Jones is an asset to the kingdom of God. Packed with eternal truth and everyday wisdom, his spirit-filled devotionals come through as Son-shine on a cloudy day. In a few short pages, he'll be in your living room discussing how sweet it is to walk with Jesus and challenging you in your Christian walk like never before!

—T.D. Mitchell
Author of *Stones Along the Path*

Ken Jones is a committed thinker whose writings challenge you to rethink preconceived notions of even the fundamentals of Christianity. *Reflections from a Grateful Heart* will alternately encourage, convict, affirm, and heal; but always cause the Word to be fresh, vital, and alive. Recommended reading for everyone from the brand-new Christian to the seasoned veterans of the faith.

—Rev. Howard Q. Stooksbury
Senior Pastor of Denver Columbine Hills Church of the Nazarene

Ken Jones serves on our staff at the Melbourne Church and is an insightful counselor and writer. You will be blessed by what he has written.

—Steve Puckett
Senior Minister of Melbourne Church of Christ

Reading Ken Jones' Christ-inspired writings is similar to being immersed into an amazing pool of encouragement, wisdom and faith. He possesses a very keen writing sensibility which works to soothe and caress the most broken and downtrodden of spirits. It is always a joy to read his insights and hints on managing the minefield called life. Mr. Jones is a true treasure.

—Regina Y. Evans
Author of *Nonnie and the Butterfly*

Ken's writin's have inspired, challenged, and fed me. I feel like I met his heart through 'em and he's as fine a Christian feller as I ever did meet. I know this here book will bless y'all somethin' fierce!

—Stevie Rey
Arthur of *The Hillbilly Bible*

A Prodigal Return

A Prodigal Return

Reflections from a Grateful Heart

Ken Jones

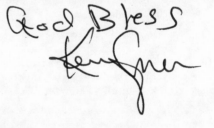

TATE PUBLISHING & *Enterprises*

Published by Tate Publishing & Enterprises, LLC
127 E. Trade Center Terrace | Mustang, Oklahoma 73064 USA
1.888.361.9473 | www.tatepublishing.com

Tate Publishing is committed to excellence in the publishing industry. The company reflects the philosophy established by the founders, based on Psalm 68:11,
"The Lord gave the word and great was the company of those who published it."

Book design copyright © 2009 by Tate Publishing, LLC. All rights reserved.
Cover design by Cole Roberts
Interior design by Lindsay B. Behrens

Published in the United States of America
ISBN: 978-1-60799-965-2
1. Religion / Christian Life / Devotional
2. Biography and Autobiography / Personal Memoirs
09.08.25

Dedication

This book is dedicated to the loving memory of my father, Ken Jones, and mother, Rita Jones-Kolb. It is also dedicated to my loving wife, Janie, and my two great sons, Kenny and Nick. This book was written for God, and to him goes all the glory.

Acknowledgments

To my wife, Janie, who is always by my side and encourages, loves, and supports me. She is the love of my life. Heaven may be short one angel. Janie, thank you for who you are. Because of you, I am a better person.

Kenny and Nick, you are the greatest. I couldn't have asked for two better sons. Thanks for loving me, warts and all. You both make me proud, and I love you both.

I want to thank Senior Pastor Jimmy Pruitt of the Morning Star Community Church in Abilene, Texas, for his encouragement, support, and friendship. Jimmy was the first one to say, "Ken, you have something to say, start writing."

My friend Eddie McGay has been by my side as a friend and mentor for almost thirty years. He has always been there. Thanks, Eddie, for your friendship, encouragement, and support.

Pat Seamon, thanks for sharing your love, friendship, knowledge, family, and time with me. Thanks for sharing the Bible and your best friend Jesus with me. Thanks for bringing me closer to God in your teachings, attitude, and mentorship. You are a wonderful elder, shepherd, and friend. Sorry about tipping the canoe.

Thanks to my Melbourne, Florida, Church of Christ family for taking me in and making me part of the body of Christ and your brother. There are so many who have shown me how to live for Jesus and one another. Thanks for all your love and support.

God bless all of my online family who have read, commented, and encouraged me. Thanks for sharing your love with me and showing me what Christians are really all about.

Donna and Tom, the best brother and sister a guy could have. I know I didn't make life easy when I was younger. Thanks for loving me anyway. I am glad we could become friends. I love you.

Henry, without your friendship, I may not have found sobriety. Thanks for leading me and showing me a better way of life.

To my recovery family, you have given me my life back and a reason to live, sober, one day at a time. Without you and God, I wouldn't be here today.

Father God, thanks for bringing this prodigal back into your fold, and sharing your precious Son, Jesus, with us. I can't begin to tell you how much you mean to me. There are not enough pages in the world to write it all. Jesus, without you, life would be unthinkable. Thank you for being my savior, friend, and brother. See you when I get home.

Foreword

Jimmy Pruitt

I have been an avid reader of devotion books for years. As a theological student at a Christian university, I found myself swimming in spiritual academia. In fact, I felt as if I were drowning in that environment. I needed a life raft. I needed something that could bring a more practical, honest, and human touch to the scriptures that I was studying from a purely academic perspective. It was in that difficult season of stretching and learning that I came upon a devotional book that brought all the dry academic elements that I was learning into perspective. I found grace again in the personal stories and anecdotes of that devotional writer. Since that time, I have continued to approach the scriptures on both an academic and devotional level.

Had Ken Jones been writing and sharing his story many years ago, I would have found life in those words as well. Ken is a man who has been on a journey of faith for many years. He has encountered setbacks and hurdles along the way. It's not uncommon for someone who has walked a mile in Ken's shoes to throw in the towel and decide that following Jesus is just not worth it. Ken realized a long time ago that everyone runs. Some run to God, and others run away. He has decided to run into the arms of Jesus. The wonderful thing about the race he's running is that he is willing to bring us along for the ride.

You will find that the love and grace of God pours through the pages of Ken's book. He's a man who is not afraid to let you see his scars and his heart. You will be challenged, encouraged, and most of all inspired by Ken Jones. Join me as we join Ken on this amazing journey of laughter, tears, victories, defeats, and life lessons learned. Welcome to the journey!

Grace and Peace,

—Jimmy Pruitt, Senior Pastor
Morning Star Community Church
Abilene, Texas

Introduction

This book is meant to bring glory to God for the love, grace, and mercy he has shown me throughout my life. This work is a collection of devotionals, thoughts, and reflections intended to share the love, grace, and mercy God has shown me. For five years of my life, I was an alcoholic and was saved from that lifestyle by God and a twelve-step program. I have not had a drink since August 13, 1978, by the grace and love of God.

My eternal life was saved by the sacrificial death of my Savior, brother, and best friend Jesus. The love he has given us all inspired me to think thoughts and transfer reflections from my heart to paper. I hope that the love and encouragement I have been shown transcends from this book into your heart through the amazing love of God. Also, as counseling and involvement minister, I am able to share the love and encouragement I have been given.

My goal for this book is to bring love and encouragement to all who read this volume and give glory to God for all that receive this gift.

A Brother of Jesus

> While Jesus was still talking to the crowd, his mother and brothers stood outside, wanting to speak to him. Someone told him, "Your mother and brothers are standing outside, wanting to speak to you." He replied to him, "Who is my mother, and who are my brothers?" Pointing to his disciples, he said, "Here are my mother and my brothers. For whoever does the will of my Father in heaven is my brother and sister and mother."
>
> Matthew 12:46–50

I don't know how Jesus' biological family felt when they were outside, but I can tell you as a disciple who is doing the will of our father in heaven, I feel pretty special. Jesus pointed at his disciples and said, "Here are my mother and my brothers. For whoever does the will of my father in heaven is my brother, sister, and mother." Imagine being there the day he actually said this and being one of his disciples. I feel a chill going through me just thinking about it. I can imagine him lifting his finger, pointing toward you and stopping, and then pointing toward me and stopping, saying, "These are my brothers and sisters." That would have been a magical moment.

Most of the people reading this are Jesus' brothers and sisters; therefore, you are my brothers and sisters. We have the same Father in heaven, and we are called to do his will as disciples of him and his Son, our brother Jesus. I would say imagine being Jesus' brother when we do the will of our Father, but we don't have to imagine the truth. Do you know how I know that? Well, I know it because Jesus said it. To be a brother of Jesus, we must do what our Father commands. Accepting and believing in Jesus as our Savior is first and foremost.

So how do we know what our Father commands? The Bible is filled with answers. We follow those commands of our Father and Jesus. We pray to our Father and seek his guidance. Jesus taught us to love God and love one another. He taught us to forgive one another and turn away from temptation and sin. Today, I pray that my wants are aligned with God's will so that when Jesus asks what man is his brother he will know I am his brother. He will know because I believe and know Jesus and with love and respect I do the will of our Father in heaven.

A Few Questions for Christians

Do not merely listen to the word, and so deceive yourselves.
Do what it says. Anyone who listens to the word but does not
do what it says is like a man, who looks at his face in a mirror and, after looking at himself, goes away and immediately
forgets what he looks like.

James 1:22–24

But someone will say, "You have faith; I have deeds." Show
me your faith without deeds, and I will show you my faith
by what I do.

James 2:18

Imagine watching the Olympics and the athletes are just sitting in
chairs, doing nothing. Imagine that no one is in the pool, on the
gym equipment, playing basketball or soccer. Imagine all the athletes are just standing around looking at the equipment and each
other. Michael Phelps won eight gold medals for swimming races.
He could never have won these races if he didn't get in the pool.
Would people who call themselves athletes be athletes if they didn't
perform? Would they be athletes just because they say they are?

How would anyone know we are Christians? What if we were
just sitting around looking at each other? What if we were silent?
What if we were rude? What if we were selfish? What if we refused
to help? How would anyone know we are Christians? What does a

Christian look like? Would someone know the good news of Jesus and the blessed assurance we have just by looking at us? Would they know we are filled by faith as we sit motionless and mundane and say, "Oh yeah, I am a Christian disciple of Jesus"?

There is action involved in the Olympics. Athletes compete in sporting events. They get up and move; they are involved in competition. They work hard, train, and they are excited about what they are doing. In team events, we see the athletes encourage and exhort one another. They cheer one another on. It is easy to discern that they are not only athletes but also Olympians by what they do, how well they do it, and the enthusiasm in which they perform.

What does a Christian do? What does a Christian look like? Shouldn't *faith* be an action word? Does Jesus want us to have faith and do nothing with it? Didn't God our Father give us spiritual gifts and his Son to use for the furtherance of his kingdom? I believe being a Christian is a call to action and time to put my faith to work. For me, faith without works isn't faith at all. Paul told Timothy we must train as athletes. We must train as an athlete because we are called to be an athlete for our Father and his kingdom. We have gifts to use and events to perform; let's get in the pool.

A Flying Leap

I served four years in the navy from 1976–1980. I arrived on my first ship shortly after boot camp. My first ship was the *USS Charleston LKA* 113, an amphibious cargo and assault ship. I was nineteen years old. I thought I was pretty cool and ready to begin my stint in the navy. When I reported aboard, I was assigned to be a cook. One of the other cooks gave me a tour of the ship. I was quite impressed and beginning to feel pretty important, but I was really quite nervous. I was wearing my dress blues, which really let everyone know I was a rookie, a mere boot. (A boot is a rookie fresh from boot camp.) After the tour, my mentor said, "Let's eat." We went through the galley (kitchen) and through to the mess hall (dining room). As we were going into this new room, my shin hit a small bulkhead (wall) which was about twelve inches high. Because I was looking straight ahead, my tray flew forward about ten feet, and I went flying after it. The crew cheered my entrance with a catcall of, "Boot, boot!"

I was never so embarrassed in my life. After I cleaned up and went back to the mess hall, I said I really wasn't very hungry after all. That was my welcome and shining moment aboard the *USS Charleston,* a moment that lived in infamy. Now that I had introduced myself to everyone, I couldn't hide the next six months I was aboard that ship, and no one was going to let me live that one down. What the heck was that thing doing there, anyway?

My chief said something about airtight doors. Hmmm. That was a time I literally fell; I have fallen several times figuratively. I have made many mistakes in my life, and I have fallen through sin.

When I fall, God gently and sympathetically lifts me up, wipes me off, and says that he loves me. He believes me when I say I want to change. He says, "C'mon let me help you." He hands me my tray, gets down, and helps me clean up my mess. He comes with me, helps me fill my tray, and says, "It is okay. Let's try this again, but don't forget the airtight fittings. Don't forget the holes in the road, the distractions and temptations. I am with you and will guide you. Keep your eyes on me."

We may all trip, stumble, and fall along the path to heaven. Don't give up, don't hide. Ask God for help. Keep your eyes open. As Hebrews 12:2 says, "Let us fix our eyes on Jesus, the author and perfecter of our faith, who for the joy set before him endured the cross, scorning its shame, and sat down at the right hand of the throne of God."

A God Thing or Coincidence

But blessed are your eyes because they see, and your ears because they hear.

Matthew 3:16

Do you have eyes but fail to see and ears but fail to hear? And don't you remember?

Mark 8:18

When I was drinking alcohol, I drank more than my share. Near the end of my drinking, I was asking God at night not to let me wake up. I wanted to die, even though I was afraid and uncertain of death and where I would go when I died. On my ship I met Henry, who was reading a book on alcoholism, and we began talking about my drinking. The next night, he took me to my first twelve-step meeting. Here I am today, sober over thirty years.

During my separation from my wife and subsequent divorce, I said to my friend Joe that I had no place to go. He asked what I meant. Joe had a three-bedroom house, lived alone, and invited me to live with him until I could get back on my feet. He even had extra room where my boys could stay. He said that he had a carpenter friend who would build some bunk beds for the boys. I can't tell you how many times things like this have happened. I have worried about something and then positive things coincidently happen.

One of the elders from my church, Pat, called me to answer some of my questions. We set up a time for him to come to my house. Pat said, "Let's see why God has brought us together." Then he showed me in God's Word about salvation, God's grace, mercy, and the road to heaven. It's all there in the Bible.

Did you ever need some money, and a check magically appeared? Or needed furniture and someone you were having coffee with said, "Hey, I have a kitchen table. You can have it"? People seem to appear out of nowhere. Things appear out of nowhere. I have heard these things referred to as "God things." I heard someone say once, "The definition of *coincidence* is where God remains anonymous." It is a kind of God thing. These things happened just when I needed them, just when I thought it was the end. Just in time, God's time.

Is this magic, coincidence, or a God thing? The Bible is filled with God's promises that he will meet all our needs. We are to take life a day at a time. God provided manna daily as Moses took the Israelites through the desert. Jesus says, "Give us this day our daily bread." Twelve-step programs say, "Live one day at a time." This is not magic as long as I have my eyes and ears open to God.

God knows what I need and provides it. All I need do is ask, pray, and pay attention. Luke 11:9 says, "So I say to you: Ask and it will be given to you; seek and you will find; knock and the door will be opened to you." When I pray and stay attentive for God's answer, God has and does provide. This is not magic; this is God answering prayers, prayers from my mouth and prayers from my heart. He hears them all, he loves us, and he meets our needs. Maybe not in our time, but always in his. I have found that reading the Bible and praying reminds me of this.

I have to stay attentive for his answers, and he sends answers through people like Henry, Pat, Joe, and many others. If I stay focused on him, I will see and hear his answers. Today, I want to be attentive to what I once considered coincidence or God things. They are God things; they are not magic. They are strategically and timely planned incidents from God. I need not be surprised by the wonderful events; I simply need to thank Abba, Father.

A New Day

This is the day the LORD has made; let us rejoice and be glad in it.

Psalm 118:24

I have always loved this verse. It gives me visions of flowers, mountains, streams, babbling brooks, and the sun shining on my face. Okay, I don't always have those visions. Sometimes I wake up grumpy. I don't feel the verse, and I feel grumpy. My wife says, "Good morning." I say, "Good morning" and mutter, "Yeah, yeah, yeah." Sometimes I wake up late, and I rush around with my head racing like the Daytona 500 track full of fast, noisy cars, thinking of the next three things I have to do. When I was drinking, I never had these scenic visions until I was quite drunk, and I may have said, "Woo hoo" with slurred speech. But the next morning, I wasn't rejoicing; I can tell you that. Sheesh, I had a headache.

Today is a new day. I get to choose how I will start my day. Now I begin with prayer, meditation, or passing a thought on to a friend or my family. There is a smile and a hug for my wife as I wish her a good day. I let the Lord know I am ready and available for duty. I like to start the day with a cup of coffee while reading devotionals that relate the grace and love of God. Then I reflect on what is said and let it spread through my mind and heart.

I know my day will be spent with God at my side. It is my choice to let him into my mind, heart, and actions. You know, my day goes a whole lot better when I do. After all, this is his day. I can rejoice or not. Rejoicing is fun. You should have seen me when the Red Sox won the World Series in 2004 and again in 2007. Woo hoo! What a party in my head and on my lips after those events. I was doing the wave alone, sitting and watching the games on my couch.

I choose today to have God with me, to rejoice in his day. I choose to remember that if God is for us who can be against us? He will be with me throughout the day and night. He will meet all my needs. I have complete assurance of his love, grace, and mercy. I will be able to meet all my human challenges because he is with me. No need will go unmet while God is in charge, and that isn't changing. So today, I choose to rejoice. Today I choose God.

A Place for Us

In my Father's house are many rooms; if it were not so, I would have told you. I am going there to prepare a place for you. And if I go and prepare a place for you, I will come back and take you to be with me that you also may be where I am.

John 14:2–3

I have visited friends and family and spent the night, or several nights, in their homes. They have always been wonderful hosts and have told me they have prepared a place for me, and they have also told me to make myself at home. They enjoy my company and I theirs; they have prepared a place in their homes and at times even picked me up at the airport. My hosts have a nice, clean room waiting for me to sleep, and they make sure I have everything I need. I have also prepared a place for friends and family at my home. I try to make them as comfortable as possible; even finding out their favorite foods, snacks, and soft drinks to make sure they are available for them. I do this because I love them and want their visit to be as pleasant as possible. I don't usually invite just anyone to my home; it is usually someone I love a great deal.

Jesus answers the question "How much do I love you?" by his atoning death on the cross. After he paid my sin debt through his death, he was resurrected and beat death. Jesus gave me eternal assurance of a life with him and our father in heaven. Imagine our belief in Jesus' sacrificial death as an act of atonement for us. Jesus paid our sin debt, and that is the answer to the question "Does God really love me?"

Okay, he gave his life, and now he says there are many rooms in his father's house and he is going ahead to prepare a place for us. Well, not only is he preparing a place for us; he said he will also come back for us. On top of all that, the King of kings, the Messiah, our Savior, the Son of God, and our greatest friend says he is coming back to take us with him so we can be where he is. Only those who believe get to go. The future looks good. Jesus himself is preparing for our arrival and is coming to get us. This will not be for a short visit; he is preparing our eternal home in heaven in his father's house. Jesus has done it all for us. Why wouldn't I do what he asks of me? I am waiting for the day Jesus says, "Welcome, make yourself at home. Because this is now your home and wait till you see the room I prepared for you." Jesus wants to spend eternity with us so much. He has a place for us.

Advocate

Whoever acknowledges me before men, I will also acknowledge him before my Father in heaven.

Matthew 10:32

From 1990–1999, I worked for the state of Florida as a child protective investigator and supervisor. My job was to investigate child abuse and neglect as well as counsel families in crisis. Children are the most vulnerable to abuse and neglect and have very little to no voice. When I would speak to the children, they saw me as an authority figure, a big guy, and an adult. I told them that if they needed help I was there to be their voice, their advocate. I told them I worked for the state of Florida and whatever help they needed I would use the full voice of Florida to get it. I would make sure the people that needed to hear them would.

Well, not a bad advocate, huh? I know an advocate with much more authority. His name is Jesus. On the day of judgment, I will not stand alone in front of my heavenly Father. My best friend Jesus will stand and acknowledge me. He will be my advocate. He will say, "I know this man, and he knows me. I will use my full authority here in heaven to let him in." He is also our advocate now. When we pray, all prayers brought to our Father in Jesus' name will be heard and answered. Not only is he my advocate; he was also my replacement on the cross and the final sacrifice required. Jesus died to make me righteous in front of our Father; he has prepared a place in heaven for me. He will come to get me, and on judgment day, he will speak on my behalf to the Creator, Father, and God. The grace of God is amazing that a sinner like me would have an advocate like Jesus. My job is to have a repentant heart, trust, and obey God's Word. Then God himself is my advocate, Jesus.

My purpose today is to be an advocate for Jesus. I am the voice that stands for Jesus. I acknowledge, believe, and speak out that Jesus was here and died for my sin. I will bring him glory by my actions. Jesus is my savior. Jesus is my friend, and he is my brother. All prayers are answered through the name of Jesus. I feel secure in knowing I have an advocate here on earth and also when I reach heaven. The state of Florida carries no authority in heaven. Jesus does, and he is my friend. He is the Savior to the world, and he is my advocate. It doesn't get any better than that.

Ahh, Sunday

> While they were eating, Jesus took bread, gave thanks and broke it, and gave it to his disciples, saying, "Take and eat; this is my body." Then he took the cup, gave thanks and offered it to them, saying, "Drink from it, all of you. This is my blood of the covenant, which is poured out for many for the forgiveness of sins."
>
> Matthew 26:26–28

Back in the Jones household, when I was about six years old, getting ready for church was no minor task. My mother had to get three children ready to go. My father loved to sleep, and she had to wake him up too. At that time, I was six, my sister was four, and my brother was an infant. We attended church; my father didn't go to church, but he did take us. My mother would be harried and have to take us to the crying room. This was a room where babies and little children went that cried. My brother was a noisy one. So we were banished to the crying room, where they piped in the service. I could hear the priest talking about God and about his son, Jesus, and those babies would howl. I remember thinking maybe these babies were possessed and they should send a priest in for some exorcisms.

Even as a young child, I loved to go to church. Somewhere along the line, I stopped for a while, started going again, and stopped again. Now, of course, I am going again. I love my church services at the Church of Christ. Even when I was a young child, I was enthralled by the communion services or Lord's Supper. When they said, "Jesus took the bread and then he took the cup, he said when you do this do this in memory of me." This is a special time during the service we are to partake in Jesus' Last Supper, celebrate this meal and his sacrifice for us. I remember when the priest took the bread, holding it up in the air, and the altar boy would ring the bells. The priest did the same with the cup. I remember this because even as a child, I was in awe of the sacrifice Jesus made for us.

Each Sunday we share in this again. The church I attend now has no bells, and we don't lift anything up in the air, but we do remember Jesus, and that is what it is all about. This is a celebration and devotional to Jesus' awesome sacrifice and reminder of his Last Supper. It conjures up thoughts of Jesus washing feet, pointing out his betrayer, and those who would turn on him. Jesus loved those men, washed their feet, and served them a meal anyway. Jesus then gave himself up to die so that we could live. Then he prayed for us. He told us he would send us the Holy Spirit; he told us he was going ahead to prepare us a place. After all of this, what did he ask us to do? Jesus had a simple request, "When you do this, do this in memory of me."

Churches all over the world will have this memorial for Jesus each Sunday. Let's memorialize Jesus every day, and whatever we do, let us do it in memory of him. As we leave the church parking lot, let's remember we are entering the mission field where the good news of Jesus can be shared daily.

Am I About Love?

Love is patient, love is kind. It does not envy, it does not boast, it is not proud. It is not rude, it is not self-seeking, it is not easily angered, it keeps no record of wrongs. Love does not delight in evil but rejoices with the truth. It always protects, always trusts, always hopes, and always perseveres. Love never fails.

Corinthians 13:4–8

I know you have seen this verse before. This verse is one of the better-known verses. Janie and I used it at our wedding ceremony; you may have used it at yours. I was thinking this verse should not just be used as a verse at the ceremony but as a marriage vow itself. This verse should also be our motto in life and our mission statement and our vision.

You may think I talk a lot about love, but so did Jesus. He told us to love God and love one another. Did you ever ask someone what his or her definition of love is? I have. I have gotten all kinds of answers. I believe the true definition of love is found in Corinthians 13:4–8 of any version of the Bible. I believe this is the love that God wants us to demonstrate toward one another. I believe this is the love we should demonstrate toward our spouse, children, parents, family, and everyone. This is the love Jesus was talking about.

Love is patient. Am I patient with others, or am I in a hurry? Do I let people finish sentences? Do I let them be themselves? Do I let them learn through their own experience and give them to God? Am I patient with God, trusting his timing? Love is kind. Am I kind to everyone, even the cashiers, waitresses, bureaucrats, those important to me, and people I disagree with? First Thessalonians 5:15 says to make sure that nobody pays back wrong for wrong, but to always try to be kind to each other and to everyone else.

Love does not boast or is not proud. Boasting and pride are something God looks down on and will bring us down for. Love does not boast. We have nothing to really boast about except the Lord. This arrogance has no beauty whatsoever. Pride and ego lead to quarrels and ultimately sin. God's love is perfect; it does neither of these things.

Love does not easily anger, nor keep a record of wrongs. We are called to forgive. What kind of love is easily angered? Is that the love God shows us? When God showed us his love by giving Jesus on the cross his blood washed away our sin. It is gone; God does not keep a record of what he has washed away. God is patient with us and not easily angered. But he has been angry with his people because they have turned away and not followed his commands. God is pure love. Jesus is pure love. We are to emulate him.

Love does not delight in evil but rejoices in the truth. God is the truth. We delight in God. We have nothing to do with evil. Love always protects. God protects us, so we need to protect others, as well as show them the truth and show them the way to salvation and help them stay the course. Love always trusts. Trusting God is easy, but do we always trust him? We need to. He is perfect truth, love, and salvation. We can trust him; we need to demonstrate that trust. Love always hopes. With God, there is always hope. It lets us look forward with conviction that we are his and he will always be with us and he will never let us out of his sight. Hope for great things to come through him. Love always perseveres. Don't let others' shortcomings get you down. Be patient, longsuffering, and hang on. Persevere with God as Job did. He is with us, no matter what.

Love never fails. What a promise! God is love, and God never fails. I need to be like Jesus. He is pure love. He gave his life for me. I can do that by not being self-serving. I need to show the qualities Paul told the Corinthians about. Paul did not make this up; the Bible is divinely inspired. It is the voice of God. If I want to know how to love, I only need to read the definition given me by God himself. Am I about love? Am I about God?

Am I My Brother's Keeper?

Remember this: Whoever turns a sinner from the error of his way will save him from death and cover over a multitude of sins.

James 5:20

Then the LORD said to Cain, "Where is your brother Abel?" "I don't know," he replied. "Am I my brother's keeper?"

Genesis 4:9

I have heard people tell me you can lead a horse to water but you can't make him drink. I have heard that you can't help people who don't ask or want help. You are not you brother's keeper. Well, some of this is sound advice if one is not trying to do the will of God. Just as the horse will eventually get thirsty and go to the water, patient and loving concern may one day be accepted by one who is available and speaks the truth through love. Look what Jesus did for his brothers and sisters who didn't ask for help or forgiveness.

When I was a child, I lived surrounded by water. I loved to sit on docks, jetties, and anything I could, and look out at the water and dangle my feet. My mother would always be close by, probably holding her breath, saying, "Kenny, be careful. Not so close." When I was much younger, she would say, "Stay out of the street; be careful. Look both ways and grab my hand." If I saw someone about to walk off a cliff who didn't see the danger, would I not tell him because he didn't ask? If I saw someone headed for physical harm, would I allow that because he didn't ask for my help?

Second Timothy 4:2 says, "Preach the Word; be prepared in season and out of season; correct, rebuke and encourage—with great patience and careful instruction." James 5:20 says, "Remember this: whoever turns a sinner from the error of his way will save him from death and cover over a multitude of sins." Loving correction of a brother or sister from going astray may save them from death or harm. Hmm, should I correct someone else? If it is me, please correct me. Don't let me stray into death or harm. Help me, hold me accountable, and let me know I am headed for danger. Love God and love one another. Would you let one you love self-destruct without sharing your concern, God's concern, and giving some loving correction? Am I my brother's keeper? I believe I am, and I believe we all are.

Amnesty

Amnesty: the act of an authority (as a government) by which pardon is granted to a large group of individuals.

Webster's Dictionary

Peter replied, "Repent and be baptized, every one of you, in the name of Jesus Christ for the forgiveness of your sins."

Acts 2:38

For God so loved the world that he gave his one and only Son that whoever believes in him shall not perish but have eternal life.

John 3:16

When I was a little kid, I borrowed some library books. I kept the books way too long and owed a hefty late fine. I was afraid to tell my mother and father because I didn't have the money to pay. One day, on our local radio station there was a public service announcement that the Suffolk County Library was granting amnesty to all those with late books. Just bring them in, and there would be no penalty. They called it Amnesty Week. They said the fines would be forgiven. What relief I felt. I gathered up the books, brought them in, and handed them to the library lady. She checked them in and thanked me. Then she asked if I wanted more books. Of course, I declined and left before she changed her mind. Phew, I love amnesty.

Our heavenly Father makes a similar offer. Have you sinned? Have you come to know Jesus as your Savior? Have you repented and been baptized? In the Old Testament, the Law was given, and the punishment for sin was death. Through Jesus, the penalty is paid. We are to believe, repent, and be baptized, and the sin will be forgiven. Ahh, I have received sweet amnesty yet again. I am not free to go and sin again, but I am free to live a life at peace, knowing I have eternal salvation. I have been pardoned by God's great love, mercy, forgiveness, and grace.

Do you have outstanding sin? Have you been forgiven? Sins can and will be forgiven. We just need to come clean and bring them to our Father through Jesus, who paid the fine for us. This is good news. Consider this a public service announcement. Every day is Amnesty Day with God. Today, relieve your mind, your heart, and your soul. Bring your sins to God, confess, and ask forgiveness through Jesus' death and resurrection. Repent and be baptized. Sweet freedom and amnesty are yours. The fine was paid for you. Phew, I love forgiveness and amnesty.

Ask

Ask and it will be given to you; seek and you will find; knock and the door will be opened to you.

Matthew 7:7

There have been many times in my life I would be working on something and struggled through on my own with no help. I would struggle, moan, and groan and may have even use a word or two that I will not mention here. Sometimes people would even ask, "Hey, can I give you a hand with that?" With a scowl, I tell them that I can handle it. Was I really handling it? Nope. In college, I never did understand algebra. I still don't know how I graduated without passing it. I just didn't get its purpose. I would spend hours trying to get it. I never did. Imagine my stubbornness and foolish pride would not allow me to do the thing I needed to do the most. Ask. Imagine six words that would have made a world of difference: will you give me a hand?

They left that place and passed through Galilee. Jesus did not want anyone to know where they were, because he was teaching his disciples. He said to them, "The Son of Man is going to be betrayed into the hands of men. They will kill him, and after three days he will rise." But they did not understand what he meant and were afraid to ask him about it.

Matthew 9:30–32

What were they afraid of? Why were they afraid to ask Jesus what he meant? If they didn't ask, they may have missed the whole thing. Are there things you are afraid to ask people about? Are there things you are afraid to ask God about or for? All through the New Testament, people were asking Jesus to heal them. Why would people ask this of Jesus? Because they needed to be healed. What does Jesus do? He heals them. Asking. Hmmm, what a concept.

If I can't do it myself, it isn't worth doing. Have you heard that one before? I will figure it out by myself. I can't do salvation by myself. There are many things I need help with from others and from God. God tells us many times to humble ourselves, to be like a child. Usually, children ask for help. Asking really doesn't hurt. Jesus says in Mark 11:24, "Therefore I tell you, whatever you ask for in prayer, believe that you have received it, and it will be yours." So I was thinking, if you or I need anything from God, do you know what we should do? I think after years of my own stubbornness, stupidity, and foolish pride, what I need to do is ask. I think I am finally getting this stuff.

Basket Hold?

Recently, I talked about the unconditional love I found. Today, I want to tell you a story about Maryhaven. When I was younger, I worked in a school and residential setting for mentally challenged and emotionally disturbed children. I learned many lessons from the children there.

There was a sixteen-year-old boy there I'll call Sam. He was emotionally disturbed, violent, and displayed some bizarre and disgusting habits. When he entered the school, no one knew what the day would bring. As behavior management specialist at the school, part of my job was to physically restrain and help the children regain some self-control, as well as process their violent outbursts with them. Sam's outbursts were almost daily. Sam called me Kim.

One day, Sam decided to run through the three-story school building, tearing things off the wall and attacking anyone he could. I ran to help him get control, and as he was running down the stairs, he turned to me as I was running up. He looked at my shoes, pants, shirt, and face, and he said, "Snagged." He then wrapped both arms around himself and said, "Kim, are you going to put me in the basket hold?" (The basket hold is a restraint hold where you crisscross the arms of an out-of-control person in front of them, swing him around, and pull him into you so his back is to you and he is off balance.) Some of the staff later asked why he would let me or want me to restrain him.

Hmm, good question. But the answer for him was almost simple. Imagine being out of control and angry. Imagine someone pulling you into them while you are off balance, wrapping his arms around you, and pulling you in snug. As you hold him, you tell the client that I am here to help you regain control and that I will hold you until you can regain control. It's kind of reassuring and also kind of resembles a hug. Maybe all Sam needed was reassurance, some love, and a hug. His behavior never said that though. He was emotionally disturbed and unable to appropriately display emotion.

Don't we see that sometimes? Or haven't we done it? We wanted to be loved but then showed anger. We didn't express our needs or desires appropriately. Have we said, "I don't care," but we really did care? We hoped someone would see through us and give us the love, comfort, and assurance we were desperately crying out for but were unable to adequately express. Wouldn't it be nice if someone during those times when we feel out of control, angry, unable to communicate properly, or off balance put us in a basket hold (gave a hug) and said, "I will hold on to you until everything is all right again. I will be here with you. Nothing can happen to you while I am here." That is what Sam was looking for but didn't know how to ask for.

God loves us. God will hold us. God can see through us. God will hold us and help us regain control anytime. He is always with us. Reach out and ask him to put you in a basket hold until you can take some control back of your life.

Be Not Afraid

Without warning, a furious storm came up on the lake, so that the waves swept over the boat. But Jesus was sleeping. The disciples woke him, saying, "Lord, save us"! We're going to drown!" He replied, "You of little faith, why are you so afraid?" Then he got up and rebuked the winds and the waves, and it was completely calm.

Matthew 8:24–26

Jesus was with the disciples when the storm came, and they had nothing to fear. They had God with them in their time of fear. They did not have to worry. When I was a little boy and was in bed, the lights were out. I was alone, and every noise scared me. I turned on the light, and my mother told me to turn off the light and go to sleep. That was easier said than done. I was petrified. I turned the lights back on. My mother said, "Turn off that light!" *Uh oh, now I'm in trouble. Now, she is sending Dad to shut me up and to turn out the light.* When he got to my room, he sat on my bed and asked why I wouldn't turn off the light. I said, "I'm scared." Dad put his arm around me and said, "As long as I am here, nothing can happen to you. You have nothing to be afraid of while I am here." He even promised. I went to sleep with the knowledge I was protected.

There are a lot of things people are afraid of, bills, real estate, falling stocks, raising prices, our kids growing up, our kids going off to school, job insecurity, debt, sickness, and many other things. God says through David in Psalm 46:10, "Be still, and know that I am God." He says, "Don't be afraid, I will protect you." We can turn off the light and go to sleep. He is our protecting Father.

Be secure in God; know he is always watching. He knows where we are, what we do, what we think, and what our situation is at all times. Don't let the fears of the world overcome you. Be strong in your faith. Know that you have a loving God who is always with you. His son died for us and secured our place with him and his father. He says, "Rest. Be not afraid. Be still. Turn off the lights. Sleep. I am here with you. I am not going anywhere. I will always be here. I will always protect you."

Be Still

Be still, and know that I am God; I will be exalted among the nations, I will be exalted in the earth.

Psalm 46:10

Be still before the LORD and wait patiently for him; do not fret when men succeed in their ways, when they carry out their wicked schemes.

Psalm 37:7

Somebody, stop the voices. The sky isn't falling. Anxious moments are tough. Projecting outcomes is hazardous to one's health. Especially mine, especially earlier in life. The outcomes in my head were usually disastrous. Well, is there a word that fits between *usually* and *always* that would be the more correct word to use? I seemed to worry about everything. What was going to happen?

When I was about twenty-one years old and had just stopped drinking, I was a very new member in a twelve-step program. I had to learn to live life without drinking. My way was not working. The man that brought me to the twelve-step program became my mentor and best friend. He would sit and listen to me. I bet it wasn't much fun at times. When I would finish my tale of woe, Henry would say, "Ken, be still." I seemed to always be in a hurry to get somewhere. Somewhere was a quite unknown and scary place for me. But I was in a hurry to get there anyway. "Ken, be still."

What does that really mean? Where did it come from? Was Henry telling me nicely to shut up? No. Over the years, I have learned what "be still" means. Let me tell you just a few more stories first. I'm a storyteller.

There was a man I knew who was a kind and patient man living in Hawaii. One time, when I was about twenty-one, I was lying by a lake while at a function; I was wearing jeans, cowboy boots, and a shirt. This same man asked me what I was doing. I told him I was working on my serenity. He laughed and smiled at me. He told me serenity comes from a spiritual lifestyle, not something you just get by magic. Another time, at a twelve-step gathering, the chairperson asked if anyone was celebrating six months of sobriety. I quickly raised my hand and said I was now sober six months. Everyone clapped and whistled. This same man later came over and said, "Ken when you said you had six months, I was waiting for you to say, 'But I am going as fast as I can.'"

An older lady in San Diego used to tell me to stop spinning my wheels. Okay, you know me better now. Of course, over the next few decades I have learned what these statements mean. I have a spiritual way of life, I have stopped spinning my wheels so much, and I learned what it is to "be still." I have added, "Be still and know that I am God." This is right out of the book of Psalms.

This verse is so meaningful to me. This is a short verse I can use constantly, when those wheels start spinning, and I am on the quick road to somewhere. Remember, for me, that somewhere can be a scary place to me without God. Knowing that God is always with me and nothing comes to me except through God, I feel much safer and secure.

This day is all I have, and God is with me. If God is for us, who can be against us? Being still is a lot easier this way. Anxiety is not something I experience when I know God is here. If I forget these things, guess what. I am on the road to somewhere that is not a pretty place.

Reading God's Word on a daily basis, reading devotionals, praying, meditating, and speaking with those on the same path makes it a lot easier to "be still." Knowing that he is God and he is here now, I am going to be fine. Kenny Chesney sings a song titled "Safe in the Arms of the Lord." God's arms are a safe place to be and makes being still a whole lot easier.

I can relax and know that God is always with me. With God's help, nothing will get to me. Whatever it is and however long it takes, I am in the best hands possible.

Beyond Forgiveness

> The people stood watching, and the rulers even sneered at him. They said, "He saved others; let him save himself if he is the Christ of God, the Chosen One." The soldiers also came up and mocked him. They offered him wine vinegar and said, "If you are the king of the Jews, save yourself." One of the criminals who hung there hurled insults at him: "Aren't you the Christ? Save yourself and us!"
>
> Luke 23:35–37, 39

I was teaching the teen class one Sunday. I asked the teens if anyone had ever made fun of them or said anything because they were Christians. Some said yes; others said that some kids believe Jesus is boring, a waste of time, and even stupid. Imagine now, kids are mocking Jesus. Jesus has been mocked and jeered since he began sharing the good news. Jesus came to share love, the truth, a way to heaven, a good life, and his own life, and how has he been treated? He was treated with jeers, sneers, and mocking by many. Until today, this still continues—apparently from people of all ages.

Even on the cross, both criminals, hanging one on each side, mocked him. "Those crucified with him also heaped insults on him" (Mark 15:32). There hung Jesus in pain after being tortured, spit at, and mocked, all because he loves us and came from heaven to die for our sins. He was even dying for those who crucified him and were crucified with him. Jesus, with more love then anyone could comprehend hanging on the cross being mocked. One of the criminals stopped mocking him and said to the other criminal, "Don't you fear God, since you are under the same sentence? We are punished justly, for we are getting what our deeds deserve. But this man has done nothing wrong" (Luke 23:40–41). While Jesus was dying on the cross, what did Jesus say to this man? "I tell you the truth, today you will be with me in paradise" (Luke 23:43).

Although there are many who continue to mock, jeer, and sneer Jesus, it appears he needs no help from us. He alone knows how to deal with these people. How does he handle this? Well here is what I understand he said: "Father, forgive them, for they do not know what they are doing" (Luke 23:34). He goes way beyond forgiveness, and we are called to be imitators of Jesus. I still have my work cut out for me.

Bible Heroes Hall of Fame

For the word of God is living and active.

Hebrews 4:12

About twenty years ago, while I was working at Maryhaven, we took a trip. This trip was the best I had been on with the kids. We took them to Cooperstown, New York, the baseball hall of fame. I am a baseball fan or fanatic depending on whom you ask. I got to see plaques, statistics, memorabilia, and all kinds of great memories while there. My favorite was the Carl Yastrzemski exhibit. Man! Now he was a ball player. Carl played for the Boston Red Sox twenty-three seasons, which is a record for playing for the same team an entire career. What a trip to see all of this great history from these retired baseball greats, especially Yaz, number eight.

This got me thinking while I reminisced, *What if they had a Bible Hero Hall of Fame?* Of course, Jesus would be the number-one attraction. What an exhibit there could be. We would see Moses parting the Red Sea, David defeating Goliath, Paul writing while in jail, Rahab hiding spies, Joshua knocking down the walls of Jericho, a talking donkey, a burning bush, and on and on. But then I was thinking the baseball hall of fame is a shrine to those who are retired and some who have passed away. Bible heroes are still very much alive and still active in the word of God.

We can't retire Bible heroes. Their work is not done; they are still on the active roster. Their work and words are still needed and used today. They are alive and continue to bring life and offer saving grace. These heroes still bring assurance, peace, warning, truth, wisdom, love, encouragement, exhortation, liberation, and eternal salvation. We can't retire these heroes. They are still in the game.

Bombardment

Then my enemies will turn back when I call for help. By this
I will know that God is for me.

Psalm 56:9

When I was a young child, in gym class we played a game called
bombardment. We would have a few kids run back and forth
against a wall while more kids threw those big red gym balls at us.
The goal was to duck, dodge, drop, and run. Those balls just kept
on coming. It seemed like the kids throwing the balls had fangs,
bloodshot eyes, and were drooling. They wanted to inflict pain, not
just get us out. Sometimes they would even gang up on one kid.
They called this a game. It seemed like torture to us and fun for the
gym teachers to watch us little urchins get creamed with balls.

Well, this may have been good training for life. At times, there seems
to be so many tough situations coming at us one after another. There
are bills, soaring gas prices, troubled kids, broken trust, and all kinds of
life's attacks. There are sure more of them then there are of us. There
seems to be no escape. What is a person to do? Duck, dodge, drop, and
run seem to be the only way to handle some of life's situations.

Keep your lives free from the love of money and be content
with what you have, because God has said, "Never will I leave
you; never will I forsake you."

Hebrews 13:5

Let the balls fly. God has said, "Never will I leave you; never will I forsake you" (Hebrews 13:5). We are not alone. Let this promise of God bring you assurance; let assurance bring you peace and calmness. Know the balls will be flying and cry out to the Lord. He will hear you, turn to you, and may just swat some of the balls away. He also may just pick you up and put you on safe solid ground. Maybe he will tell us to duck, dodge, and drop and run faster. I am not really sure what he will do, but he sure will help us. Believe that God won't forsake you or leave you. Why should we believe that? God said so.

But I Am Afraid to Try

Have you ever said, "But I am afraid to try?" I have heard that at least three times one particular week. Over the course of years, I have heard a lot of this. I am afraid to get married, buy a house, make a commitment, go to college, make an investment, ask someone out on a date, make a phone call to a creditor, or even ask a loved one a tough question. This list goes on of course, and you know your own boogeyman. The reasons given for this paralyzing fear are being laughed at, failing, past failures, being overwhelmed, negatively projecting the future, looking stupid, worrying that people will think you are ridiculous, and this list goes on as well. I have done this very same thing, and some of these reasons may just be mine.

What if the worst happens, and I fail, or some unforeseen event occurs? What if I do get laughed at? What if I don't look graceful? What if pigs could fly? Two or three years ago, my wife and I were convinced by others that real estate was the way to go as an investment and a way to make money for retirement. Housing was booming in Florida, and people were making money hand over fist. Not much of a risk, right? Wrong! When my houses were ready to be sold, the housing boom went *whoosh,* like the sound of a flushing toilet. Our financial future looked bleak. We had to rent out the homes we bought for less than the mortgage we were paying.

Well, we still had some money in the stock market that was doing well according to the guy at our investment agency. A couple of months later, *whoosh*. Now there were increasing bills, unforeseen expenses, normal expenses, etc. I thought, *See, I shouldn't have tried.* You may be thinking or even saying, *Well, Ken, you have really encouraged me to try something new now. Great example, my man. I am going right out and give something a try I am afraid of. Yeah right!*

Well, as a Christian, I did what the Bible suggests with burdens and problems. I took them to God. The words *be still* rang in my head. God is with me. He will come through. I asked him what I should do. I was convicted to increase my tithe. Increase my tithe? I can't afford what I have now. Well, I increased my tithe. I would love to tell you new money is rolling in. But I am now trusting in God's investments and not mine.

Can anyone relate to any of this or a situation that is similar? How about you, Job? He had it far worse than I. So do you know what has happened because of all this? Believe it or not, I feel peace. I believe I feel peace and assurance because it is in God's hands. I have followed his commands. He said tithe more. At first I said, "What?" Then I said, "Okay."

> God is our refuge and strength, an ever-present help in trouble. The LORD Almighty is with us; the God of Jacob is our fortress. "Be still, and know that I am God."
>
> Psalm 46:1, 7, 10

Well, I tried investment ideas, and they just didn't work out my way. But many other things I have tried have gone well. Other things have not. But the Lord Almighty is with me. He has not let me fall. He is my strength and refuge; he is my fortress. I am safe in the arms of the Lord. I am not afraid to try anything when I know he is with me. Experience shows me that when I do as the Lord instructs, I am in safe hands. In his time, this whole investment thing will work out one way or the other, but he will be there for either outcome. I have learned to live one day at a time and not harp on the past or project the future. I have a sense of peace knowing I am in the fortress of God.

What have I got to lose when I have God? I have lost no friends or family. As a matter of fact, I have more friends. I have learned that dependence on God is the right place to put it. God is ever-present and knows what is going on always. Life is better than ever because I tried. I am at peace and have the assurance that I am safe in the arms of my loving father. God has everything under control, and I have no fear of trying.

Called to Forgive

Then Peter came to Jesus and asked, "Lord, how many times shall I forgive my brother when he sins against me? Up to seven times?" Jesus answered, "I tell you, not seven times, but seventy-seven times."

Matthew 18:21–22

I was sixteen when my father died of cancer. I can't tell you how angry I was at God. I was young; I didn't understand why my father had to die at fifty-six years old. He was a great guy, the greatest guy I have ever had in my life to date. I said some very cruel and vicious things to God. My drinking cost me family, friends, and self-worth. I hated myself. In my limited understanding, I believed that God would never forgive me for the things I said and did, especially the things I said to him and against those who belong to him. At one point, I didn't even care. I was lost. I thought no one could help me, and I didn't even know how to help myself.

I have since wanted forgiveness, especially from God. But I believed he would never forgive me, How could he? Why would he? I have learned because he loves me. The story of the prodigal son in Luke 15:11–32 gives me the answer. I learned he forgave me before I asked. He knew my heart; he knew I was sorry, he knew I was repentant and that my heart changed before I said a word. He ran to me. He was waiting; he loved me and wanted me home. His arms were open and waiting; he knew my pain better than I did. Why? Because he loves me, he wants me with him. He created me. I don't quite understand this love, but I can tell you the mercy, love, and grace that God has for me can only make me rejoice. His grace humbles me and literally brought me to tears and my knees.

Now that I have been forgiven, I am called to forgive others. In Luke 11:1–4, Jesus teaches his disciples to pray. The part that gets me is in verse four: "Forgive us our sins, for we also forgive everyone who sins against us." Wow, I have to forgive everyone, but what if I don't want to? Again, wow! I sure have become pompous. God has forgiven me great debts and now I don't want to forgive the wrongs people have committed against me. Another parable told by Jesus about the unmerciful servant is in Matthew 18:21–35. He tells of the servant forgiven a large debt who would not forgive a smaller debt by another. Because of his unmerciful act and heart, he was punished.

Is it the fear of being punished that makes me forgive others? At first, maybe. Now it is the desire for me to please God. He forgave me of so much. When someone comes to me and asks forgiveness, I want to give it as freely as it was shown me. This can be tough at times. God paid a big price so that I would be forgiven. I need to show mercy to others who come and ask for my forgiveness. I am learning that love, through reading God's Word, watching, and listening to him in the Bible, praying, meditating, and watching others who are better at this than I am.

Today, I want to have a heart that forgives. I want to use Scripture and learn that to forgive is what I am called to do. The grace shown me can never be repaid. I am to share that love with others and that forgiveness so others can experience a portion of what I have. I continue to go to God for forgiveness. He always does, and I need to stay open to do the same.

Can You Really Get Enough?

Mercy, peace and love are yours in abundance.

Jude 1:2

Can you really get enough of Jesus? I have been thinking a lot about Jesus lately and thought that maybe I should think of something else. Then I thought, *Why?* I had lunch with a young man, and we talked about church, the Bible, and Jesus: three really great things to talk about. He told me he also loves talking about these topics most of the time. He said he was surprised when others didn't share his interest, especially other Christians. I have to agree. I love these topics.

I was counseling a man the other day, and we were discussing how prayer and depending on God could assist him. I also talked about the assurance I feel when putting my problems in God's hands and the love and gratitude I have for Jesus. He said, "So is Jesus your homeboy?"

I said, "Well, yeah, sure he is. Jesus is my homeboy." *Homeboy* is a slang word used for a really good friend, someone you can count on and someone who has your back. Jesus is not only my homeboy; he is first and foremost my Savior whom I treat with love, respect, and reverence.

God has given me mercy and love in abundance. Why wouldn't my thoughts and conversation be on Jesus? Although I talk about lots of other stuff, I seem to always go back to Father God and his Son Jesus. I just love those guys. Without them, I would have no life at all.

Carry the Cross

As they were going out, they met a man from Cyrene, named
Simon, and they forced him to carry the cross.

Matthew 27:32

Learning God's will as I read the Bible seems to be what life is all
about. As I read, I am always learning more of what God wants me
to do. Every line in the Bible has a new lesson. I am usually the
kind of person that has learned things the hard way. Since reading
the Bible and taking in its life lessons, I have learned a great deal,
and it is a lot easier to learn. In this particular line from the Bible,
I learned two different lessons. How do you like that? Two for the
price of one.

The good news is a message that must be carried. After Jesus
was beaten severely, mocked, and ridiculed, he was tasked with carrying the cross to Golgotha, the hill where he would be crucified.
He was put to death by the Jewish and Roman citizens, and more
importantly, he was sent to Earth from heaven to die for our sins.
The good news comes through Jesus' death, which atoned for all of
mankind's sin. On the third day after his death, he was resurrected,
and he beat death. Jesus went to that cross to pay for everyone's sins
through his death. That cross had to get to the top of the hill so
God's plan for salvation could begin. Simon carried the cross with
Jesus. Now we must carry the cross by spreading the good news

of Jesus' death and resurrection. Our sin debt was paid and our eternal salvation assured because Jesus submissively, willingly, and lovingly died for all of us.

The second message I learned is that we need to help carry each other's burdens when we are weak. Simon helped carry the cross to the top of the hill, but that was the end for Simon. Or was it the beginning? Jesus had to be nailed to the cross to die. Simon helped Jesus at his weakest physical moment. We too must help carry each other's burdens. Simon helping carry that cross taught me two lessons: first, we should help each other with burdens and second, we need to carry the cross by spreading the good news.

The good news is really great news. We must carry and spread it wherever we go. Helping each other with burdens is an act of love toward those we help and toward God himself. So today, let's all be like Simon and help Jesus carry his cross.

Carving the Mountains

And why do you worry about clothes? See how the lilies of the field grow. They do not labor or spin. Yet I tell you that not even Solomon in his entire splendor was dressed like one of these. If that is how God clothes the grass of the field, which is here today and tomorrow is thrown into the fire, will he not much more clothe you, O you of little faith? So do not worry, saying, "What shall we eat?" or "What shall we drink?" or "What shall we wear?"

Matthew 6:28–31

I attended a mountain retreat in South Carolina. It was a men's retreat, with about one hundred in attendance, with ages ranging from twenty to eighty-five years old. Each man there had, at one point in his life, suffered from alcohol and drug addiction. All of these men's lives had been transformed by God. These men came to grow closer to God and see his beautiful and scenic views of mountains and lakes. You could also see God's creation in the men, as they expressed in their words, actions, and eyes that they had been changed. These men had been transformed by God. This was true beauty.

As we looked into the mountains and the rock that formed them, we could see how the mountains had been carved and changed over time. One could look at the beauty in the colors of the changing tress. You could see at six a.m. one hundred men coming to the outdoor chapel in the very cold weather to share in silent prayer, mediation, and gratitude for the transformation and recovery each had experienced. Later, while having coffee before the warm fireplace in the lodge, men shared laughter, tears, and stories of total transformation as a testimony to God's magnificent grace and the sacrifice of Jesus.

As I looked over the magnificent carved mountains and changing rocks and leaves, all I could say aloud was, "Wow. Good work, God." I also said to a few of the men who were struggling, "If God can shape these hard rocks and beauty, imagine what he can do in your heart if you go humbly to him and simply believe and ask."

Caught Up in Grace

I have been attempting to share some thoughts each day by e-mailing them, blogging them, and just sharing what's on my heart and mind with others. With that in mind, grace will be at the heart of this writing. I seem to be caught up in it.

I don't use the word *awe* very often because I feel it is overused. With that being said, I am in awe of God's grace. I feel *awe* does not sufficiently express how I actually feel about God's grace. The fact that God loves me and forgives me unconditionally gives me solace, assurance, and motivation. Grace seems to be my motivating factor in all I do. I want to be different, I want to be better, I want to grow and mature, and I want to learn to love and forgive others because of God's awesome grace.

When I fall asleep for the last time and return home, the Bible tells me I will be held accountable for what I have done here on Earth. God's Word gives me instructions on how to live. He tells me to love and forgive others, to give of my time, money, self, and the gifts he has given me to help those in need. He tells me to repent and be baptized, to believe in Jesus Christ as my savior. I am told to practice spiritual disciplines. I am part of Jesus' body, the church, and am active in ministries and service to others and him. I pray with others, counsel others, and continue to study and ask questions. The commands God gives sometimes are hard because my human nature doesn't always want to do some of the things commanded. I do them anyway, and since God asked, I am happy to do them. I suppose at this time in my life I am caught up in grace.

Forgiving and loving doesn't always come naturally. There have been instances someone is mean to me, belittles me or what I do, puts me down, and cheats me. It has been hard to love and forgive. Sometimes I just want to lose my temper, be as ugly as I feel someone has been to me. God commands I not do these things. I will be held accountable. That doesn't seem fair sometimes. Don't I deserve to get mad, hold a grudge, and spew some ugliness? No. Why? Because God commanded it. That being said, grace is what motivates me.

How can I show ugliness when I am shown grace, mercy, and love? Jesus died and was resurrected so I could be reconciled with our Father. His death made it possible for me to be given a home in heaven. I have acted poorly on several occasions, but he has forgiven me. Grace says to me, "Be baptized and repent." Grace says to me, "Give your time, money, and yourself to others." Grace says, "Give forgiveness to those who hurt you." Grace says, "Use the spiritual disciples in your life so you can become a mature Christian and not drink just milk but eat solid, spiritual food."

I want grace to be my compass, on my mind, heart, and lips constantly. I want what I do in life to be guided and directed by grace. I know I will continue to grow and mature in my Christian walk, but grace seems to be my compass to get there and the cornerstone to my faith.

Change Your Way of Thinking!

The Lord your God will change your heart and the hearts of all your descendants, so that you will love him with all your heart and soul and so you may live!

Deuteronomy 30:6

At one of my first twelve-step meetings I heard an excellent speaker. The speaker, whom I'll call Joe, was a friend of a friend. Joe was speaking about being in San Quentin prison and a speaker from a twelve-step program coming to speak there. Joe said the speaker talked about change. He then pounded the podium, and in a room full of people pointed at Joe and said, "Boy, you better change your way of thinking, or you will be back here."

Joe said that after the gathering, he smiled and said to the speaker, "When you said the 'change your way of thinking' thing, you pointed right at me. Why?"

He replied in a booming voice, "Because, boy, you better change your way of thinking."

When Joe shared this, he pounded the podium also, then pointed directly at me and said, "Boy, you better change your way of thinking, or you will drink again." After the gathering, I said to Joe, when you said, *change your way of thinking,* you pointed right at me. Joe said in a booming voice, "I pointed at you because, boy, you better change your way of thinking."

I have learned over the years that changing people, places, and things is not enough. Changing whom I associate with, where I go, and how I do things is not enough to change. I have grown to understand my entire way of thinking about life has to change. I am not a victim of circumstance. I have the ability to think things through. I don't have to do things any longer that used to get me into trouble. I have to have a fresh perspective, a different outlook on life. I have changed my way of thinking.

I have also learned I cannot do this on my own. I need the help of God. In prayer and meditation, I ask God to help me change my way of thinking. I was a selfish person, only thinking of me. Even if I helped someone, there was a motive. I hung around people who thought as I did. I didn't want anyone to disagree with me. I was angry and full of fear and reacted accordingly. This all needed to change. The only way I could do this was by asking God's counsel in all my decision making.

As a Christian, repentance is similar to changing my way of thinking. Repentance to me not only means changing my way of thinking but changing my heart. Turn away from sin and turn toward God. I need to have a contrite heart. I need to admit when I sin and ask God for forgiveness and the willingness and wisdom to change. I need to turn to God, to see God's, love, grace, mercy, and omnipotence. I need to follow the example set by Jesus, in my decision making and all my actions. It's like looking at life through God's point of view.

I realize I need to study to learn what God would have me do. My goal is to bring God glory in all I do. This is a new way of thinking. I work on this, in my life by reading God's word in the Bible. I achieve this by putting to use what I have heard God say and what I have seen him do. This again is found in the Bible. It's found through study, prayer, meditation, being accountable with relationships, and wise counsel. My outlook on life can change. I can be a loving and giving person. This is a stark contrast to the person Joe told to change his way of thinking. I can love, forgive, and be a servant to others simply through love and God's command. I can love God because I choose to.

Changing my way of thinking, and repentance are keys in my life today. It won't all happen this week. I need to be patient and continue to move forward. This is only possible when I ask God to change my way of thinking and my heart. This is a one-day-at-a-time process, made possible by a desire to change my mind and heart and direct intervention by our heavenly Father.

Cheerleaders Wanted

Praise be to the God and Father of our Lord Jesus Christ, the Father of compassion and the God of all comfort, who comforts us in all our troubles, so that we can comfort those in any trouble with the comfort we ourselves have received from God.

2 Corinthians 1:3–4

Therefore, since we are surrounded by such a great cloud of witnesses, let us throw off everything that hinders and the sin that so easily entangles, and let us run with perseverance the race marked out for us.

Hebrews 12:1

I have watched sporting events where cheerleaders are spurring their teams on to greatness. I wonder when a sports team chooses its cheerleaders what the qualifications are. My guess is when one reads a help-wanted ad for cheerleaders the requirements might read: cute, petite, perky, athletic, strong voice and smile. That seems to be the benchmark for the cheerleaders of the sports teams. But really, who are the real cheerleaders? I think the real cheerleaders are the people sitting in the stands and at homes on their couches. These people are invested; they are lifelong fans and live and die with each down, each point, win, and each loss. They brave the cold, sit through rain and snow, and sweat in the summer's heat. Oh yeah, they cheer, oh do they cheer. I am not trying to run the paid cheerleaders out of work. They have a place in cheering on the team.

The cheerleaders we should be are the ones that encourage and cheer each other on to greatness and in times of strife. What are the qualifications for the cheerleaders I am talking about? Okay, here is what we are looking for, only two requirements: 1. Do you want to encourage others? 2. Can you breathe? If you can do these two things, you are in. When things are good, we need a cheerleader, when things are bad, we need a cheerleader, and when things are just okay, we need a cheerleader.

I am blessed with encouragers and am grateful to have them. I don't have to be alone. God of course is my biggest cheerleader, and I love the ones he sends to me in human form as well. Encouragement, cheering up, spurring on, and even exhorting at times keep me going along the right path and most of the time with joy in my heart. These cheerleaders make it all okay, good and bad. When it's bad, they remind me I will grow and they are by my side, cheering me to move a few more yards. With smiles, hugs, words of encouragement, and a caring heart, cheerleaders are what everyone needs. Are you interested in the job? You are qualified.

Choose Love

Even before he made the world, God loved us and chose us in
Christ to be holy and without fault in his eyes.

Ephesians 1:4

I would love to tell you that when I was a child, I was a world-class
athlete and the most popular kid in school. But that would be a
lie. When I was young, I was shy and tried to blend into the wood-
work. Kids could be mean, and I was an easy target because I was
quiet and wouldn't stick up for myself. When teams were chosen
in gym for baseball, football, and basketball, I was pretty close to
last to be chosen, and sometimes dead last. That was a painful and
embarrassing experience. Sometimes I made a joke out of it and
laughed. But there was no laughter on the inside.

Since second grade, I have had a friend named Chris. He was
very athletic and was one of the more popular kids. Chris was a
kid other kids looked up to. Though other kids drifted away to
popularity and forgot me, Chris never did. I don't know why, but
Chris nicknamed me Duke. Sometimes Chris was chosen to be a
team captain. In sixth grade, we were choosing sides for baseball
one day in gym, and Chris had first pick. There were some guys
that could hit the ball over the fence, some could run like gazelles,
some that could throw like cannons, and some that could catch
like a vacuum, and they of course knew they would be chosen first.

Chris and the other team captain trash talked each other about who would get the better team, they flipped the coin, and Chris chose first. Without hesitation he said, "I want Duke." My heart pounded as he slapped me five. Chris chose friendship over a power hitter.

I don't even remember the score; who won that day; how anyone hit, caught, ran, or threw, but I remember Chris choosing me. He did it again several times later. In ninth grade, Chris was one of the school's best basketball players. We had tryouts. Chris said, "Duke, you need to go out for the team. You have a good outside shot." I was a bit scared to try out, but I did. As I ran around the court, I could always steal the ball from Chris and his other friend Timmy, who was also a starter on the team. I didn't have to wonder how I could get it from them; it was love.

I still talk to Chris, and he is still a hero. Chris is a New York City fireman. He was at the World Trade Center on 9/11. I called him the very next day. He said I was the first one to call, and he said, "I knew you would be first to call me." Each firefighter was given two official commemorative T-shirts. I have one of Chris's hanging proudly in my closet. Chris has always chosen friendship and love over everything.

God chose me and loved before I was born. I have not been the best of candidates at times for his love. But his amazing grace, forgiveness, mercy, and love have never stopped. He has chosen me for a job in life. I feel my gift is encouragement; I just love encouraging others. I have learned this from others, and I use this gift because I know how important it is to need love and encouragement.

Jesus didn't choose the best and brightest to associate with. He didn't hang out with the stiff-necked or conceited. God chose the downtrodden, the sick, the weak, the least, the sinners, and the ones who needed him. He chose me. We all need him, but some do not believe they do. Jesus said in Mark 10:31, "But many that are first shall be last; and the last first." Jesus chose the last, the least. Jesus chose our love and obedience. The underdog has a chance in this one.

God knew and loved us before we were born. We have a choice to love and obey him. Today I choose love, today I choose to obey, and today I choose you. I want to thank you, Father. Thank you, Jesus. Thank you, Holy Spirit. Thank you all for being my friend and loving me.

Christianity Is Not
a Spectator Sport

Therefore, since we are surrounded by such a great cloud of witnesses, let us throw off everything that hinders and the sin that so easily entangles, and let us run with perseverance the race marked out for us.

Hebrews 12:1

I have played many sports throughout my life, especially as a kid. My favorite was Little League baseball. I remember going to try-outs and the manager asking, "what position do you play?" You know what? I don't remember one kid saying, "Just give me a uniform and let me sit on the bench and watch."

I said, "I like to pitch, and when I am not pitching, I will play anywhere." Recently, I watched the Major League Baseball All-Star game. It was long, fifteen innings. The guys who were no longer on the field as the game progressed were on the top step of the dug-out chomping at the bit, wishing they could get back in there and hit that game-winning home run. Me, I fell asleep around inning twelve. I was not playing in that game.

Being a Christian is like that. Each morning, I go to my heavenly Father and say something like this: "Put me in, Coach. Father, I don't just want to wear the uniform and sit on the bench watching. I want to run the race, and I want to be in the game, and I am ready." I ask my Father each day what I can do, how I can do his will and his bidding each day. How can I bring another person to Christ, or how can I encourage my family? Father, what can I do to please you?

I don't want someone to ask what position I play in church and have to say, "I play spectator, back row, left out." I want to say, "I play centerfield." I am a scrappy gamer. I am not a star, but I suit up, show up, and ask where I am needed. The game and life's rules are in the Bible. I get personal hitting and fielding instructions from my coach, God himself, through prayer and meditation. I also get great tips as I fellowship and work with all of those in the body of Christ. We are all connected at the Spirit. We are a team, and we all need to be in the game. Christianity is a team sport. What position do you play?

Closing Out the Day

Praise be to the Lord, to God our Savior, who daily bears our burdens.

Psalm 68:19

Be joyful always; pray continually; give thanks in all circumstances, for this is God's will for you in Christ Jesus.

1 Thessalonians 5:16–18

I begin my day with Bible reading, devotionals, prayer, mediation, and solitude. It is an awesome way to set the tone for the day. In 1 Thessalonians 5:17 (NIV) it says, "Pray continually," and in the King James Version it says, "Pray without ceasing." So prayer is the way I start my day. What should I do after that? Well, Paul says we should be praying all day. Everything I do should be bringing glory to God. I am to pray all day, continually and without ceasing. I should be thinking of God continually and without ceasing.

So in the morning, I say please, and at the end of the day, I say thank you. So what if the day doesn't go so well? What if I had a bad day? What do I do about that? You are not going to believe this, but God has an answer for this one too. First Peter 4:16 says, "However, if you suffer as a Christian, do not be ashamed, but praise God that you bear that name." So if I have some suffering through the day as a Christian, I am to praise God because I am in Christ. Following Jesus sure is a mature way to live. Giving thanks and praise for anything that happens, wow. God will teach me through all situations, good and bad.

So how do I close out my day? I close out my day with prayer, meditation, and solitude. I take a look at my day, the good, the bad, and the ugly. I ask forgiveness where needed, and give thanks for another day. I ask God to help me improve tomorrow and make restitution where needed. I thank him for Jesus and all he has given me. I thank him for letting me do his will and share my gratitude for all he has done for me. I rest easy, knowing I can slumber under the eyes of God and his angels while I sleep. God is with me continually and without ceasing.

Come Back, Amazing Grace

So this is what the Lord says: "If you change your heart and return to me, I will take you back."

Jeremiah 15:19 (NVC)

While the son was still a long way off, his father saw him and felt sorry for his son. So the father ran to him, hugged, and kissed him. The son said, "Father, I have sinned against God and against you. I am no longer worthy to be called your son." But the father said to his servants, "Hurry! Bring the best clothes and put them on him. Also, put a ring on his finger and sandals on his feet get our fat calf, and kill it so we can have a feast and celebrate. My son was dead, but now he is alive again! He was lost, but now he is found!" So they began to celebrate.

Luke 15: 20–24 (NVC)

When I was sixteen, my father died. I did not understand death. All I knew was my father was gone, and I would never see him again. I was crushed. I cried for weeks. The pain was unbearable. All I could do was get angry; I took it out on God. I yelled, screamed, and cursed him. I told him I hated him, and I told him all he ever did was take people. My grandmother had died four years earlier, and she and I were very close. I hated him for taking them. I had no understanding of death. The only understanding I had was that it was permanent.

Around the time I was sixteen, I was introduced to beer. Beer took away pain. Beer took away fears and insecurities. It made me bigger and stronger. It also made me better looking and made the girls love me (so I thought). I drank until I was almost twenty-one and was in the navy. Then, beer was taking away my family, my money, my self-esteem, friends, closing in on my job, and my desire to live. Dying was more attractive to me than waking up one more day and having to face life. I hated what I saw in the mirror. I wanted to spit at the reflection. I hated the angry, selfish, violent, arrogant person I had become. I was not raised to become a drunk who hated himself.

I got involved in a twelve-step program over thirty years ago, which entirely changed my life for the better and brought me to a belief and love for God. I got reinvolved in the Catholic Church and went to the seminary. But I left. Something was still missing. I got married had two great children, Kenny and Nick. My wife and I divorced after nine years. I began living a life on the wide road, doing as I pleased. I had many friends, but I was still lonely and knew something was missing.

I met Janie. We dated a few years and then married. Janie is one of the best blessings that ever happened in my life. She is the best friend I have ever had. She and I are a team. I am blessed to have her as a wife. We both love each other, each other's children, and Janie's grandchildren, who call me Grandpa Ken and Kenpa.

Something was still missing. I was still afraid of death, still not sure where I was going. I felt I had done things in my life that would surely keep me out of heaven. I knew God was forgiving, but I did sinful things anyway. What arrogance. I turned my back on God's commands. I had cursed him and did not think there was any turning back.

I had nothing against my original Catholic upbringing, but I began to attend the Church of Christ. I went a few weeks and liked what I saw. I prayed to God. I told him I wanted to give my life to him and continue to serve others. I was a counselor and had my own business at the time. I knew I was going to hell and understood why. I sent an e-mail to one of our elders, Pat, who called me. He said he was glad I e-mailed and he wanted to get together and see what plans God had in bringing us together.

Pat came to my house one Sunday morning after church. He brought his Bible. I had the coffee ready. I confessed to him my past and told him I was sure I was going to hell. He told me it wasn't up to him to forgive me. Then he told me the words that would change my life and give me what I was always missing. He said, "Let's look in the Bible and see what God has to say." It was as if I heard the good news of Jesus Christ for the first time. My eyes, ears, and heart must have been opened wide. I had heard this a thousand of times before but never like this. We talked about a contrite heart and repentance; for sure, I was there. I wanted to change. I wanted Jesus' blood to cover my sins. I wanted to repent and turn back to God. Pat read me many passages on repentance and baptism.

I then said to Pat, "Can you baptize me now?" Pat baptized me that night. The people that were there sang to me and welcomed me to the family. My life has never been the same. Pat and his wife, Bonnie, have become very cherished and close friends. I meet with Pat weekly for lunch. Pat has become my mentor. Pat tries to keep me in line. I now work at the church as an involvement and counseling minister, for almost four years now as of 2009.

When Pat opened that Bible, he opened a new way of life. I go to it daily. I go to it for all my answers. The Bible teaches me how to live, love, forgive, and be a husband, a father, a brother, and a friend. The Bible teaches me how to act at work and in the community at large. Jesus' example is the one I strive to follow. I am God's work in progress. I have given him everything.

Commercial Fishermen–Apostles

As Jesus was walking beside the Sea of Galilee, he saw two brothers, Simon called Peter and his brother Andrew. They were casting a net into the lake, for they were fishermen. "Come, follow me," Jesus said, "and I will make you fishers of men." At once they left their nets and followed him.

Matthew 4:18–20

He got up and rebuked the wind and the raging waters; the storm subsided, and all was calm. "Where is your faith?" he asked his disciples. In fear and amazement they asked one another, "Who is this? He commands even the winds and the water, and they obey him."

Luke 8:25

Jesus' first choice for disciples and apostles were commercial fishermen. Have you ever met a commercial fisherman? I know a few. If I were gathering holy men, my first choice would not be commercial fishermen. Have you ever heard them talk? Their language, jokes, and some of their actions can make a salty sailor wince. The only thing stronger than their vocabulary is probably the smell of fish on them. Now don't get me wrong, these are dedicated, hardworking, strong, quick thinking, and team-oriented men. I guess these were the characteristics Jesus was looking for.

These men spent three years with Jesus. I am guessing that they didn't become instant holier-than-thou types but remained just a little rough around the edges. I don't think they started out with King James Version speech. They were not quite ready to get up and speak about the kingdom of God; they had quite a bit of training to undergo. Miss Manners wasn't around back then to teach them etiquette. Pop psychology wasn't around either to help them get in touch with their inner child. No Henry Higgins to teach them pronunciation.

Remember when the apostles were out in their fishing boat and the storm broke out? That scene captivates me. I can see Jesus, curled up asleep, maybe with an old sail as his blanket, the water rushing into the boat, the sound of thunder, the sight of deadly lightning, fishermen scurrying around, bailing the large, floundering craft. What do you suppose the fishermen-apostles were saying? "Oh gee, thou art in quite a predicament. Please, Peter, passeth me thine bucket." You think they added, "If we art saved from the storm, it is God's will"? Not from the sound of the text. They were freaking out; they were being hard-edged, commercial fishermen. I am guessing the language of these men may have gone back to earlier days, and it might have curled some hair. These guys were hollering and screaming, trying to save each other's lives. They woke Jesus, who watched the insanity and heard the fear in the men's voices. Jesus stood up and rebuked the storm. He told it to stop. The men were stunned. Then, Jesus looked at the men in the now still waters and said, "What's wrong?" No, he said, "Where is your faith?" I can imagine the looks, the questions, and the glazed-over eyes. "Huh? Who is this guy?"

Well, you may or may not believe this, but I am still a little rough around the edges at times. I am a work in progress. Coming to Christ is what I needed, although I didn't and haven't become a saint overnight. There are times when there are storms in my life. If Jesus were in front of me, he might ask, "Where is your faith?" I might have asked him questions like "Were you sleeping? Did you see what was happening?" He would have watched me run around, reacting with no clear direction. I might have even sounded like a salty sailor, through fear and panic.

Like the apostles, we have all had storms in our lives. I don't know about you, but I know there have been times I worried and panicked before calling on Jesus for rescue. He is right here; the key to peace in life during these storms is faith in God. Our Father is here for us, which is part of Jesus' message." So far, my best decision is to turn to God. Why don't I always think about that? Do you? Am I alone in this? Jesus showed us what to do in a storm. Turn to the Father, ask for peace, ask for quiet, and ask the waves to stop coming over the boat.

After the storm had quieted, Jesus asked, "Where is your faith?" Do you suppose they were embarrassed? Do you suppose some of them said, "Ahh, we knew you would come through? We were only kidding"? Do you think they beat themselves up a bit for their lack of faith and that Jesus even had to ask? I get like that, although God always comes through. God loves me, and Jesus said if I come to the Father in his name, my prayer will be answered. How do I forget that?

Today, I will put my faith in God. Through the storms I may encounter, I know when I ask the storm will be under God's control. I have nothing to worry about. The sun will come out; the sea will be calm. Then I will be able to go to God and say, "Thank you" and not have to answer the question "Where is your faith?"

Congregation Goes Wild

Bring the fattened calf and kill it. Let's have a feast and celebrate.

Luke 15:23

It is the bottom of the ninth at Fenway Park, and the Red Sox are down two to one. With a man on second and two outs, up comes David Ortiz. The pitch, the swing—he's done it again! A home run and the crowd goes wild. Two seconds left at the Amway Arena, the Magic are down 101–100. Dwight Howard, running down the court, jumps, dunks, and then the buzzer. Magic wins! The crowd is on their feet. There is bedlam in the arena. With a tie score, the Oilers need one point to win. With three seconds, Gretzky skates. One second, the puck goes past the goalie. The game is over. Gretzky does it again; the fans are in a frenzy. There is one second on the clock, Giants ahead of New England. The ball is hiked, Manning kneels down. The game is over. Giants win! What an upset. And the crowd is on their feet. This place is out of control with excitement.

Imagine if we did that in church. We have plenty to cheer about. A few years ago at a service at my church, our preacher, Steve, was talking about the gods of other religions, all of whom had died and been placed in a tomb. He went down the list, naming them. Then he said, "And Jesus, that tomb is empty. He is alive." For some reason, I wanted to jump up, wave my fist, and yell, "Yes!" That is exciting. Jesus beat death. He beat more than a buzzer, a clock, or a strike count. Jesus was crucified. He died. He was put into a tomb with a giant boulder in front of it and guards watching it. On the third day, that rock moved. Jesus had beat death. I jumped out of my seat for the Ortiz homerun but sat quiet in church. My insides were going wild.

Other moments in the Bible where I want to cheer: when God parted the Red Sea for the Israelites as the Egyptian soldiers were close on their heels; when the Egyptian soldiers tried to cross, *swoosh,* the sea came back together, and the enemy was drowned. How about when Jesus called the dead Lazarus out of his tomb and he walked out? How about when he called legions of demons out of a man? When he gave sight to the blind man? When friends cut a hole in a roof and lowered their friend down to be healed? How about when Jesus, dying on the cross, said, "Father, forgive them. They know not what they do"? No fish, no problem. Jesus said, "Lower your net on the other side." Peter was so excited to see Jesus he jumped out of the boat. David swung the rock, *bam,* right between the mighty giant Goliath's eyes. There are so many miraculous stories in the Bible, and when they are told in church, it is almost like we could do the wave. The preacher could be yelling, and the congregation would be going wild. Jesus just keeps on doing the seemingly impossible.

Today I want to be excited by God's Word. I want to share it. I want to read it. I want to savor every word. It is an amazing book. It is more than a book. If you like adventure, you got it. Suspense, poetry, love stories, mystery, intrigue, murder, war stories, deceit, agriculture, farming, the list goes on. It is a book for everyone. Most of all, it has love and salvation for those who trust in Jesus and obey God's Word. Imagine after just a few of the examples I have given what God will do in our lives if we just ask. He takes care of those who pray to him and brings home those who believe, accept, and obey Jesus. Sinners can be saved through God's great grace. And the crowd goes wild.

David's Confession

Come and listen, all you who fear God, and I will tell you
what he did for me. For I cried out to him for help, praising
him as I spoke. If I had not confessed the sin in my heart the
Lord would not have listened. But God did listen. He paid
attention to my prayer. Praise God, who did not ignore my
prayer or withdraw his unfailing love from me.

Psalms 66:16–20 (NLT)

Do you remember the story of David watching Bathsheba on her
roof while she was bathing? He sent for her, and she was brought
to him. One problem for David: Bathsheba was married to a lieu-
tenant in David's army. That did not stop David from commit-
ting adultery with Bathsheba. David knew how to fix the marriage
problem through manipulation, treachery, and murder. David sent
Uriah, Bathsheba's husband, to the front lines of battle, where
fighting was the fiercest. Uriah was killed in battle. David not only
committed adultery, but he committed murder so he could have
Bathsheba for his own. God was angry with David for his sinful
actions.

In this psalm, David praised God and gave thanksgiving for
forgiving him after he had confessed and asked forgiveness. David
uses this psalm to not only give praise and thanksgiving to God
but to share with all who fear God. David bore his heart, confessed

to a nation his sin, and shared through confession to God that his prayer for forgiveness was not only heard but also granted. God did not hold back his love or grace from David when he came to God with a contrite heart and confessed.

David shared all of this with us so that we could witness the forgiving heart of God. He also shared this to warn us that without confession God may not listen to our prayer. David shared because he confessed God heard his prayer and did not ignore him. David is telling us we need not carry around the guilt of sin or hide it from God. David tells us to go to God with a contrite heart and confess our sin to God. God will listen to our confession and prayer. God will not ignore us, nor will he turn away from such a prayer. Through confession to God, we will find the peace and forgiveness we are looking for through God's mercy and grace. Do you have sin in your life you have not shared with God? Bring it to him today, and know the gratitude, joy, and peace David found when he brought his sin to God.

Dazed and Confused

When he saw the crowds, he had compassion on them
because they were confused and helpless, like sheep without
a shepherd.

Matthew 9:36

Okay, back to Maryhaven. While there, I met two boys. Both were
in their midteens. The first was a slim teen, emotionally disturbed,
developmentally disabled, and had one arm which was atrophied,
which swung in front of him. He also had seizures. The first time
I was with him he had a seizure. I went over to him, and my goal
was to comfort him. As he came out of the seizure, he jumped up,
hit and kicked me, then ran. I was later told that when he came
out of seizures, he became violent each time. Hmm. A little more
communication may have been helpful.

Next, let me tell you about the other boy. He had a brain
injury when he was younger. He could not handle change. If there
was a substitute teacher, his eyes would glaze over; he would start
swinging and kicking, scream, and run. He had no destination,
but we weren't to get in his way, or he would see us as trying to
hurt him and would attack. The slightest change would trigger this
response.

Both boys would have to be held in a basket hold to help them
regain self-control. There were times I would have to hold them

down on the floor until they could calm down enough to move to my office. When I first responded to these outbursts, I would be quiet until they regained some composure. I would speak to them calmly with compassion and assurance. Most times, I would get a sincere apology; next, they would cry and hug me. They had no recollection of what had happened, nor did they know why they had become so violent.

They needed to be still. They needed to hear a calm and controlled voice to let them know everything was going to be all right. They needed to know they were safe. They needed to know I understood what had just happened and I was there to help them through it. They were given assurance. They also needed understanding.

God gives us compassion and assurance when we are dazed and confused and when the world seems to be whirling around us, out of control. I don't know about you, but I know I have said more than once, "Why is this happening to me?" I can talk about it with another person, and even better, I can go straight to God in prayer, meditation, and his Word, and I can find out what happened as long as I have the eyes to see, the ears to hear, and a tender heart to respond.

As Paul said in Acts 9:18, "Immediately, something like scales fell from Saul's eyes, and he could see again." Saul was able to see clearly again. When I go to God, this is what happens for me. I can see and think clearly again. Being still, calm, and reassuring for these teens helped them to see and think clearly again.

Did That Frog Say
Ribbit or DYRYBT?

Then the LORD opened the donkey's mouth, and she said
to Balaam, "What have I done to you to make you beat me
these three times?"

Numbers 22:28

Hmm. *DYRYBT* sounds just like *ribbit,* so which does the frog
really say? Is the frog telling us something? Well, why not? In the
book of Numbers, we have a talking donkey. On TV, we have had a
talking horse, Mr. Ed. We had My Mother the Car, she could talk,
and she was a 1928 Porter. Yogi Bear talks, Scooby Doo talks, and
many others. Okay, enough silliness, maybe the frog does have an
important message for us though.

One of the elders at our church, Don, speaks fluent frog and
he knows exactly what they are saying. He is kind of like a frog
whisperer. I was at an elders' meeting one Sunday morning that
the ministers were invited to. Don told us the amazing message
from the frog. He told us exactly what the frog is telling us. He
said it was the same message that the elders have been asking us for
months now. I was amazed at the wisdom and insight of the frog.

Well enough suspense, Don explained to us that the frog
actually says, "DYRYBT." And being able to speak fluent frog
and spending much time in the woods, Don explained the exact

interpretation of *DYRYBT*. It is, "Did you read your Bible today?" Imagine, just as Balaam's donkey spoke wisdom to Balaam, the frog asks, "Did you read your Bible today?" Don is a true frog whisperer. Well, Don did use the acronym DYRYBT, and I just let my head do the rest. So all that being said, the frog has a question for you today. "DYRYBT?"

Do Over

In reply Jesus declared, "I tell you the truth, no one can see the kingdom of God unless he is born again."

John 3:3

I remember as a little kid playing baseball a strike wasn't always a strike. If the swing didn't feel right, the sun got in your eyes, there were bugs flying around, you didn't have your Wheaties, or you just wanted another try, you could shout, "Do over!" Sometimes, you were only allowed a certain amount of do overs. You may get seven or eight strikes that way. Who knows? Those were the days when a mistake could simply be corrected by saying, "Do over." As an adult, that isn't always possible. Drive into the back of another car sometime and say, "Do over." It doesn't work. Air traffic controllers don't get do overs.

I have made many mistakes in my life where others were affected. They were hurt. If I said, "Do over," would that change things? Nope. Sometimes, I would try the old standby, "I am sorry." But after a while, that got old. No one believed me anymore. It sure would have been a lot easier to yell, "Do over!"

I don't like playing word games. So when I say this, I am not playing with words here. God would not give me a do over. God gave me a fresh start. When I came to God with a contrite heart, a repentant spirit, and humbled before him, I was given a new life. No do overs necessary, or do over limits. I thought the life I lived had done me in. There were several passages in the Bible that set me straight. Here is one that has given me the assurance from God that I had been given a fresh slate: "For God so loved the world that he gave his one and only Son, that whoever believes in him shall not perish but have eternal life" (John 3:16). I have been forgiven, and it is time for me to move forward.

So if I believe in Jesus, I can have eternal life. Ahh, there is the catch; I have to be become a whoever. After close examination and prayer, it turns out that I am a whoever. Good news: we are all whoevers. I have also repented and have been baptized for the forgiveness of my sins. This is way better than a do over; this is total cleansing, a fresh start, and a rebirth into Christ.

The mistakes I make now and the sins I commit can be forgiven, and I can start fresh. Peter asked Jesus how many times we should forgive someone. "Seven times?" Jesus said, "No, seventy times seven." That comes straight from Jesus, the Son of God. That shows the patience God has for me and you. I can go to him when I err and when I sin. I can be forgiven. Peter denied Jesus three times and then was brought back into the fold by Jesus; later, Jesus called Peter a rock. He was solid. That's not a do over, that's a fresh start.

I have been given a fresh start as a Christian. No do over or a do over limit. That doesn't give me carte blanch to go out and sin. It just takes into account my humanness and his knowing that I am not perfect. I will do my very best in life to follow Jesus and to follow God's commands. I will love God and love others, as well as serve and make disciples in the world. I will continue to study God's Word, pray, and meditate on his Word. If I make a mistake, I don't have to freak out and yell, "Do over!" I will turn to God with a contrite heart and repentant spirit, and through God's grace, I will receive a fresh start. Do overs are nice, but you can't beat a clean slate and a fresh start. Ask God for a fresh start and clean slate, and you will find peace and assurance.

Do You Feel Like
a Crushed Grape?

For every house is built by someone, but God is the builder
of everything.

Hebrews 3:4

Have you ever popped a grape in your mouth? A sweet, delicious
grape? Maybe two or three at once? I am drooling thinking about
it, mmm. Do you know how they make wine? They take those big
delicious grapes, put them in a giant barrel, and then they step on
them, kick them, push down hard with their feet, trample, tromp,
jump on, and pulverize them; well, you get the picture.

Since I no longer drink alcohol, I don't drink wine, but I do
like grape juice. I have been told there is nothing better than a
good glass of wine. Have you ever watched wine connoisseurs?
They pop the cork, sniff it, swirl the wine around in a fancy goblet,
put a little in their mouth, swish it around like they just brushed
their teeth, and they drone on about the bouquet of the wine. It
looks like they are enjoying that wine with great pleasure. All this
from some squished grapes that someone stepped on. So I guess the
grapes have become better and something new after they have been
crushed and healed?

Have you ever felt like a squished grape? Have you ever been
stepped on, kicked, knocked down, pulverized, mocked, hurt,

abandoned, ridiculed, gossiped about, joked about, or just really beat down? Do you know you can come out the other end even better and something new? I don't think anyone will smell you, swish you around, and talk about your bouquet, but they will see a stronger person. We can grow by giving all this to God, by forgiving the other person, by knowing we have a Father who will build us back up into someone even better.

Don't let anything keep you down. Turn to God. He loves us and builds us back up and will make us a whole new creation. Grapes aren't the only thing that can become better after being crushed. With God's help, so can we.

Do You Know My Father?

Father, glorify your name!

John 12:28

As I mentioned earlier, at age sixteen, I lost my best friend to cancer. He was the greatest person I have ever known. His nickname for me was Champ, and my nickname for him was Dad. My father was also named Ken Jones. He was a man filled with love. He loved his family, friends, and neighbors, and, it seemed to me, everyone. My uncle once said of my father that when my father walked into a room, the room would light up and you knew there would be fun coming. In my eyes, he had a big red cape with a big letter *S* on it as big as his smile.

When I was nine or ten, my father was the commander of the local American Legion. He was a World War II navy construction battalion veteran who served in the Tinian Islands in the Pacific. Each year, the American Legion in our town sponsored a carnival where they operated all the booths and sold tickets. My father gave me a roll of tickets and said, "Have fun." I went to every ride, but before I got on each ride, I would stop at the booth and say hello to the legionnaires and say, "My name is Kenny Jones, do you know my father?" They would all say yes and tell me what a great guy he was. After a while, they would just say, "Hey, there is Kenny Jones's boy." I wore that title with great pride and still do today.

I have learned more and more about my heavenly Father, God. The more I read his Word, pray, meditate, listen to sermons, and talk with others, the more I learn just how much he loves me. I have learned that God loves me more than my earthly father did. The first time I heard that, all I could think was, *That is impossible.* My father helped me deliver newspapers in the rain and snow; my father protected me just by his presence in the house when I was afraid of the dark. I always knew when he was there nothing could happen to me. How did I know that? He told me.

Well it turns out it is true. I have been a sinner, one who has been away from God. Alcoholism, greed, selfishness, self-centeredness, all kinds of sin, and I have even cursed God in the past. I turned away from him. God has never turned away from me. In fact, I am one of the whomevers he sent his Son, Jesus, to die for. He sent Jesus to pay my sin debt, so when I believed in Jesus as my savior, I could be reconciled to my heavenly Father and have eternal life. My heavenly Father also sent the Holy Spirit to dwell in me. God meets all my needs, he hears all my prayers, and he knew me and what I would do before I was born and loved me anyway. That is amazing grace and amazing love.

This Father, God, gives light where it is dark. This Father makes it possible to do all things. He has given me an abundance of blessings. He has given me gifts and talents to be of service to others. This father has his son preparing an eternal home in heaven for me right now. My Father, God, means everything to me. I want all I do to glorify his holy name. He is the one who gave me my earthly parents to care for me until I could be with him.

My heavenly Father has never left me. He has been with me all my life. He has been here and will always be here. Through all my sufferings and tribulations, he has been here to comfort me, through my joys to applaud and through trials to cheer me on. He listens to my prayers and praise whenever I utter them, whether by word, deed, or in my heart. My Father, God, has carried me when I could no longer go on. He has loved me when I could not love myself. He has given me reason to go on, rejoice, praise, sing, and serve him and others. He has shown me what real love, mercy, and grace are.

Do you know my Father? Would you like to? There is a book all about him. The authors were even inspired by him telling them what to write. My Father's book is titled the Holy Bible. It is written in many languages and translations. My Father is very well known and well loved. When discussion of him begins, the room lights up, and the fun begins. It is a great privilege to be Kenny Jones's boy. However, it is only with awe that I am graced to also be the son of our Father, worthy of all the praise and glory. Do you know him?

Do You Know Their Story?

Part One

> For God so loved the world that he gave his one and only Son, that whoever believes in him shall not perish but have eternal life. For God did not send his Son into the world to condemn the world, but to save the world through him.
>
> John 3:16–17

Have you ever seen a biker filled with tattoos, bearded and wearing his bandana? What did you think? Have you ever seen the ladies of the evening walking down the street in their short dresses, swaying back and forth? How about those who are pompous, those who laugh a lot, those who don't speak, those who put on airs? Who are these people? What are their stories? Don't they all have a mother and father? Do they have children? Are they hiding from something? What about the drug addicts, alcoholics, those who hide behind food, gambling, and porn addictions? What is their story? Are you afraid of some of these people? Are you disgusted by them? Are you one of them? Am I one of them?

When we walk down streets, into stores, schools, work places, and churches we see these people. What do we think? Do we know their story? Do we know their history? Are some of these people hiding from something? Maybe themselves? There was a time in my life where it was easier to laugh than cry. It was easier to talk than endure the silence. It was easier to say nothing and become invisible, that way maybe no one would notice me. Do we know people like that?

There are so many people out there that have been battered physically, emotionally, and sexually. There are people from broken homes and people who have never met their parents. There are people who have experienced extreme grief. There are people walking around with tons of guilt and shame for what they have done with and in their life and for what others have done to them. God tells us not to judge, and to leave the judging to him. God knows the heart of every man and woman. No one is without sin; God made provisions for those he loves, and he loves all of us.

There are so many people out there that need to be recognized and loved back into the human race. Those tattooed bikers are filled with love. Just look at the Santa runs they put on for the kids at Christmas with their bikes. Many tattoos tell a story. Ladies of the evening, why are they out there? God wants them back, and how can we get them back to him? All the addictions and fears people hide from, how do we get them back? Love, kindness, mercy, and the truth are the answer. That is what brought me back to the arms of Jesus. Giving people a smile, a nod, and recognition that each of us is a person loved by God. Our testimony is our best way of letting others know they are not alone. Be gentle. Do you know their story?

Do You Know Their Story?

Part Two

Do They Know Our Story?

Praise be to the God and Father of our Lord Jesus Christ, the Father of compassion and the God of all comfort, who comforts us in all our troubles, so that we can comfort those in any trouble with the comfort we ourselves have received from God.

2 Corinthians 1:3–4

Many of the people I spoke about in part one of this writing think those of us who attend church and are Christians are just a bunch of pious, holier-than-thou holy rollers. Some of the people I wrote about actually attend our churches. Some of them are even members already and are afraid to confess or repent because they may think there is no hope for them. At first, I was one of them. Maybe those people need to know that they are already one of us and we are one of them. Don't we all have the same Father, the same Brother, and Savior? Aren't we all God's children? Don't some of us need to be found and brought back to God?

Do the people who think we are holy rollers know some of us have exactly the same story they do? Do they know that some of us have similar stories? Have we told them? In many of Paul's letters, Paul lets people know he is one of us. He even goes as far as to say he is the worst sinner. Paul shares this so that all who read will know that there is no one who cannot be saved by the blood of Jesus. Do we open up with one another? I mean really get to know each other? Or is it just a "Hello" and "God bless"?

I know before I was saved my perception of churchgoers were they all thought they were perfect and looked down their nose at me. Once I actually met Christians and they opened their hearts and shared their testimonies with me, I found out they had needed saving too. Jesus came for all sinners, and there is no sin too big or too small that wasn't paid for on the cross. Do we let people know we are a grateful bunch? Do we look grateful? Do we act grateful? Do we share our gratitude with others through love and service? Jesus said, "Love God, love each other." And he even said, "Love your enemy." So let me see, I have to love my neighbor, my friends, my family, and my enemies. Wow, that is everyone.

The good news is for all. When we share it, does it sound like good news, or does it sound like an insurmountable obstacle? When we share the good news, do we let folks know we will help them and help them grow spiritually? And then, do we? Not only do we need to know their stories, we have to ask ourselves, "Are we doing a good job of sharing ours? Do they know our stories?"

Do You Know Their Story?

Part Three

Hiding in the Status Quo

I pray also that the eyes of your heart may be enlightened in order that you may know the hope to which he has called you.

Ephesians 1:18

Earlier, I asked if we see people for who they really are. I used examples such as addicts, alcoholics, tattoos, prostitutes, and easy-to-spot people who may not be part of the status quo or what one may consider "normal." Now the big question: what is normal? *Normal* is an interesting word. Normal seems to really be what is normal for a group. If I was part of a biker group with leather and tattoos and I showed up in a suit and tie, would I be normal? Or are tattoos and leather normal for that group? So I want to talk about what society may consider normal and what that is. My friend Craig says, "Normal is a setting on a washing machine."

Just for purposes of this writing, let's look at the people who dress like all the rest, act like all the rest, you know, the social norm, your neighbor, church members, preppies, and folks who just don't stand out, the status quo. Phew, that's a lot of explaining for what I want to say. Do you know that some people hide behind the status quo, titles, jobs, families, and masks they wear? Just about anyone can have a past and a present they are not proud of. There is guilt, shame, pain, grief, illness, addictions, and all sorts of issues they do not want to get out. I am talking about people we know, the people next door, coworkers, the people sitting next to us in school and church. Can we see them? How can we if they don't tell us? Which eyes are we using?

Are the eyes in your heart working? Can you see beneath the masks these people are wearing? Maybe we do, but they aren't asking for help, so we tell ourselves we should mind our own business. If we saw someone drowning and they weren't yelling for help, would we just let them drown because they didn't ask for help? How well do we know the people around us? Relationships and building trust opens the hearts, minds, and mouths of others. Getting to know people on more than a surface level is so important for all of us. When we say to some people, "How are you?" They say, "Fine." On the inside, they are screaming, "Please ask me more. Please talk to me."

Are you hiding? Do you know someone hiding? Our relationships of course take time to build and open up to one another. Is it worth it? Oh yeah, we can be as sick as our secrets, and that can lead to loneliness, addiction, deviant behavior, and suicide. Let's show love, concern, and patience toward one another. When we look at someone, let us look with the eyes of our hearts and look beneath the status quo and the masks others are wearing. Let's remove our own masks, and let's share our stories with one another. None of us have to be alone.

Do You Love Me?

When they had finished eating, Jesus said to Simon Peter, "Simon son of John, do you truly love me more than these?" "Yes, Lord," he said, "you know that I love you." Jesus said, "Feed my lambs." Again Jesus said, "Simon son of John, do you truly love me?" He answered, "Yes, Lord, you know that I love you." Jesus said, "Take care of my sheep." The third time he said to him, "Simon son of John, do you love me?" Peter was hurt because Jesus asked him the third time, "Do you love me?" He said, "Lord, you know all things; you know that I love you." Jesus said, "Feed my sheep."

John 21:15–17

Have you ever been asked by your husband, wife, boyfriend, girlfriend, parent, or child, "Do you love me?" What is their answer? Mine would be, "Of course I love you." Imagine if they ask you two more times. My thought would be, *What in the world? Why are they asking this? Of course I love them.* Now they comment saying, "It is not enough. I want you to show me with your actions."

Peter had denied Jesus three times before Jesus was put to death. After Jesus was resurrected, he came back to the apostles, and on this occasion, Peter was to be brought back into the fold. To show his love for Jesus, Peter was to feed his lambs, take care of his sheep, and feed his sheep. Peter was to come away from his fear and take the lead to share the good news with God's people at that time. Peter loved Jesus and was forgiven his sin. He was to repent and show his love by following Jesus' commands.

I am a sinner and have been forgiven through the blood of Jesus. I wonder if Jesus came to me and said, "Ken, do you love me?" What would he command when I said, "Of course I love you?" What if he asked three times or as many times as I have denied him? It may take a while. I do know what he has said. "Love God, love one another, and serve the world." He has told me to share the good news and to make disciples. I am to glorify him in all I do and say.

What would he ask of you? What would he ask of me? Are we doing it on a daily basis? What if he asks us? He has already proven his love for us.

Do You Play Solitaire
with Christianity?

Praise be to the God and Father of our Lord Jesus Christ,
the Father of compassion and the God of all comfort, who
comforts us in all our troubles, so that we can comfort those
in any trouble with the comfort we ourselves have received
from God.

2 Corinthians 1:3–4

Let us not give up meeting together, as some are in the habit
of doing, but let us encourage one another—and all the more
as you see the Day approaching.

Hebrews 10:25

I was in the hospital for four days. Hospitals can be very lonely
places. The only people you see are the medical professionals, and
there is really no conversation, love, or encouragement. Of course,
they try. My wife came and sat with me. Now that was love, encouragement, and reassurance. I also know that while I was in the hospital, my church family was praying for me, and also the Christian
friends I have met on online were praying. I received phone calls
and visits from some of my church and spiritual family. When I
got home, I received phone calls and visits from many of the same
people. I did not go through this experience alone. I had God, and

I had God's people with me every step of the way encouraging, comforting, praying, and loving me back to health.

As Christians, we are not called to believe Jesus is our Savior and then just hang out by ourselves all the time. Some believe they do not even need a church family. Right or wrong, I believe what it says in Hebrews 10:25, "Let us not give up meeting together." As the day approaches for Jesus' return, we need to be awake; we need to be doing his will. Jesus tells us we are to make disciples, encourage, and comfort one another. We can't interact with one another if we are playing a game of solitaire. We are to teach and call each other back when we start to go astray. How can one do that alone?

It is easy for me to think of myself as a great Christian when I am alone reading and thinking how wonderful the Bible is. I can really get into a mindset where I think I am one with God. Well, I am because prayer and meditation are so necessary. But as a Christian, I am to put that knowledge and love to use and be involved with others on many levels. So forget the game of solitaire, put the cards away, meet together in the church with its many activities, get involved in the community and our families, and let's do as God commanded. He said, "Meet together, encourage, comfort, exhort, love, and pray for each other." It feels great on both ends and fulfills the commands of God. What a cool command, fellowship with others. Deal me in.

Do You Want to Be Happy?

Blessed is he whose transgressions are forgiven, whose sins
are covered. Blessed is the man whose sin the LORD does not
count against him and in whose spirit is no deceit.

Psalm 32:1

Did you ever watch the TV program *Who Wants to Be a Millionaire?*
Did you ever think about the title of the show? Isn't that title a rhetorical question? It seems my chapter title and the question I pose is
a lot like that show's title, extremely rhetorical. Okay, that said, let
me get to the point. In 2003, I bought a new car, a 2003 Mustang
GT, eight-cylinder, five-speed, with leather seats. A midlife-crisis
mobile.

Well, one morning about a week after buying the car, I pulled
onto the highway, moved from the right to left lane, and zipped
past a slow-moving car. Shortly thereafter, a state trooper decided
to pull me over and express how good the acceleration was on my
new car, so I thought. He came over to my window and said, "You
made that car look like it was standing still." (I sure did.) He asked
me where I was going in such a hurry and then said, "Slow down.
I will give you a break this time."

Don't you love getting a break? One time I called a company
when I got a bill with a late fee. I spoke to the representative who
was very kind and seemed to enjoy our conversation. He said, "You

know what? I am going to waive your late fee this time." Hmm, another break. I have had many breaks in my life. I always feel relieved and grateful when I get a break. My transgressions have been forgiven. I will tell you what, speeding tickets and late fees are expensive. So when they are waived and forgiven, I am both grateful and happy.

The price of sin is death. It is also a one-way ticket to the lake of fire, eternity with the father of lies, and eternal separation from God. My sin debt must be paid. No one will say, "I will just cut you some slack." There is something I must first do; I must believe that Jesus took on my sin. Jesus was beaten and mocked, and he submissively gave up his own life for me. He paid my sin debt. I now believe that Jesus died for my sins. My one-way ticket to the lake of fire has been torn in half, and I was told that my trip was cancelled because of Jesus' sacrifice and my faith in him. I now get to spend eternity with God, the author of life and love. I will spend eternity with Jesus, the Savior of the world. I have again been pardoned, this time on an awesome and phenomenal level. I have been given assurance in eternal salvation, I have been pardoned and forgiven, and I have been given grace and mercy. You know what? I am extremely grateful and happy. So let me ask you again: do you want to be happy?

Don't Forget to Turn
On the Lights

Be joyful always; pray continually; give thanks in all circumstances, for this is God's will for you in Christ Jesus. Do not put out the Spirit's fire.

1 Thessalonians 5:16–19

One Sunday, when my friend Pat was preaching, he read a passage that really caught my attention: "Do not put out the Spirit's fire" (1 Thessalonians 5:19). God's will for me is to be joyful always, pray continually, and give thanks in all circumstances. Therefore, as a master of the obvious, I figured out that if I practice joy, continual prayer, and give thanks in all circumstances, I would not put out the Holy Spirit's fire. Okay then, easy enough. Yeah right.

Well as a master of the obvious, I also can deduce that when I don't practice joy, continual prayer, and giving thanks in all circumstances, I am putting out the fire. I am turning out the lights on the Holy Spirit. I am alone in the dark. The dark is a scary place to be when I am all alone. I have no sight, focus, or direction. I am not seeing or hearing God; my heart is calloused.

When discouraged, depressed, let down, abandoned, fearful, self-conscious, or isolated, I am again alone in the dark. The fire has been put out. When ego takes over and I tell God, "I've got it from here," there is usually trouble. Ego is easing God out. No light equals no God. I have shut him out. When one believes that God can't help me, God won't help me, God is just a fantasy anyway, a crutch for the weak; that, my friend, is darkness. Which is a quiet, sightless place. That is the devil's playground.

The fire needs to be constantly stoked. The fire needs to be bright and ablaze. God calls me to be joyful always, in continual prayer, and giving thanks in all circumstances. Wow, that is a tall order that takes maturity. That is what we are called to do, mature. We are called to pray, meditate, read God's word in the Bible, and participate in mature Christian relationships that are filled with love and accountability. This task may not be easy, but it is more than worth it. Knowing God personally is better than just knowing of him.

Jesus gave his life so I could be reconciled with our Father. Jesus also gave his life to pay for my sins; his resurrection gave me life, eternal life, with him and our Father. The Spirit was sent to me by God to have him live within me always. That should bring me, not only joy, but great joy. Praying continually, giving what I am doing to God throughout the day. Giving him glory in all I do, saying please and thank you throughout the day, and talking to the one who loves me most, God. If I come upon tough circumstances, God is there with me. If he brings me to it, he will bring me through it. This I have been assured of. So why do I find this so difficult?

My job now is to live one day at a time, meditating and soaking in this beautiful passage from Paul to the Thessalonians. I need to make it part of my life. I need to change my way of thinking and incorporate this as part of my thinking. I don't need to regret the past or fear the future.

Today, I want to remember to turn the lights on. Stoke the fire; make a big blaze of the Spirit. I want to remember to live in joy for the blessings in my life. I want to talk to God continually, giving him praise and glory in all I do. I want to practice his kindness with all I meet. When the going gets tough, I thank him for being right by my side. This is spiritual maturity at its finest.

Don't Give Up

Are they servants of Christ? I know I sound like a madman, but I have served him far more! I have worked harder, been put in prison more often, been whipped times without number, and faced death again and again. Five different times the Jewish leaders gave me thirty-nine lashes. Three times I was beaten with rods. Once I was stoned. Three times I was shipwrecked. Once I spent a whole night and a day adrift at sea. I have traveled on many long journeys. I have faced danger from rivers and from robbers. I have faced danger from my own people, the Jews, as well as from the Gentiles. I have faced danger in the cities, in the deserts, and on the seas. And I have faced danger from men who claim to be believers but are not. I have worked hard and long, enduring many sleepless nights. I have been hungry and thirsty and have often gone without food. I have shivered in the cold, without enough clothing to keep me warm.

2 Corinthians 11:23–27

I am a baseball fan and was amazed at a player named Don Baylor. Don was hit by pitches more times than any other player in the history of baseball. Don would get hit but never look hurt; he wouldn't even flinch. He would just trot down to first base. I thought, *Wow, he is pretty tough.*

Don is tough but no comparison to Paul. Paul endured great hardships in being a Christian. Paul never stopped preaching the good news of Jesus. When Paul was arrested, he kept writing and preaching. When the beatings stopped, he trotted down to first, and he continued to write and preach. After he had been stoned with rocks, what did he do? He wrote and preached. Paul never gave up. Talk about determination and persistence. Talk about persecution.

Paul is the same man who was known as Saul. Saul was a fire-breathing Christian hater. He took Christians right out of their homes. He arrested them and sometimes had them put to death. They were stoned to death right in front of him. After all that, what did God do? He called Paul to lead the Gentiles to salvation. Huh? God decided Saul, a.k.a. Paul, was the man for the job. Paul's persistence, strength, and faith were just what God wanted, and he transformed some of Paul's other qualities into the man Paul became. Paul was shown grace.

Paul was given grace. Imagine that this killer, torturer, and kidnapper of Christians was given God's grace. Grace is an unmerited gift from God through Jesus Christ. God's grace was given freely to Paul. What did Paul do with this grace? He shouted it from the rooftops. He was grateful. He was willing and endured anything and everything that came his way. Why else would this man want to endure such punishment? He loved God. He loved the good news of Jesus Christ. He loved grace, that's why.

So are we here in this country persecuted for spreading the message of Jesus Christ? Am I personally persecuted? Do I get my feelings hurt? Do I get discouraged? Things don't go my way? Is it too hard for me to be a Christian? I need to look at Paul as an example of a man who was given grace and despite it all never stopped preaching, teaching, and writing until his dying day. He was only a man, and I am a man who has also been given grace.

Today, I want to share the good news of grace. I won't let the little things discourage me. I am so grateful for being forgiven. I don't want anything to stand in my way of passing on the good news of Jesus. Jesus died on the cross so I could be reconciled with God. He was resurrected so I would have eternal life. After all I have done, God loves me enough to give me an unmerited gift of grace. It is yours for the asking as well. Don't give up. Trot down to first.

Duplex Cookies

But blessed are your eyes, because they see; and your ears, because they hear.

Matthew 13:16

As I mentioned earlier, I have become a master of the obvious. Now that may sound easy, but not for me. Sometimes I just don't see the obvious. Sometimes I have to learn things the hard way. I am a graduate of the University of Hard Knocks. Do you know if you don't drink you won't get drunk? Insightful, huh? Took me a while to get that one. Do you know you can only live in this day? Uh huh, that took a while too. I spent some time regretting the past and worrying about the future. I have even tried to put the wrong shoe on the wrong foot. Hair wax is not good on a toothbrush.

When I was in kindergarten, we always had snack time. I loved snack time (still do). We usually had milk and duplex cookies. Duplex cookies are the ones with a chocolate top and a vanilla bottom, depending on which way you want to hold it. They also have vanilla cream in the middle. I always hated those cookies. They tasted and smelled like clay. Even into my twenties, I wouldn't eat them. One day, it just came to me, when I was in kindergarten before snack time was playtime. I usually played with clay; I didn't wash my hands before I ate my cookies. Do you know, when you thoroughly wash your hands, duplex cookies are delicious and smell like cookies? Eureka! An "ah ha" moment. I am a master of the obvious.

In my life, I have had times where life just seemed overwhelming. I have also harbored anger and resentments. I thought nothing was going right and probably never would. I could be such a victim. There has been pain that I thought would never subside. Do you know when I pray, meditate, and study God's word in the Bible, worry, resentments, anger, and fear seem to vanish. Isn't that incredible? So let me see, if I study God's Word, put his word into my actions, thoughts, and my life, things get better and more manageable. When I pray and meditate on God's Word, I am assured I am not alone and God will help me handle anything. He will not leave me nor forsake me. I am having another "ah ha" moment. Hey, I have a great idea. Why don't I study God's Word, pray, and meditate every day? Wow, I am a real genius. Insight at its finest. Now I am thinking, *See that? Another stroke of genius from my master-of-the-obvious skills.*

Today, I will pray and meditate; I will also study and live God's Word in my life. I will take life one day at a time, and I will wash my hands thoroughly before eating any duplex cookies.

Faith without Works

But wilt thou know, O vain man, that faith without works is dead?

James 2:20 (KJV)

I am a man who has been saved by God through the death and resurrection of his Son, Jesus. My faith is demonstrated through my works, which are an act of love to me. Grace is the price Jesus paid on the cross. When I reflect about Jesus, I see his attributes: love, mercy, teaching, and his selfless act of becoming a man and dying for all of us. I am awed. Works become a joy. When I read James 2:20, I think, *Why wouldn't I share the gifts that God has graciously blessed me with? Why wouldn't I love those around me as Jesus demonstrated?* For me, it does not even have to be a command. I do it out of sheer love for our Father, Son, and Holy Spirit.

I have been baptized through emersion because I love Jesus. All I do is out of love for him. Works, actions, and love are all my desire due to the grace given me. Jesus suffered persecution, torture, and hatred and was ridiculed, mocked, spit on, and nailed to a cross because he wore my sin. Our Father could not bear to see the sin on him and had to turn from the sin his Son bore. Jesus did this all for me and you. Sin, I did it, we did it, and he paid for it. Why? Because of a love that is beyond my comprehension. Is my work a chore? Is my ministry a chore? Is my forgiving and loving a chore? It may be difficult at times, but I do it because I love God. He doesn't even have to tell me. I am willing. I want to; I want others to see what I see when I look at the grace of the cross.

If I do no works, I consider myself ungrateful and taking my Savior for granted. I love him and will do all I can. Please, Father, help me to see where I can help, where I am needed, and where I can do your will. What should I do next? Please make my works pleasing to you. Not for brownie points or because I am afraid not to, simply because I love you and want to please you, and in my own small way thank you. Thank you for loving me. Thank you for loving us. Thank you for saving me and one day bring me to your awesome presence, to find me and us pleasing in your sight. I come to you in Jesus' name.

Feed Your Heart

But solid food is for the mature, who by constant use have
trained themselves to distinguish good from evil.

Hebrews 5:14

How many times have you heard, "Eat healthy and exercise"? I
have heard that a lot lately after recently spending some time in
the hospital with chest pains. I think doctors, nurses, friends, family, and well-meaning people have to take a class practicing these
very words. "Eat healthy and exercise" is a mantra of sorts, and
people seem to enjoy saying it. The body needs proper nourishment, it needs to move, and it was built to move. The body is like
a well-oiled machine; it needs to be maintained. Do you think we
can come up with any more clichés on what the body needs? Well
apparently, eating right and exercising is the healthy and mature
thing to do to get the best results.

What about Christians? Are we eating right and exercising? I
don't mean caloric intake; I mean spiritual food. We know how to
get the most out of our bodies by feeding it right. What are we feeding our hearts, minds, and souls? Television, movies, politics, pornography, media's anger with government, boredom, self-righteous
anger, the need to be right, resentment, old wounds, and the list
goes on. If this is all it is being nourished with, our hearts, minds,
and souls won't be very healthy. How do we exercise what we take

in? What are we putting out? Is it the same as the list above? Are we putting out what we are taking in? If that's what we are taking in and demonstrating, we won't be very spiritually healthy.

Imagine taking in the Bible daily, the love story from God. Love, grace, forgiveness, peace, sacrifice, submission, and service will be our byproducts. If we take in proper spiritual nourishment and practice spiritual disciplines, we will be treating ourselves well. So watch what you feed your heart, because your tongue will let you and others know what it has been fed. Our attitudes and behavior will also be affected by a well-fed heart.

Finding the Narrow Road

Enter through the narrow gate. For wide is the gate and broad
is the road that leads to destruction, and many enter through
it. But small is the gate and narrow the road that leads to life
and only a few find it.

Matthew 7: 13–14

When I was camping in Canada, on two occasions there were some
very narrow paths through the woods and hills that took us from
one lake to another lake. This is called portaging. Me, I just call it
insanity. We had to carry our backpacks, canoes, and all our gear
through these winding narrow paths, and it seemed to me all uphill
paths. My friend Don named two of the many paths we took Big
Agony and Little Agony. There is nothing little about agony. Well,
to get to the next lake, these trails are necessary to get where you
want to go. They were not easy, but when we got to the lakes, we
could see crystal clear lakes and beautiful mountains.

Have you ever thought about the path to heaven? A small gate
and narrow road lead to life, and only a few find it. When we were
on our camping trip, we had maps to get us where we wanted to
go. On our trip through life and on to heaven, we have our Bible,
the Word of God, as our map. We are told our path is narrow. Jesus
is the small, narrow path. He is also the narrow gate we must enter.
Jesus is the only way that leads to life. Find him, and you have

found the right path. Sometimes the narrow path is not easy; there are temptations and distractions along the way. There are sin and temptations calling out. There are times we just want to give in. There are times we do give in, and we have to find that small gate and narrow path again.

Heaven is even more beautiful than what I have seen on my camping trips in Canada, I am told in the Bible. I can only imagine what it will be like. So I will continue to portage the road to my happy destiny, slowly and deliberately following the path that leads to Jesus. Sometimes our burdens are many and heavy, so we can help each other carry the burdens and we can also bring our burdens to God. Don't let your burdens stop you. Trudge if you have to. Don't let sin, temptation, and distractions stop you on the road. Keep your eyes fixed on the road and on Jesus. The portage to Jesus is well worth it.

Follow Me

Come, follow me," Jesus said, "and I will make you fishers
of men.

Matthew 4:19

There was a time in my life when I could not go without drinking
alcohol. I hated myself. My family and friends were afraid of what
I was doing to myself. They really didn't know how to stop what
I was doing to them or me. I was hurting all who loved me. They
didn't understand what I was going through. They didn't believe
me when I said I was sorry, but I truly was sorry; I just couldn't
stop doing what I was doing. My apologies got old and stale. I felt
life was no longer worth living. I asked God at night to let me die;
I was hurting those around me and those who loved me. A man I
met on a navy ship who was a member of a twelve-step program
and personally knew God said, "Follow me, and I will show you
a life without alcohol. I will show you a better way of life. I will
show you a life beyond your wildest dreams. I know where to find
recovery and God." My meaning for life has changed; I enjoy life
and the gifts I have been so richly blessed with because I followed
this man. I have found a life beyond my wildest dreams.

The apostles followed Jesus when he said, "Come, follow me
and I will make you fishers of men," (Matthew 4:19). Some were
fishermen and understood his metaphor. Jesus sought men to assist

him in bringing other men and women to our Father. God loves us and wants us with him. He wants to help us and encourage us. He wants us to love him and each another. He wants us to help others, encourage others, but most of all, he wants us to share the saving message of Jesus with others. We are the fishermen. So strap on your fishing vest, get your best fishing bait, put on your fishing hat, and follow Jesus. His words are found in the Bible. We can use them, and we can use our testimony as a witness from our hearts. Let people know they don't have to hurt. They don't have to be alone, and they don't have to carry guilt and resentment any longer. Let them know they don't have to die; they can have eternal life with our Father.

Jesus said in Matthew 16:24 to his disciples, "If anyone would come after me, he must deny himself and take up his cross and follow me." As you make a life of loving, serving, and helping one another, you will find peace and joy in your life and theirs. This can be a full-time job, but it is the best one. It is like a feast: eat it up, drink it up. Love feels great.

There are many fish out there. They are everywhere, so cast a net and use good bait. Don't use judgment and fear, use love, grace, joy, and mercy. Being a Christian does not have to be scary and solemn. Life with Jesus in your heart can be a party. Follow him. Although the world may not share this sentiment, they are not living in my heart. My heart is where God lives, the counselor lives, and his Son's atoning death and resurrection live.

We share with those who have ears that will hear, those with eyes will see. In John 10:27, "My sheep listen to my voice; I know them, and they follow me." We are also likened to sheep. We know his voice; we should follow him. I want to follow Jesus to the cross. He gave his life so that I could have a life. He made it possible to be closer to his Father, our Father. He made it possible to share eternity without pain, suffering, anger, guilt, shame, hatred, and so on. If you want what the Bible offers, then Jesus invites us to follow him.

Friendship

Some men came, bringing to him a paralytic, carried by four of them. Since they could not get him to Jesus because of the crowd, they made an opening in the roof above Jesus and, after digging through it, lowered the mat the paralyzed man was lying on. When Jesus saw their faith, he said to the paralytic, "Son, your sins are forgiven."

Mark 2:3–5

Imagine having a friend who is paralyzed and hearing Jesus, a man who performs miracles, is in town. You and some other friends believe his message and have faith Jesus can heal your friend. You put him on a mat; you all smile and tell him, "Today is the day. You are going to walk again. We are going to take you to Jesus, who can heal you." Can you imagine the look on your friend's face? Is he excited or just in disbelief? Maybe he has never walked before. But he anticipates being able to walk today. You get him to the destination, and there is no way in; the crowds around the doors are like trying to buy Super Bowl tickets on game day. Your friend says, "Oh well, you tried." Or he is just discouraged and says, "Thanks anyway" or "I knew it was too good to be true." Who knows what the man or woman might say? But the friends are real friends, and they look at each other; then one smiles mischievously and says, "I have an idea. Let's go up on the roof, dig through it, and lower him down to Jesus. He will have to see him." Jesus saw him all right, but he also saw the love of the friends and the faith they had. Jesus said, "Pick up your mat and walk." Dancing, the five of them walked off together. Probably hugging, skipping, and running with joy and tears in their eyes, thanks on their lips and in their hearts.

Friendships run deep in the Bible. David and Jonathan had quite a friendship. Jonathan, the son of Saul, who was trying to kill David, served with his father but was true to his friendship with David. They made covenants together. Jonathan told David whatever he wanted he would do. David took care of Jonathan's crippled son when Jonathan died. Jesus asked his friend John from the cross to care for his mother, Mary. Of course, John said *yes*.

Jesus gave the command to love God and love one another. He said, "Love one another as yourself." I have to ask myself what length I would go for a friend. Jesus is my friend. He gave up his life, he took on my sin, and he took my place. When it was time to pay for my sin, Jesus said, "I will pay. I am aware of the payment needed. Despite the torture, cruelty, taking on the sin of the world, and a slow horrible death, I will pay. Ken Jones is my friend. I will pay his price. Jesus doesn't love my sin, but he loves me. There is no greater love than giving your life for another. Wow, what grace, mercy, forgiveness, and love he has for his friends.

I ask myself how deep my friendships run. What am I willing to do? Jesus taught me he was willing to die for me. Friendship also means picking up the mat, carrying my friend, digging through a roof, sliding my friend down, having faith, going to any length, being available to care for someone's mother, washing feet, and even giving my life for my friends. What an example. What a benchmark.

I want my friends to know about Jesus. I talk to them and send them e-mails like this. I want them to know they don't have to live in the dark, they don't have to be paralyzed, they don't have to ever be alone, they don't have to do things on their own, learn that fear is their choice, see that death does not have to be a mystery or something to be feared. I love my friends. I want to get to know my friends better. I want to love more, forgive more, and show mercy more. I want to know how they are, what they are thinking, what I can do to help, how I can celebrate with them; share meals, ideas, and insights; and share their joys as well as sorrows. I want to be available. Do I call my friends enough, see them enough, and give of myself enough?

So today, I will make this a priority to follow Jesus' command to love one another as myself, reach out, and to pay attention to where I am needed and to not think of my needs first, but my friends'. Who are my friends? My neighbors are. Who are my neighbors? You know, Jesus told us, everyone. You are my neighbor. You are my friend. Reach out to a friend today. Make a new friend today. We all need them. Grow in Christian fellowship and help the fellowship grow. Bring glory to God in your friendships today.

Fuzzy

Turn your ear to listen to me; rescue me quickly. Be my rock
of protection, a fortress where I will be safe.

Psalm 31:2

When I was about four or five, I had a good friend named Fuzzy.
Fuzzy was a neighbor about my age. We were always together. I
don't know if that was his real name, but that is the name I knew
my best friend by. Fuzzy couldn't speak clearly. He must have had
slow speech development, because he had a speech impediment
although I didn't understand his words we sure could communicate. That was okay with me. I like to talk, and Fuzzy liked to listen. Fuzzy would just sort of follow me around and smile. Also at
that age, I was quite the adventurer. One day, I took Fuzzy on one
of my adventures.

Today's adventure led us to a hole, where a house was going to
be built. My plan was to go into the hole and play, then go home.
Fuzzy was too chicken to go into the hole with me; he was not
quite as adventurous or maybe just a bit smarter than me. Well,
I couldn't get out of the hole. I knew my mother or father could
figure this out. So I sent Fuzzy after my mother. Dad was at work,
and Mom was at home. I imagine Fuzzy knocked on the door,
tugged on her shirtsleeve, and somehow convinced my mother to
go with him. My mother, having no idea what Fuzzy was saying,

instinctively knew she should follow him. Now it was Fuzzy and Mom to the rescue.

There have been many times I have gone in prayer. Just like Fuzzy, I don't know how to ask for what I need. I just tug, and what I am trying to say makes no sense. I loved Fuzzy; I always knew what he was saying. God loves us. He knows what we are saying and what we need. The Holy Spirit interprets for us. He listens to our hearts. He comes to the rescue even though I am not sure what to say or quite how to say it. Sometimes the prayer is simply, "Help." I am safe in God's arms.

Of course, when I go to God, sometimes I want to be specific and help him out with deciding my needs. But he knows better. When I was in the hole, I really didn't care how my mother got me out; I just wanted out. That is how I need to go in prayer to God. I have situations where I need his help, guidance, and rescue. I have no suggestions, just a need. I grunt, groan, and tug. He knows exactly what to do and when to do it. I simply need to go to him.

God has rescued me on more than one occasion. When I am lost and don't know what to do, when I am in one of life's holes, when fear sets in, when anger takes over, when I am hurt, depressed, mired in self-absorption, or I see no way out, I go to God. God loves me. He is all powerful. He knows all my needs. He knows exactly where I am. He can hear my innermost desires and comes to the rescue.

Today, when I take one of my ill-advised adventures into my head alone, I will turn to the one that loves me for rescue. God knows the way around in there and the way back out. He will then help me decide my next move, bringing glory to him in all I do. God bless Fuzzy, wherever he is.

George

I would not forget you! See, I have written your name on the palms of my hands.

Isaiah 49:15–16

A number of years ago, I had a good friend named George. George and I were in the same organization. He was in his late seventies. George was originally from the Bronx. He worked as a bagger at Publix grocery store and as a school crossing guard. He had a great sense of humor and was quite gruff. George and I had lunch and breakfast a few times in the year I had known him.

One night, I was chairing a meeting with about one hundred in attendance. I had asked George to read something. So when it was time, I announced that my good friend George was going to read. He got up, and everyone laughed. He got to the microphone and said, "Hello, my name is Charlie." My good friend George was named Charlie. I was quite embarrassed, not only because from my slip at the meeting, but because I had been calling Charlie George for about a year. He never corrected me.

I asked Charlie later why he never corrected me. He said he had been called worse things. He said, "George is fine. You can call me George or Charlie, just not late for supper." It didn't seem to matter.

Isn't it good that God knows who we really are? In Isaiah 49, God tells those in Jerusalem that he will never forget them. He has their names written on his hand. God also said in Jeremiah 1:5, "I knew you before I formed you in your mother's womb." God will never call us by the wrong name. God will never leave us, forsake us, or forget us. God always knew George as Charlie.

When we go to our Father, he knows us. He knows our needs, our desires, and our sins. He knows all about us. He knows what we have done and what we are going to do, even with the free will he has given us. He doesn't have to guess. So when we go to him, we don't have to be ashamed. He already knows and is patiently and lovingly waiting for us.

Today, I will go to my Father, knowing he always knew me and still does and always will. I will never surprise him. I can go to him with anything. If he knows already, why do we have to go to him? We go to him because he loves us and wants our fellowship with him. He knows our name, and we know his. Prayer is our conversation with our all-knowing and all-loving Father.

GIGO

The acts of the sinful nature are obvious: sexual immorality,
impurity and debauchery; idolatry and witchcraft; hatred,
discord, jealousy, fits of rage, selfish ambition, dissensions,
factions and envy; drunkenness, orgies, and the like.

Galatians 5:19–21

Do you remember the old computer expression GIGO, Garbage
In, Garbage Out? If you input garbage data, you will get garbage
information. The idea of input got me thinking of what I put into
my heart and mind. There was a time in my life I put bad data in.
The data had nothing to do with God, and it simply had to do with
my pleasures. What are we watching, looking at, reading, listening
to, and who are we spending time with? What information are
we feeding ourselves? GIGO. If we put garbage in our hearts and
minds, that is what comes out of our mouths and what we demonstrate in our actions.

A life of reading the Bible, attending church, being around
godly people, prayer, meditation, and following God's will gives us
words and actions that have to do with God, and this is what we
will demonstrate. Accepting God in our lives, Jesus in our hearts
and letting the Holy Spirit dwell in us and do its work in our soul
will produce a good lifestyle. Therefore, what we take in, we will
put out. GIGO—God in, God out.

But the fruit of the Spirit is love, joy, peace, patience, kindness, goodness, faithfulness, gentleness and self-control.

Galatians 5:22

Whatever is true, whatever is noble, whatever is right, whatever is pure, whatever is lovely, whatever is admirable—if anything is excellent or praiseworthy—think about such things.

Philippians 4:8

If we take God into our hearts, minds, and souls, we will put out love, grace, mercy, forgiveness, and the fruits of the Spirit. This is because we are becoming more like Christ and emulating him. My friend Jimmy Pruitt says we leak out what we are full of. If we are filled up with love and grace, that's what we will leak out. Leaking is demonstrating and speaking. My goal is to leak God. GIGO—God in, God out. I want to speak of God's love and grace and want that to show in my actions. If that is what I am putting into my life, that is what is going to come out.

So GIGO takes on a whole new meaning, God in, God out. Now I am reading God's Word, praying, meditating, surrounding myself with godly people, and reading godly material. This will help me put out the fruits of the Spirit in my speech, actions, and lifestyle.

Gilligan the Encourager

Joseph, a Levite from Cyprus, whom the apostles called Barnabas (which means Son of Encouragement).

Acts 4:36

After Paul and Silas came out of the prison, they went to Lydia's house, where they met with the brothers and encouraged them. Then they left.

Acts: 16:40

Do you remember the skipper's little buddy, Gilligan, on *Gilligan's Island?* Any problem Skipper, the Professor, Mary-Ann, Ginger, or the Howells had, Gilligan was always there to cheer them up and encourage them. Whenever anyone was losing hope of never getting off the island, Gilligan would be there with encouragement and his smile. No matter what the problems: the Professor turning a coconut into a radio, Ginger worrying about her looks, Mary-Ann worrying she wasn't as pretty as Ginger, the Howells worrying about their money, or any of the Skipper's concerns, Gilligan was there to encourage them.

In the Bible, Paul was an encourager. Even after getting out of prison, getting whipped, shipwrecked, and beaten, he encouraged Christians to follow Jesus. Paul never stopped encouraging. He called people saints, he told them he was praying for them, and he told them he couldn't wait to be with them. Paul also let people know when they were not being obedient to God. But he always let them know they could change. He reminded them of the awesome grace of God and the sacrifice he made of his own Son, Jesus. He told them the good news that Jesus came to Earth to teach, show people who God was, and ultimately die and be resurrected so that we could be with our Father, God.

Don't we all need some encouragement sometimes? Things don't go well. We get lost in the daily ho hum. Bills, traffic, work, problems at home, divorce, problems with children, and all kinds of hurts. Do we sit and worry? Do we sometimes ask, "Does God really care about me and my problems? Is God listening? Is Jesus really coming back? Was he really here?" There are those who have asked these very questions over the years. I have been one of them at times. God's love and encouragement from others have gotten me through all those times.

Loving people also means I need to encourage them. Encouragement that God really does care. He cares a great deal. How much? Look to the cross. He loves us more than we can possibly comprehend. He is always listening. He always knows what to do, how to do it, and when to do it. Trust in him. He will come through. He always does. We get encouragement when we study God's Word, when we speak to him in prayer, and when we listen to him through his word in the Bible and through meditation in prayer. Encouragement comes when we attend church fellowship, Bible study, and small groups. Encouragement comes when we obey God's commands, serve him, and when we encourage one another. Encouragement comes when we love God, love one another, and serve the world.

Today, I will look to see where encouragement is needed. Today I will encourage others to know that God loves them. I will help others find hope. Hope is something we all need. So is faith. I will help encourage others to find faith and hope. I will bring a smile, a handshake, a hug, a kind word, and encouragement with me wherever I go.

God Can Use You

Josiah was eight years old when he became king and he
reigned in Jerusalem thirty-one years.

2 Kings 22:1

When I was eight years old, I was in the second grade, anxiously
waiting for the final bell. I would go home and run around some
trees in the front yard with my little, long-haired, black mutt,
Spooky, hot on my heels. I would play with either of my friends,
Ray Ray or Fuzzy, or my imaginary friend, Toto. When I was eight,
my mother or father still cut my meat and I had a bedtime.

Josiah was eight years old and was the king of Jerusalem. God
picked him and led him. God used an eight-year-old boy to rule
a nation. Being from the United States, we don't have kings, and
I guess God just didn't need me to be king. I have thought in the
past that God couldn't use people like me, that I was just a common, ordinary guy. Well, I found out God uses common, ordinary
guys and gals.

God used a murderer, Moses, to free the Jewish slaves from
Egypt; a murderer and adulterer named David to rule nations; and
used another murderer, Paul, to preach to the Gentiles and write
a majority of the New Testament in the Bible. There are many
examples in the Bible. God used a common, young girl, Mary,
to mother God himself in the form of man. As a matter of fact,

he used an ex-drunk to write these reflections. It doesn't matter what we have done. God can and will use us if we let him or if he chooses. God changes lives, God makes kings, and God makes the common extraordinary. Give your life to God. Be prepared. You could be next.

God Loves Me, Warts and All

> For you created my inmost being; you knit me together in
> my mother's womb.
>
> Psalm 139:13

My friend Harold used to say, "God loves me, warts and all." I used to think that was a funny thing to say. However, isn't it true? There was another man I knew, Terry. He used to say, "God is nuts about me." What interesting comments to come from two men who at one time struggled with their demons, whose lives were ruined and then God brought them back to the world of the living and a world of sanity, to help others in their struggles.

When I look in the mirror, I see some extra weight. I have tried to look good in front of employers, girls I tried to impress when I was single and younger, and other people I wanted to look good in front of. And I just generally felt that I didn't meet their standards. I am now leading a small group. I was in another one for over three years. That leader is so much better, and I know there are people in my group that could step up and do so much better than me. I love the line, and I realize I am still a work in progress in everything I do. God does get a kick out of me. That's my line.

I don't know what Jesus was thinking when Peter said, "I would fight to the death for you." Jesus knew that Peter would deny him three times. Jesus also knew Peter's heart. Do you suppose he knew

Peter really meant it when he said it? When Moses was called to lead the Israelites out of bondage, he had five excuses why he wasn't the guy for the job. Who me? God said, "Yeah, you." Well, that isn't exactly the way the conversation went, but that is how I heard it. When Jesus washed the feet of the apostles, Peter seemed embarrassed. He must have felt as if he should be washing Jesus' feet.

I am a work in progress. I am on a journey with a long way to go. I am striving daily for progress. People have been gentle and patient with me, which I appreciate. God has been patient with me. I have been patient with others.

Just who is it I have to please? It is God. He knew me before he knitted me in my mother's womb. He knew my sins, my failures, and my shortcomings before I even got here. He was ready. He sent Jesus over two thousand years earlier to atone for the sins of my life. God knows me and loves me. He is patient. He isn't concerned what my waist size is or how many wrinkles I have. He cares that I suit up and show up for life and bring glory to him in all I do. He knows me at my shabbiest. But God doesn't mind, because I am coming to him and thanking him for planning my day with him.

So today, I place myself in front of my Creator, our Father, who loves me, warts and all, as I do my very best and expect that the progress of the day will be sufficient for this day. I will remember I am a work in progress and not strive to be the best, but the best I can for now. I am on a journey. I will take it one step and one day at a time. Just keep suiting up, showing up, and be ready for duty.

I am glad God is patient with me. I know he gets a kick out of me, watching me whirl all around, trying to do better. I am his, he knows me, he knows my heart, and he knows what I am doing. He is the one I want to please. I am accepted, warts and all.

God, Are You Sure?

"What was it he said to you?" Eli asked. "Do not hide it from me. May God deal with you, be it ever so severely, if you hide from me anything he told you." So Samuel told him everything, hiding nothing from him. Then Eli said, "He is the LORD; let him do what is good in his eyes."

1 Samuel 3:17–18

There have been times in my life I have brought different problems and situations to God because I didn't know what to do. I have read the Bible and listened for answers I wanted to hear that I didn't think were right. Imagine me thinking I might know better than God. That said, and no lightning, I will proceed. I would ask myself, "Does God have all the details on this one?" As I have gone through life's problems and situations and have given them to God, not only was the problem or situation solved, I have come away a better and stronger person because of God's intervention. God can and should be trusted in all situations. He does know all the details even better than I do, imagine that.

God has been trusted throughout the Bible in situations when I have thought, "Well why would he do that?" Abraham brought Isaac to the mountain to sacrifice him just as God asked. Abraham trusted God without questioning him. Isaac was not sacrificed, and God taught us all a valuable lesson on faith through him. Job went through terrible trials. Job didn't lose faith, and God rewarded him tenfold for his faith. There are many examples such as these in the Bible. Even more notable is Jesus, who sacrificed himself for the ones he loved, us.

Imagine Eli, whose sons were cheaters and scammers. God not only held the sons accountable, but Eli himself for doing nothing about it, his sin of omission. When God told Eli he and his sons would be punished and put to death on a given time, Eli understood. Did he accept this? Oh yeah, he loved and trusted God. When Samuel told him of the conversation with God that the time had come, Eli didn't wail and complain. He said, "He is the Lord, Let Him do what is good in His eyes" (1 Samuel 3:18). Today, I have to ask myself, "Do I have the faith of Abraham, Job, and Eli? Will I trust and have the faith that is needed when the situation presents itself?"

God's Country

I really enjoyed my most recent seven-day trip to the great out-doors. Five guys from my church and I went camping, canoeing, and fishing in the Canadian boundary waters. We traveled from Ely, Minnesota, into remote Canada, past waterfalls; clear, crisp lakes; rocky mountains; trees; and scenery beyond one's wildest dreams. Good thing my travel mates were my friends, because I am not the greatest outdoorsman.

We had great fellowship and fun. I will tell you, it was cold most of the time. We even saw some ice and snowflakes. At night, I was sleeping in four layers of clothes and a wool cap. Most of the days were fairly warm. Canoeing through the lakes was beautiful, and we had visited many different lakes. At times we would have to portage to get to the next lake. My personal definition of portaging can be summed up in one word, *torture*.

Portaging is when you carry your canoe and gear on your back and walk up and down mosquito-infested hills of rocks, mud, and very narrow paths. This was very difficult for me, stumbling, bum-bling, and mumbling (the other guys didn't mind this as much). I even fell once with the pack on my back, and I got back up and trudged forward again. But when we portaged to the other side, there were waterfalls and the most beautiful lakes and country one can only imagine. The trek was well worth the effort.

But small is the gate and narrow the road that leads to life
and only a few find it.

Matthew 7:14

Narrow is the road. The road can also be bumpy through life,
with hills and valleys, rocks, mud, and all sorts of things that can
trip us up. There have been many times I have gone stumbling,
bumbling, and mumbling through life on the narrow path that
leads to eternal life. I have even fallen and been helped up by my
loving Father, God. He loves me and is very patient. At the end
of this narrow path is heaven and eternal life. I believe this narrow path can be like a portage. I believe it can be a tough trudge
through life at times, but when we get to the other side, we will see
God, Jesus, and our eternal home. It is well worth the portage.

Grandma's Shadow or Black–and–White Cakes

At that time the sign of the Son of Man will appear in the sky, and all the nations of the earth will mourn. They will see the Son of Man coming on the clouds of the sky, with power and great glory. And he will send his angels with a loud trumpet call, and they will gather his elect from the four winds, from one end of the heavens to the other.

Matthew 24: 30–31

For the first twelve years of my life, I had one of God's angels with me. I called her Grandma. I lived in Patchogue, New York, and she lived in the Bronx. She would come to visit us every few weeks and stay a few days. She would usually come by train, and Grandpa would stay home. My anticipation of her visit was at fever pitch. I loved when she would visit. Although things in my home were great, when she came it was even greater. If she came during the day, Mom would walk us to the train station to meet her. In the evening, when Dad was home, we picked her up by car. She was my maternal grandmother, and I loved watching her tell Mom what to do.

My younger sister and brother and I would stand and wait for the train. I couldn't wait to hear the train whistle. When she got off the train, I raced to get to her first and give her a big hug and a kiss. She had her suitcase and a white box with string around it of black-and-white cakes (chocolate icing on one side, vanilla on the other, mmm) from Horn and Hardart's. When we got to the house, we settled her in. Then, as the days went by, she would always read me the comic section of the paper and let me watch her pray if I was quiet. This usually lasted about one hour. She had her rosary beads, prayer cards, and Bible. I was her shadow for the days she was there. I remember sitting, eating social tea cookies with her, and seeing her giving a couple to the dog because he looked at her. She said he had sad eyes. Having Grandma around made my world pure heaven. But what is heaven really like?

> Jesus spoke to them again in parables, saying: "The kingdom of heaven is like a king who prepared a wedding banquet for his son."
>
> Matthew 22:1–2

> And I heard a loud voice from the throne saying, "Now the dwelling of God is with men, and he will live with them. They will be his people, and God himself will be with them and be their God. He will wipe every tear from their eyes. There will be no more death or mourning or crying or pain, for the old order of things has passed away."
>
> Revelation 21:3–4

Jesus will come in the clouds, and we will hear a trumpet. All tears will be wiped away. No more pain or death. Feasts, buffets, treasures. Jesus will be there, and God our Father will be there. If you read Revelation, there is a great description of heaven. Heaven is our home, our final destination. Living in obedience and faith in Jesus is our way in. Jesus told us he is going to prepare our mansions, or rooms, depending on which version of the Bible you have read, and said he will come back to get us. We will not know the hour. We must be ready. Study, prayer, and meditation will teach me what I am to do. My mission statement is to love God, love others, and serve my church, community, and the world.

I am now at fever pitch anticipation for Jesus to return. I love my life, don't get me wrong. I love my wife, children, brother, sister, their families, and my friends but, heaven ... With Grandma, I listened for the train whistle. With Jesus, I am waiting for the trumpet. While I wait, there is work in his name to be done. All my work should bring God glory.

Today I will do the work that God has prepared for me; I will not waste a minute. I will spread the good news wherever and whenever I can. I will love people and serve them. I will obey all of God's commands and repent when I fail. I have looked down the tracks, listening for the whistle. Now I look to the clouds and wait for the sound of the trumpet. I don't know the day or hour, but I know I will hear it. Listen. Do you hear it yet?

Growing in His Trust

For everyone who has will be given more and he will have an abundance. Whoever does not have, even what he has will be taken from him.

Matthew 25:29

When I was about twenty-five years old, I went to a comedy club with some friends. The comedian was a man named Bob. He was hysterical; he made me laugh all night. I laughed so hard my side hurt. I had tears coming out of my eyes. I was sitting at a table in the front row, and the comedian could see me. As he started telling a joke, I started taking a drink and began to laugh. The soda shot right out my nose. The comedian saw this and pointed at me. He said, "Do that again." Later, he started to talk. I went to take a drink, and he looked at me, paused, and said, "I will wait." If I had already taken that drink, I would have given him a repeat performance. He could tell I was having a great time and that I was involved. He singled me out and drew me in the rest of the night. The more I laughed, the more he drew me in. By the end of the night, everyone knew me. At the end of the show, he shook my hand, smiled, and thanked me for being so involved.

God does that. When we get into our faith, when we begin to study, pray meditate, and serve, God gives us more to do. When we serve him, God knows we can be trusted with more, as the parable of talents discusses. God has given us gifts to use for his service to others. We are his hands and feet here on Earth. I notice the more involved I get, the more involved I get. Did you catch that I wasn't repeating myself? When I first started at my church, I just attended. Now I serve in several ministries and counsel in the church as a full-time minister. I believe as the people get to know me and God sees he can trust me with small things, I will be doing more things. Already, he has entrusted me with the counsel of his children. I must respect that trust and give godly counsel.

I love being loved and trusted by God to serve people. They are his children. When they come to me, he trusts me to lead people in his direction. I also love serving God and serving people. Turning back to God and having faith in Jesus has been the best move I have ever made. Over thirty years ago, as a practicing alcoholic, I couldn't be trusted. As the years have gone by, I got closer to God. I have become a Christian. Being a Christian means having faith in him and obeying his commands. James said, "Faith without deeds is not faith at all" (paraphrase). As I continue to grow in my relationship with God and in knowledge of his Word, the more service and ministry he allows me to perform. Service to God and others brings me great joy.

Today, I will continue to serve God, serve others, and be ready for God's next assignment. When he gives it to me, I will thank him for his added trust and love. I will also continue to thank him for allowing me to do these things as they bring me and him great joy.

HKU Alumni Reunion

You may be an alumnus and just don't know it yet.

It's a school of hard knocks for those who leave God's path, a dead-end street for those who hate God's rules.

Proverbs 15:10 (The Message)

Did I ever tell you that I have an advanced degree and graduated with honors from HKU? What a great school. Do you know they don't even need advisors there? I did so well there they have asked me back to teach some of the core classes. Oh by the way, there are no diplomas either, but you do get some bumps, bruises, and scars along the way. Are you also an alumnus of Hard Knocks University (HKU)? Isn't it great that some of us have had to learn things the hard way? No.

Come on, who needs MapQuest, a GPS, or directions? We will find it. I don't know why they put directions in a box of something you have to put together. If I look at the picture on the front of the box, I can figure it out. I know what the experts said, but hey, I can do this. The experts just spout a bunch of mumbo jumbo anyway. I don't need to read the Bible; I can decipher who God is on my own. It is too hard to figure out what those two-thousand-year-old guys were saying anyway. If I am a good guy, they will just let me in heaven anyway. Yeah, right.

Even when I was a young child, it seemed I had to find things out the hard way. When I was about four years old, I was at a place I referred to as the "big pool." My mother always told me to stay close to her, but I would always sneak off and find some adventure. Well, one day, I saw one of the bigger kids jump off the diving board into eight feet of water. Mom said, "Stay away from that." It looked like way too much fun to stay away from. Two lifeguards and a rescue swim later, I realized it probably was not as much fun as it looked. When I was around that same age, Mom said, "Don't go by the stove" and "Don't touch. It is hot." Maybe she shouldn't have said that. The next thing she said was, well, not exactly G-rated, but it was panicked, something about ice and a towel, and I was screaming. She said on another occasion, "Don't play with that knife." The next thing you know, the bandages are out, and Mom and Dad are wondering if we need to go get stitches. They said, "Stay in the yard." Well I have to tell you it was a nice ride home in the police car. Shall I go on?

With all my bumps, scrapes, and scars, HKU wants me back. I know all about trying things the hard way. The hard way and my way seem to be one in the same. No matter what they say, I have a better idea. Usually after I say that, bandages are needed.

The Message version of the Bible actually uses the words *hard knocks* twice, once in Jeremiah 48:11 and then the one I used from Proverbs 15:10. Leaving God's path leads one to hard knocks. The Bible gives directions and commands to live by. God's way may not always be easy, but it is simple. My way is usually the hard way. It also says it is a dead-end path for those who don't follow God's rules. You are not going to believe this, but in my life I have left God's path and didn't follow his rules. Well, a belief in Jesus as my Savior, a baptism, and much ongoing repentance later, I am back on his path and following his rules. Life is so much simpler, wholesome, peaceful, loving, and filled with God's grace and mercy when I simply follow his path and directions.

So, my fellow HKU alumnus, we are holding a class reunion at church this Sunday. Alumni are also meeting between the pages of the Bible, in prayer, meditation, and in wise counsel. Read the directions. Follow Jesus' path and commands. There may be a few bumps and bruises along the way as well, but you are not alone, and God himself will be with us every step of the way to assist and carry us when asked.

Handling Fear

Adam and Eve defied God's command not to eat from the tree of life, and then they hid. God was looking for them and of course knew where they were. God called out to them, and they said they were hiding because they were naked. They knew right from wrong and realized they had chosen wrong. God said, "You ate from the tree I forbid you, didn't you?" Adam blamed Eve, and Eve blamed the snake. Fear caused hiding, lying, and blaming others. On one occasion, David was afraid of his enemy and acted crazy. Did he not trust God? Was that why he felt he had to be deceptive? Abraham was afraid of Abimelech and told him Sarah, his wife, was his sister. More deception and lies. Peter denied knowing Jesus three times out of fear, lying and denying his good friend.

When I was a child, I blamed others for my mistakes, or I just lied and said I didn't know how something happened. I didn't want to fess up. As an adult, I don't always want to fess up, still at times saying, "Hmm, I don't know" or "I didn't know." Fear causes me to freeze, tighten up, obsess sometimes, and sometimes lie.

Jesus knew the fear of his eminent death. In the garden, he sweat blood and asked his Father if he could pass this cup. He knew how his end would come and that it would be tortuous. Jesus took this fear to his Father in prayer. He prayed for strength. It was given. Alone on the cross, he said, "Father, why have you forsaken me?" He is God. He could have gotten down at any time. But out of great love, mercy, and obedience to his Father, he stayed and faced the fear of death for us.

Fear is a motivator—not always a good one. If you are being attacked by an animal and you run, that is a good fear. Staying out of dangerous situations is good. But fear can cause lies, deception, manipulation, loss, and not doing things God would have us do. Fear has cost more lost opportunities than anything. Follow Jesus' example, go to God with fears, pray for strength and wisdom, and especially pray for God's will and power to get through any fearful situation.

Hang On

After six days Jesus took with him Peter, James and John the brother of James, and led them up a high mountain by themselves. There he was transfigured before them. His face shone like the sun, and his clothes became as white as the light. Just then there appeared before them Moses and Elijah, talking with Jesus.

Matthew 17:1–3

Moses led the Israelites through the desert for forty years and never was allowed to enter the promised land. Imagine, this man, who was faithful to God, listening to his very voice and following his direction, was told that because of some lack of faith along the way, he would not be allowed to enter the promised land. Centuries later, on a mountaintop, there he was with Elijah and a transfigured Jesus, in the heart of the promised land, talking to Jesus. Moses' faith had been rewarded, and he was called into service once again.

I wonder if a young shepherd named David ever thought he would be a king? Did Saul, a young Jewish boy, ever imagine being confronted by our Savior Jesus and chosen to be the apostle that led the Gentiles to Jesus' movement? Do you think a rough and tumble fisherman named Peter ever thought he would be walking on water with his hand stretched out to the King of kings? And what about

Abraham? As a child, did he ever think God would promise him a child and deliver on that promise when he was ninety years old?

Hope, belief, and faith have led many to tasks beyond their wildest imaginations. When God has a task for us, he can do anything and will. Are we open to the will of God? Have we followed his commands to believe, repent, and be baptized? Are we fishing for men and making disciples? Do we love God and one another? Are we following the commands of God? What can faith do, and where can it get us? If we turn our will and our lives over to Jesus, hang on, for we are in for the ride of our lives.

Have You Ever Felt as If You Were Strawberry?

Everyone who calls on the name of the Lord will be saved.

Acts 2:21

I am a big ice cream eater. I love the stuff. My favorite is Häagen Dazs caramel cone; okay, I like all ice cream. But that's an aside. Have you ever had Neapolitan ice cream? That is vanilla, chocolate, and strawberry. I don't know about you, but when the ice cream is almost gone that means only strawberry remains in my box. Strawberry is often overlooked and doesn't get the credit it deserves. I say three cheers for strawberry. Hmm, do you think strawberry feels left out, overlooked, ignored, and alone? Does strawberry need therapy?

Well as a child, when I was with other kids, I always felt neglected and left out, kind of like strawberry. As I grew into teen years, you guessed it—strawberry. Even into young adulthood, strawberry. I felt alone, left out, ignored, and sometimes even picked on. Strawberry has had a rough time of it. Most of my life I have wanted to be chocolate or vanilla, not strawberry. I tried everything to appear chocolate and vanilla to no avail. Everyone could tell I was strawberry.

I even asked God to make me chocolate or vanilla and remove me from a life doomed to being strawberry. You know what? God loves strawberry. If he were dipping a bowl of ice cream, he would take a level scoop of chocolate, vanilla, and strawberry. Then he might even mix it all together with his spoon. God loves all flavors. He has no favorite flavor. Now I know this may not seem biblical, but it does say in Acts 2:21, "Everyone who calls on the name of the Lord will be saved." God will save everyone who calls on the name of the Lord. He loves everyone. He has never changed me to chocolate, vanilla, or even Häagen Dazs caramel cone. God loves us. He will save everyone who calls on the name of Jesus, even strawberry.

Have You Talked to Your Donkey Lately?

> Then the LORD opened the donkey's mouth, and she said to Balaam, "What have I done to you to make you beat me these three times?" Balaam answered the donkey, "You have made a fool of me! If I had a sword in my hand, I would kill you right now." The donkey said to Balaam, "Am I not your own donkey, which you have always ridden, to this day? Have I been in the habit of doing this to you?"
>
> Numbers 22:28–30

I am going to use a phrase you may not have heard in a while; let's make believe. Let's make believe God gave me the gift of prophesy and I can put a curse on people. I can make people weak for an evil dictator to completely annihilate. This dictator sends his men to get me. They say I will receive one billion dollars to curse this dictator's enemy. God says, "Don't go." I tell them, "No, I can't go." So the evil guy sends back more distinguished people. They promise me land, a castle, a fleet of cars, and now five billion dollars. So, off I go. Now I did it; I have disobeyed God.

I get in my Mustang, put it in first, and there is an angel in the road. The car sees it, but I don't see it. All I see are dollar signs. The car is in first; it stalls. *C'mon!* I punch the dash. I start it again, put it in first. It stalls; now I am mad. I kick the floorboard and hurt my foot. One more time I start the car up, and the car goes backwards and stalls. The jolt jerks my neck. Now I've had it. I punch the steering wheel. The radio comes on and says, "Hey, quit it. Why are you beating me? I am your car, whom you drive daily, and I have given you no problems." Then I see the angel. He says, "You have angered God. Didn't he tell you not to go?" Now, he wants you to go and tell the evil dictator guy exactly what he tells you. Since you are a prophet with cursing powers, you are to do what the Master desires you to do. You haven't been given these powers to benefit yourself. Make believe is over, now wasn't that fun?

Look at Balaam. Here is a guy whom God told not to go to Moab, meet with Balek, or curse anyone. Balaam was a prophet no less. Did he listen to God? No. So off Balaam goes to meet Balek, curse the enemy, and collect his reward. Balaam was set to receive riches from Balek. God told him, "Don't go." What part of *don't* didn't Balaam understand? God could have handled this many ways. But you know our loving God. He tried it the nice way first, but Balaam wouldn't listen. He sent an angel to stop Balaam. The angel stood in the path; the donkey could see the angel and tried everything to stop. Balaam, with only riches in sight and a long journey ahead, got mad at the donkey; he beats the donkey three times. Then the donkey started talking to him and pushed Balaam's foot to be crushed against the wall and said, "Hey quit it. I am your donkey, you ride me every day, and I have never given you any trouble." It is probably not every day the donkey talks to him. Now Balaam sees the angel. The angel tells him he has angered God and he has to go tell Balek that God told him to tell him and curse no one. Also, Balaam will have a limp from his crushed foot, reminding him to lean on God, not on his own thinking and greed.

So, how does God get your attention? Have you talked to your donkey lately? Maybe you have and just don't know it. There may have been signs telling me not to do something I know it is not God's will, or maybe I haven't gone to God with an idea first. I know right from wrong; it tells me in the Bible. It also tells me I have been given gifts to benefit others and my church. These gifts are not to be used selfishly. Do you hear the little voice inside saying, "I wouldn't do that"? How about some of the little hints that things may not be going well? How about the warnings from mentors, people we trust in the accountable relationships we have established? The donkey is talking to you.

The Holy Spirit has been given to us to help us make sound, godly decisions. I need to listen. By reading the Bible, praying daily, meditating on God's Word, and having accountable relationships, I will make better decisions. Is my donkey talking? These disciplines are here for us to show us God's will. The gifts and talents God has given me are to be used to bring glory to God, not me. What will it take to get my attention? In Genesis, God broke Jacob's hip. In Numbers, we have a talking donkey and a crushed foot. Failure in my life comes from not going to God with my ideas first. I also have the Bible to see if the idea is biblically sound. I have other spiritual disciplines to ensure I hear my donkey. When God wants to get your attention, he will. Don't be surprised if your donkey starts talking to you.

Today, I will listen to my donkey. The donkey had more wisdom than Balaam. My donkey reminds me to use spiritual disciplines before I use my spiritual gifts or make decisions. Listen and watch for the cues of your donkey.

He Has Risen!

He is not here; he has risen, just as he said. Come and see the place where he lay.

Matthew 28:6

Don't be alarmed, he said. "You are looking for Jesus the Nazarene, who was crucified. He has risen! He is not here."

Mark 16:6

Jesus said to her, "Mary." She turned toward him and cried out in Aramaic, "Rabboni!" (Which means Teacher).

John 20:16

Three sweeter words have never been said than *he has risen*. Jesus had been put to death two days earlier, and he arose on the third day. Jesus is alive. Can you imagine the decibel level of Mary crying out *Rabboni?* What must it have sounded like? Jesus had been resurrected from the dead, just as he had said he would. Amen.

For a Christian, every day is Resurrection Day, or Easter as we like to call it. It is not just a day for chocolate bunnies, jelly beans, marshmallow peeps, and cards; it is a day many people choose to celebrate the resurrection of our Savior, Jesus Christ. People all over the world are standing up and taking notice of our Savior.

Six words and two sentences are music to the ears of those who can hear. In John 19:30, it says, "When he had received the drink, Jesus said, 'It is finished.' With that, he bowed his head and gave up his spirit." Jesus died. Why would these words be music to anyone's ears? Well it isn't a pretty picture to me either. It was a brutal and gruesome scene and not the first one I want to remember. Throughout the Old Testament a blood sacrifice for sin was necessary for forgiveness. Jesus was God's sacrificial lamb for the atonement of our sins, my sins. Jesus' death meant the end of all blood sacrifices. Our sin debt was paid the moment Jesus said, "It is finished," bowed his head, and gave up his spirit. Jesus is now the path to eternal life through his own sacrifice. Our sin debt is now paid in full. "It is finished." The sacrificial lamb was sacrificed, Jesus. There is no greater love.

So you can imagine why I now say those were great words. But here are some more great words in John 20:16: "Days after the death, Jesus stood and called to Mary. Mary turned and cried out to Him, Rabboni!" How about the words *he has risen?* How about the ones we use, *he is alive?* We now have eternal life with God our Father in heaven. We have eternal life, and our sin debt was paid with those six words: *it is finished* and *he has risen.*

There will be many celebrating Easter just as they celebrate Christmas. These are two days of the year more people will think of Jesus. More people will attend church. On Easter, let's welcome them and share in praise and worship to our Father in heaven for making his son Jesus a sacrificial lamb to pay our sin debt, and to Jesus who wore that role and gave up his own life so that our sin debt would be paid in full. Let's worship this day with those who come to celebrate the resurrection of our Lord and Savior. Let's share the love, gratitude, and joy we have for Jesus. Let's share the good news of Jesus Christ. They are open to hear. Isn't every day Easter?

The gratitude I feel for the sacrifice Jesus made for me and his resurrection for my eternal life are beyond words. As I think about Jesus, bowing his head, blood-soaked, saying, "It is finished," and knowing it is me who should have paid that price chokes me up. There are no words to describe the feeling of his resurrection and the scene with Mary turning and crying out, "Rabboni!" I want to turn and shout, "Jesus, you are alive!"

He Hears My Cries

> I waited patiently for the LORD; he turned to me and heard my cry.
>
> Psalm 40:1

I'm thinking God is a busy guy. There is war, world hunger, natural disasters, zillions of people with mega-zillions of problems. What makes me think God will listen to me? Well the psalmist says here that he waited patiently and God heard his cry. Not only did God hear his cry amongst all the noise, but it also says God turned to him and heard his cry. God gave him one-on-one attention. Get this: do you know what God did next? Check this out, in Psalm 40:2: "He lifted me out of the slimy pit, out of the mud and mire; he set my feet on a rock and gave me a firm place to stand." Okay, so God, the Creator of everything, heard one individual, David, cry. He is just one guy. God turned to him, lifted him up, and set him on solid ground. God listened and answered one guy.

As if that weren't enough, it says in Psalm 40:3, "He put a new song in my mouth, a hymn of praise to our God." So, after being lifted out of a slimy pit and placed on a rock, God puts a song of praise in David's mouth, a hymn of praise. God changed David's whole attitude and outlook. God changed David's heart from one of fear and worry, being in a slimy pit, to one of being slimy on a rock with a song of praise and gratitude to God who saved him.

Why did God save him? God saved him because he was crying out.

Do you know that we talk to that very same God? There is fear and worry in our lives at times. We are in a slimy pit at times and need to be lifted out and placed on solid ground. Sometimes I am not as patient as David was, and I am not sure that God will come to my rescue, but David assures me he will. God not only assured David but also came to him. So let me get this straight. David cried out, was patient and trusting in God to come to his aid, and God came and aided. Okay, I know what I need to do. I need to cry out and trust God. I need to call out and reach out. This is what David said in Psalm 40:3: "God knows me and my cry and will come to my aid." God is beyond awesome.

He Won't Forgive Me This Time

The idea that I couldn't be forgiven for this one probably started as a child. Coming home with a bad report card I would think, *Oh man, they are gonna kill me.* When I broke the neighbor's window playing baseball, I got that sinking feeling. You know the crimes, the sins against the family. You have your list.

As I get older, I am introduced to God; he is that unforgiving Father I heard about as a child. God sent his only Son, Jesus, to atone for our sins and save us from death and guarantee those who believe a place with him in heaven. Until I commit that sin I can't be forgiven for. Come on, you know the one. Maybe two, hmmm, maybe more. Alcoholism, drug addiction, adultery, stealing, lying, cheating, jealousy, anger, cursing, staying away from church; this could become a long list given our conscience. I have heard some say, "God will never forgive me for this one," or that one or many of them. I felt the same way until my friend said "Let's look at the Word and see what God has to say."

Further study into God's own words shows many examples of his forgiveness. Moses killed an Egyptian guard. He was a murderer, and God had him lead the Israelites out of bondage. David, the king, the giant slayer, and author of Psalms, committed adultery with another man's wife, and then sent the man to the front line of battle to die so he could have Bathsheba all to himself. God loved David, and David wrote of that love. Saul, who became Paul, dragged Jesus' followers out of their homes, put them in prisons, and to death. He held the cloak of Stephen while he was being stoned. Paul, of course, was a chosen apostle by the resurrected Jesus to bring the good news of forgiveness to the Gentiles.

Peter denied he knew Jesus three times after saying he would die for him. All but one apostle ran and hid (John), and when Jesus had been resurrected, he came through the door, and his first words were, "Peace be with you." Thomas wasn't there that day and doubted. He needed proof. Jesus returned and gently told Thomas to touch the wounds in his hands and feet. How about the adulteress about to be stoned? Jesus said, "Those without sin cast the first stone." No stones were thrown. Since no one stoned her, Jesus said, "Go, and sin no more." He took one of thieves being crucified with him to paradise because he asked to be forgiven.

God loves us. He is waiting for us to come to him. With Moses, David, and Paul, he went to them; he had plans.

> That everyone who believes in him may have eternal life. For God so loved the world that he gave his one and only son, that whoever believes in him shall not perish but have eternal life.
>
> John 3:15–16

> Peter replied, "Repent and be baptized, every one of you, in the name of Jesus Christ for the forgiveness of your sins. And you will receive the gift of the Holy Spirit. The promise is for you and your children and for all who are far off—for all whom the Lord our God will call."
>
> Acts 2:38–39

Wow! Forgiveness for all sin when we ask in Jesus' name. The death on the cross was painful, the torture before painful. Jesus took on the sin of the world for all time. Why? Because he loves us. He created us; he knew we would fall, make mistakes, and sin. Come to our Father in Jesus' name. Forgiveness is for the asking. Don't let pride or your own misunderstanding of God's forgiveness get in the way. Grace and mercy are God's way of forgiving. He loves you. He loves me. Let's do this together.

He Will Not Be Evicted

When it was almost time for the Jewish Passover, Jesus went up to Jerusalem. In the temple courts he found men selling cattle, sheep and doves, and others sitting at tables exchanging money. So he made a whip out of cords, and drove all from the temple area, both sheep and cattle; he scattered the coins of the money changers and overturned their tables. To those who sold doves he said, "Get these out of here! How dare you turn my Father's house into a market!"

John 2:13–16

I watch television, read papers, and listen to the radio. I have been hearing that they are kicking God out of the schools and out of our federal buildings. All I can think is, *Oh, really? Who kicked God out? They must have a pretty big foot.* God has more than squatters' rights. He is the Creator of everything and everyone. He isn't going anywhere; he is here to stay. God has not left the schools or the federal buildings. He is still there. They took out the symbols, but they can't get rid of God. God always was and always will be. He was here before schools and federal buildings. The naysayer schools and federal buildings will be gone one day, not God. No prayer allowed in school? Watch the kids before a test.

I have read, watched, and heard that children are not permitted to pray in schools. They say there can be no signs of God whatsoever. Again I say, "Oh really?" Aren't we the light of God? Did our lights go out? People see the joy and love we bring. Exuding the fruits of the spirit wherever we go, we shouldn't check them at the door. We are Christians. Wherever we go, we are contagious. We are Christians in all our words and deeds. I can talk to God anywhere; my heart should have constant contact with him.

I don't think God is surprised by the actions of some who try to kick him out, but I know it doesn't make him happy. This is the sort of thing that happened throughout the Bible, people turning away from him. As a Christian, I need to show his love. When the shopkeepers turned the temple into a flea market, Jesus evicted them. Noah built an ark when God decided to evict the whole world. God evicted those who turned against him in Sodom and Gomorrah, also in Jerusalem and Judah. God and his Son, Jesus, do the evicting. They are not evicted. God is all powerful, the Creator of everything and everyone.

I am not condoning the actions of those who want Christianity gone or want God gone; I am saying we need to shine our lights brighter. We need to set the examples by bringing our contagious joy everywhere. Apparently, the government doesn't find itself responsible to follow God's commands. We should be doing that anyway; we are the body of Christ.

In Revelation 3:20, Jesus said, "Here I am! I stand at the door and knock. If anyone hears my voice and opens the door, I will come in and eat with him, and he with me." He won't barge in anywhere he is not wanted. He is a gracious guest. But who is really the guest here on Earth, and who is the Creator? God will not be evicted.

Today, I will not hold anyone else responsible for spreading the Word of God and the good news of Jesus Christ. I will take that beautiful responsibility upon myself. I will do it out of gratitude and love for God, who gave his Son, and to Jesus, who gave his life. No one can evict God from my heart, mind, or soul. Jesus will evict anyone from his Father's house that does evil. Today, my heart is his Father's house; Jesus has knocked, and I have let him enter. God's Spirit is also within me. Wherever I go I bring God. I don't leave home without him. I will let my light shine wherever I go. God has promised in Hebrews 13:5, "I will never leave you or forsake you." He will not be evicted. He loves us and isn't going anywhere. He is and will always answer those who call his name.

Headlines: AD 33

Can you imagine the headlines back around the year AD 33 after the death on the cross?

Rebel Leader Put to Death Today.
Jesus, the Head of a Radical Group, Crucified.
Man Claiming to Be the Actual Son of God Can't Even Save Himself.
Governor Pontius Pilate Sentences Imposter to Death.
Radical Group Scatters as Their Delusional Leader Is Put to Death.
Man Claiming to be the King of Kings of Some "Netherworld" Is Sent There.
Last Words of Supposed King of Kings are "It Is Finished." He Sure Is.
Executioner Held for Contempt as He Claims Dead Rebel Leader Truly Is the Son of God.

How about the headlines three days later?

Rebels Steal Body of Rebel Leader Jesus to Perpetuate the Resurrection Hoax.
Body of Man Claiming to Be the Son of God Is Missing.
Which Way Did He Go?

Jewish Leaders Angered and Confused as the Body of Jesus Is Missing.

Radical Group in a Frenzy as the Body of Their Leader Has Been Stolen.

All the while, Jesus is walking through walls, visiting his disciples, saying, "Peace be with you." Indeed, he has risen.

I guess there are some things the press has never really gotten right.

Heart of the Creator

From Mount Zion, the perfection of beauty, God shines in
glorious radiance.

Psalm 50:2

Have you ever seen a picture that was taken underwater? Have
you seen pictures of the fish and their surroundings? The colors
are magnificent. Better yet, have you been there? Take a walk and
gaze at the mighty ocean with its waves crashing, or a serene lake,
a majestic mountain range, green plush grass on the hillsides of
Ireland. God painted all of this. Where do you take your vacations?
Why do you go there? I love the mountains of North Carolina; I
have seen Pike's Peak in Colorado, the Pacific and Atlantic Oceans.
I swam in the crystal clear waters of Hawaii and camped on its
mountaintops. I have fished in the clear lakes of northern Canada;
these views are breathtaking.

Where have you been? What have you seen? Can you believe
that God created all of this beauty, majesty, and power, and it is
all here for us? God is an awesome Creator. He is the Creator of
perfection. He uses love to create us. Look at the animals, the birds,
the fish, the people, all different, all from the heart and mind of
God. Our minds are amazing. Computers give a lot of information, but all programmed by the complex brain of a human being.

God created human beings. God's beauty and love surrounds us. Have you taken it in? Thought about it? Meditated on it?

Look at a painting, car design, clothing design, home designs, pottery, just look at anything that was created. It is all beautiful. However, the creators got the inspiration somewhere. Was it from their hearts? The creation is nothing without the Creator.

God created us. He is still creating us, daily. He is giving us love, new ideas, new prayers, and new people in our lives, new inspirations, gifts, talents, and new encouragements. We are not finished. There is much to learn. We are a work in progress. Ask God for answers, ideas, ministries, missions, strength, wisdom; we can even ask for much more. Let him continue to create. His creation is beautiful. Keep an open mind, a blank canvas. Let him use his magnificent colors, imaginative ideas, genius, and power to mold you and shape you. Wait until you see what you can become.

A creation made with love is beautiful, powerful, awesome, and magnificent. Ahh, but the heart of the Creator I cannot even begin to express. Heaven is even more beautiful. Can you imagine?

Today, I will ask the Creator to work on me. I will ask him to use his creativity to make me what he wants. I will ask him to use his love to mold me. I will ask his will to be done in my life. Beautiful things can happen when I choose to remain available and open to him. I cannot even imagine what he can still do with me if I remain open to his love.

Here to Serve

For even the Son of Man came not to be served but to serve others and to give his life as a ransom for many.

Matthew 20:28

For you have been called to live in freedom, my brothers and sisters. But don't use your freedom to satisfy your sinful nature. Instead, use your freedom to serve one another in love.

Galatians 5:13

I used to work with a guy named Chuck. When asked to do something, Chuck would say, "Here to serve." On the side of police cars, it says "Serve and protect." Even some grocery store bags say, "Service with a smile." In some twelve-step programs they say, "Show your gratitude by service to others."

Jesus came not to be served but to serve. Even the night before his death, at the Last Supper, he served. He also washed the disciple's feet, a servant's job. He served the meal, and he served a lesson. He wants us to serve. Jesus also served himself up as our Savior. He served our death sentence for our sin. Jesus was all about serving.

Jesus gave us commands to serve one another and to go out and make disciples of the world. Jesus gave us the command to serve.

Mature Christians serve. We feed the hungry. Not just the hungry for food, but the hungry for God. We serve them God's Word.

Just like newborn babies, new Christians need to be fed. They need God's Word fed to them. Mature Christians can feed themselves through God's Word. They understand God's Word because they read it, study it, pray, and meditate on it. Hebrews 5:14 says, "Solid food is for those who are mature, who through training have the skill to recognize the difference between right and wrong." As mature Christians, we can't wait for someone to feed us. It is our job to use spiritual disciplines to mature.

Am I eating? Am I being challenged enough by others? As I study this thought as a maturing Christian, I am not called to be fed. The Bible has challenges, and I am called to feed as I meet the challenges of the Bible. Unbelievers, new Christians, and the young are fed. I am called to serve. My reward is in heaven, not here.

The food is on the table; I can cut my own meat and feed myself, and with the help of the Holy Spirit, digest. I can't always depend on others. In Timothy, we are called to be like an athlete, soldier, and farmer, one who trains, studies, and works hard. Timothy 5:3–7 says, "Endure suffering along with me, as a good soldier of Christ Jesus." Soldiers don't get tied up in the affairs of civilian life, for then they cannot please the officer who enlisted them. And athletes cannot win the prize unless they follow the rules. And hardworking farmers should be the first to enjoy the fruit of their labor. Think about what I am saying. The Lord will help you understand all these things.

This writing is written to me and shared with you. Because today I have to remember, I am not called to be served or fed. I am called to love, serve, and feed. I am called to be mature, not to depend on someone else for my spiritual growth. Of course others can help, but they are not responsible for me. No one except Jesus will stand with me in front of his father. There are no excuses for me because I wasn't fed enough. Bible reading, study, prayer, meditation, and wise counsel are all necessary to me for growth.

Today, I am here to serve.

Hey, It's Monday.
Let's Go Fishing

"Come, follow me," Jesus said, "and I will make you fishers of men."

Matthew 4:19 and Mark 1:17

Hey! It's Monday. Let's go fishing. I would love to be doing the kind of fishing I did late May and early June 2008, when I went to Canada with five other guys and camped out. We fished off canoes, which was our only transportation for eight days. The fun, fellowship, food, and fishing were great. The portaging wasn't as much fun, but the fellowship and camaraderie was my favorite part. But I won't be taking that trip again soon, and I am talking about another kind of fishing. Jesus wants us to be fishers of men and women. Jesus wants us to bring our catch to him. Let's get our tackle boxes ready, go out into the world today and every day, and start fishing.

Sunday is over. The churches are closed, the pews are empty, lights are off, preachers are icing down their horse voices, and we are back in the world. Some people don't like Mondays, but today is a great day for fishing. In church, we got the bait we need to bring along, the Word of God, fellowship, joy, a spiritual boost, and love. Love seems to be the best bait out there. Love with a non-judgmental attitude catches the most fish. Putting the good news of Jesus Christ on the line along with love seems to catch the most. Kindness and understanding needs to be in our tackle box along with the Word of God and truth.

Imagine the joy we can share with all those we come in contact with by our words and actions toward them. This is a great time to fulfill the great commission, making disciples. Loving God and loving one another leads us to the biggest catches. We can bring more to Jesus, and then they can enjoy salvation, assurance, and fishing alongside us, shoulder to shoulder. Hey, let's get excited about being a Christian today. No really, let's get excited, enthusiastic, and grateful. Come on; grab your tackle box, fishing pole, and Bible. It's Monday. Some of the best fishing is Monday. Okay, the best fishing is any day. So let's go.

Hey, Look at Me

Your attitude should be the same as that of Christ Jesus.

When I was a child, my family was involved in many things: American Legion, Boy Scouts, Girl Scouts, and baseball—all sorts of events that had dinners. At all the dinners my father went to, I stood with him. My father always waited until everyone was in line and all had been served at buffet dinners; then he would go through the line. We were always last. After the dinner, he would always be last to leave because cleanup was needed; garbage needed to go out, floors mopped, and people spoken to. You would think he was the janitor. With the American Legion, he had two terms as commander and was the Boy Scout leader. He ate last, took out trash, and mopped floors. He never made a big deal about it. He just did it with a big smile and a desire to serve and share a kind word with others. I could never figure this out. Shouldn't the commander eat first and leave first? Shouldn't he be exalted and appreciated? Well he was none of those things, but one thing I do know and learned, even more at his funeral, was that he was loved by many. Grown men, tough, old, World War II veterans had tears in their eyes.

Of course, I now realize he was an imitator of Jesus. He was the one of the best examples I have ever had. In Paul's letter to

A Prodigal Return **187**

the Philippians, he told them their attitude should be the same as Jesus'. Paul was also writing that letter to me. He said my attitude should be the same as that of Jesus Christ. Jesus is King of kings, Son of God, and washer of feet. Jesus laid down his life for all of us. He never said, "Here I am, look at me, serve me, take care of me, and do for me" or anything like that. He served others, taught others, loved others, and met the needs of others; he loved and forgave freely.

So today, I want to be more like my dad. I want to be more like Jesus. I want to put the needs of others first. I want to put their needs before my own. Being a humble servant will be my code today and every day as a disciple of Jesus. I want to thank my dad for the great example he set for me while he was here. I want to wish you all a beautiful day and ask you to join me in imitating the attitude of Jesus. I thank you for your beautiful, tender heart, and for your service to God and others.

Hey, My Hand Is On Fire

> When they become aware of the sin they committed, the assembly must bring a young bull as a sin offering and present it before the Tent of Meeting.
>
> Leviticus 4:14

In 1977 my favorite watering hole was in Norfolk, Virginia. I was a regular, kind of like Norm and Cliff on *Cheers*. I had a lighter that needed to be filled, so the bartender gave me the fluid to fill my lighter. I filled it and got some fluid on my hand, but I didn't know it. Did I mention I used to get a little drunk? Well, a pretty lady was sitting next to me and had a cigarette that needed a light. Just like any knight in shining armor would do for a damsel in distress, I clicked my lighter. My hand caught on fire, and she lit her cigarette off my thumb. I think I made an impression.

So here is my battle cry today; awareness is a call to action. Well, my hand was on fire, and the lady next to me lit her cigarette with it. Well, that's one response. Nick, the owner of the bar, had a better idea; he threw a wet towel on my hand. What is awareness without action? Of course, we all need the awareness of a problem, bad habit, sin, shortcoming, defect of character, and burning hand before we can do anything. But do we always act?

I know I should start exercising. So someone says they have been exercising. I say "Yeah, I need to start exercising." Yeah, this drinking problem is pretty bad. I need to stop this. This smoking is bad for me, sinning needs to stop, interrupting others isn't nice, I need to forgive more, I need to stop judging others, I need to stop gossiping, I need to encourage more. I need more time in Bible study, prayer, mediation, and the list is endless. Do you have a list? Are you aware that you need more discipline, self-control, kindness, patience, etc.? So, now we have become aware. What's next?

Here are some things I have thought about. You know I have always wanted to write a book. I have wanted to learn to play an instrument. I really need to call that friend or family member. I need to turn my will and life over to God. I should be baptized into Christ. I should get to church. Again, these are all good insights and awareness, but where is the action? Hmmm, my hand is on fire.

It says in James 1:23–24, "Anyone who listens to the word but does not do what it says is like a man who looks at his face in a mirror and, after looking at himself, goes away and immediately forgets what he looks like." So do we know the Word and walk away and forget what it says? Do we do live the Word? Do we see the problem? Are we aware of it? Do we see something very important that needs to be done, and do we walk away and forget about it? Do we need more action?

We can start by asking God how we can change, and we can ask him to help change us. We can read God's Word, meditate, and seek wise counsel. The answers are there. Now we need the motivation. We can't always just wait till we get around to it.

This is my call to action. This is my battle cry to you and me. What changes need to be made? What are you aware of? Is your hand on fire?

Hey, Why Are You Laughing?

Our mouths were filled with laughter, our tongues with songs of joy. Then it was said among the nations, "The LORD has done great things for them." The LORD has done great things for us, and we are filled with joy.

Psalms 126:2–3

For it is with your heart that you believe and are justified, and it is with your mouth that you confess and are saved.

Romans 10:10

On my most recent camping trip, I asked a friend, "Am I ruining things by being so slow?" He said, "We keep you around for comedic relief." You know I laugh and try to make others laugh as much as the next guy. Okay, I probably do it more than the next guy. You will never guess why I do this. Go ahead take a guess. Did anyone say, "Because you are happy"? *Bing, bing, bing.* You are a winner. Yep. I am happy.

The laughter in my mouth comes from a grateful and happy heart. Why is my heart happy? Because the Lord has done great things for me and I am filled with joy. Do you know that others are watching us as Christians? Some think we are an odd bunch believing in the unseen and what they consider a fairytale. They watch to see what we are doing. They have read the Bible or heard of it, and they think it is gloom and doom, all fire and brimstone, and they ask, "What in the world are they laughing at? What are they singing about? What do they have to be happy about?"

How is it supposed to look to be a Christian? A long face, serious looks and judgmental attitudes—is that what we look like to others? Jesus died for all of us. He gave all who believe assurance in heaven with him and our Father. We have been freed from sin and self-hatred. We are free from all that binds us through Jesus. He has given us a confident and loving life. I am saved. I am going to spend eternity in heaven. I have God, who loves me and created the universe, listening to my prayers all day every day, and the King of kings who is coming back to get me on that day. Why wouldn't I be happy? Let's laugh, sing songs of joy, and show our gratitude through love and service to one another and to God. When others ask what we have to laugh about, let's not make them wonder. Let's tell them.

Hmmm, What's Next?

Shout for joy to the LORD, all the earth. For the LORD is good and his love endures forever; his faithfulness continues through all generations.

Psalm 100:1, 5

Holidays are great. The Fourth of July is a wonderful memorial to the day we were freed from British tyranny in 1776. We have so many holidays like that to memorialize great events. When I was a child, I didn't understand all that was being memorialized and celebrated. I just knew there were presents involved in some holidays. One Christmas day, I received my gifts and said, "I can't wait until Easter."

Holidays have come and gone since that day. If this Fourth of July is over and gone, you will be able to buy half-priced red, white, and blue cupcakes, cookies, and cakes, maybe have some leftover barbecue, get some Fourth of July sales at the stores, or enjoy the rest of a three-day weekend. These well-planned holidays just seem to come and go.

Now what? What's next? How about today? Hey! It is today and a good day to remember Psalm 100. The Lord is good. His love endures forever, not just on holidays or when we remember. His faithfulness and love endures all generations; that's forever. Shout for joy. God loves us today. If you ever have post-holiday blues, you know what? God loves you that day too. Today, let's just share in God's eternal love. Enjoy your day today and every day, knowing no matter what God loves you. No, really, he does. This isn't a cute feel-good thought; this is a tried and eternal truth. Enjoy holidays. Memorialize and celebrate God's love today. Nothing half price tomorrow, this particular holiday continues.

How's My Stance?

But for that very reason I was shown mercy so that in me, the worst of sinners, Christ Jesus might display his unlimited patience as an example for those who would believe on him and receive eternal life.

1 Timothy 1:16

In 1983, the unthinkable happened. My hero, Carl Yastrzemski, retired from baseball. Number eight, Yaz, Carl Yastrzemski, was finished with his baseball career. Yaz was my childhood baseball idol. I love baseball, and as a young child, I played it daily. I loved to hit. I would step up to the plate and hold my bat way up in the air just like Yaz. He batted lefty. I was a righty, but that bat would stick way up there, and I would announce to all, "Now batting: number eight, the leftfielder, Carl Yaz Yastrzemski." Hit or no hit, I would ask how my stance was and if I looked like Yaz. The year 1983 was the end of an era for me.

Today, I also want to emulate my hero. His name is Jesus. He gave his life for you and me. He also gave us many examples to follow. The fruits of the Spirit are a fine example of what Christ is. Galatians 5:22–23 says, "But the fruit of the Spirit is love, joy, peace, patience, kindness, goodness, faithfulness, gentleness, and self-control." Jesus was also merciful, forgiving, and so unselfish that he gave his life for us. The fruits are gifts we receive as the Holy

Spirit dwells within us. Jesus had all those qualities. Jesus was the most giving and loving man to ever walk the earth.

As a Jesus follower, I am called to be like him. To copy him, I am called to hold my bat way up just as he did. I am to look like Jesus in my words and deeds. I am to treat all I meet with love and kindness and to treat others as Jesus would, even when things don't go my way, when a waitress has a bad day and takes it out on me or gets my order wrong, when the grocery checker is snippy, and in all such instances. That is tough sometimes. But as a mature Christian, this is my call.

I am called to be a seven-days-a-week-twenty-four-hours-a-day Christian and emulate Jesus. I am to serve others, use the spiritual disciplines, walk the talk of the Bible, use the fruits of the Holy Spirit with all I encounter, use my workplace as my pulpit, and glorify God in all I do and say. I am called to make disciples of all people, everywhere. As a fisher of men, having the fruits of the Holy Spirit and emulating Jesus make up the lifestyle I want to live.

Today I will work on emulating Jesus. Whenever I have the opportunity, I will hold my God high. I will ask my heavenly Father, "How's my stance?"

Humpty Dumpty

Scorn has broken my heart and has left me helpless; I looked
for sympathy, but there was none, for comforters, but I found
none.

Psalm 69:20

Do you remember the fairy tale of Humpty Dumpty? Humpty
Dumpty sat on a wall; Humpty Dumpty had a great fall. All the
kings' horses and all the kings' men couldn't put Humpty together
again. Poor Humpty, he was now just a giant, broken, scrambled
egg. Have you ever felt broken? Has someone ever broken your
heart? Have you ever felt as though all the kings' horses and all the
kings' men couldn't put you back together again?

Throughout my life, I have suffered through hurt. At sixteen,
I was with my father when he died. For over fifteen years, I waved
good-bye to my children at the end of my every-other-weekend visits due to divorce. I went to my mother's funeral over eleven years
ago. I almost drank myself into oblivion thirty years ago. There
have been several broken relationships over the years. Friends have
come in and out of my life, and miles and death have separated
us.

Nothing hurts worse than a broken heart, or hurt feelings from
being jilted, divorced, left, put down, dumped, or cheated on, and
the death of someone close. Counseling helps the brokenhearted

a great deal, but nothing works better than prayer. Jesus said in Matthew 7:7–8, "Ask and it will be given to you; seek and you will find; knock and the door will be opened to you. For everyone who asks receives; he who seeks finds; and to him who knocks, the door will be opened."

If you have been hurt, if you have or are brokenhearted, seek counseling if the pain is too much. As a Christian, we can seek Christian counseling. Call out to God. Your prayers will be answered. God has excellent vision and hearing. He misses nothing. God sees the inner reaches of our hearts. When we fall, God will pick us up and put us back together again—even stronger than before.

I Am Going on a Retreat

Therefore the prudent man keeps quiet in such times, for the
times are evil.

Amos 5:13

I have been on several guided retreats throughout my life. I have
been on some retreats for sober alcoholics in recovery. I have been
on church retreats and college retreats when I was in the seminary.
All were run extremely well. There were speakers, time for prayer
and meditation, and time for study. It was a time I could come out
of the world and just slow down. On one retreat, they even took
our watches; we didn't know what time it was. Retreats provide
a much slower pace where I can refresh from the rat race of the
world. They are a time to be quiet and listen, a time to get away
from temptations, bad news, work, schedules, deadlines, phones,
television, and all things that distract from time with God.

With so much going on around us, don't we all need this type
of retreat? Doesn't this sound relaxing? Closing off our mind from
all the distractions and temptation of the world? To just retreat
and get away, to be still, to feel safe, calm, and quiet. This is a very
refreshing and invigorating time. If you are told about a retreat
or you are invited, I suggest you go. They are a great chance to
spend time alone with God in quiet prayer, mediation, studying his
Word, and listening in meditation.

I invite you to go on a fifteen-minute retreat today. Go to a quiet place with a Bible and pray and meditate on it. Turn off phones, television, radio, Internet, and find peace. Close your eyes and go to a place you find peaceful. Sit at the cross, the throne of God, by a babbling brook, the ocean, or wherever you feel at peace and just meditate and pray. Ask God to slow down your thoughts, slow down the pace around you, help you focus on him, ask what you can do to better the world today and how you can bring him glory.

My goal is to retreat for a minimum of fifteen minutes, maybe up to forty-five minutes, depending on how much time I have available. I might read the Bible for thirty minutes, pray, and meditate the next fifteen to twenty minutes. I have not done a retreat like this before. I think it will take patience, training, encouragement, preparation, determination, and desire, but I believe that the time at my short retreat will be well worth it. I am looking to be refreshed and invigorated. Who better to spend this time with than God, in quiet study, prayer, meditation, and contemplation? Do you want to join me?

I Am So Right I Am Wrong

Pride only breeds quarrels, but wisdom is found in those who take advice.

Proverbs 13:10

I have found I can be so right I am wrong. Since I was a child, I find myself in quarrels I have no business in. I have argued because I am right, so the other person must be wrong. Then I back myself into a corner because of my ego, and pride won't let me out. These discussions start out mellow enough, and then someone may have the audacity to disagree with me. When I am wise, I let it go by and let it be no big deal. Sometimes I must make my point, apparently no matter the cost.

I have met people over the years that are foolish and have stubborn pride. This can destroy families, friendships, and marriages. These people, like me, have found it necessary to be right. Our defensive postures have also led us to foolish pride that causes quarrels. Once I have completed the argument and have become the champion, I feel like an idiot. I feel deep guilt, knowing I have not shown love. I have not shown the mercy and grace that has been given me by my heavenly Father. Now I owe apologies. But wait, I thought I was right, justified? Self-righteous anger and pride only lead to shame and guilt. But how come I am so unhappy? I was right.

Early on in my adulthood, someone asked me if I wanted to be right or happy. That is wise advice, which I have used many times, but sadly not every time. When I feel this knot from my ego and pride kick in, I have to ask myself some questions. Will what I am about to say bring glory to God? Will what I am about to say show love and concern for the other person? Do I remember whom I am talking to? Will the other person leave the conversation feeling destroyed? Will what I am about to say lead me to shame and guilt? Will this discussion destroy a relationship?

I love what Proverbs 17:28 says. "Even a fool is thought wise if he keeps silent, and discerning if he holds his tongue." So when pride and ego show their ugly heads and we feel that fire burning inside ready to pounce, we need to think first. Don't destroy a friendship, family, or marriage over trying to be right due to foolish and stubborn pride.

Here is another verse that tells me what God thinks of pride and arguments: 2 Timothy 2:23. "Don't have anything to do with foolish and stupid arguments, because you know they produce quarrels." Foolish and stupid arguments say it all. So I have to ask myself, "Do I want to be right, or do I want to be happy?"

I Can See Clearly Now

Part One

When he had gone indoors, the blind men came to him, and he asked them, "Do you believe that I am able to do this?" "Yes, Lord," they replied. Then he touched their eyes and said, "According to your faith will it be done to you"; and their sight was restored. Jesus warned them sternly, "See that no one knows about this." But they went out and spread the news about him all over that region.

Matthew 9:28–30

I don't know about you, but I am not crazy about the dark. As a child, I was terrified of the dark. As an adult, I am still a bit cautious in the dark. I just don't like not being able to see. Believe it or not, I have lived a good portion of my life in the dark. I wasn't able to see where my life was going, but I continued to walk around feverishly in the dark, trying to find my way out. In a room, there is a light switch, and in life, there is a light. Jesus is the light.

When I came to Jesus and asked him to be my Savior, the light came on. The fear diminished. I am not going to say I am fearless, but I will say I know where to bring my fears, to God. Today I know I face my fears with the help of God. There is no darkness with Jesus as my Savior. The light is always on, and I can see my direction. I can see Jesus. I can see my heavenly Father, and I can hear the voice of his Holy Spirit. The Bible adds light. It's like turning up a switch that has a dimmer, which I can make brighter. Through prayer and meditation, the light gets even brighter.

Like the blind men in Matthew 9:28–30, I have asked Jesus to be my Savior and to help me see. Do I believe Jesus is my Savior? Do I believe Jesus can do this? Yes, I do. My faith has set me free and turned the light on. I was blind and now I see. My life has been paid for by Jesus' sacrifice and resurrection. Following God's commands brightens my day and my way. I see exactly what to do and where I am going. Jesus is my light. I keep my eyes fixed on him. I follow him and his example.

Are you in the dark? Do you like the dark? If not, turn on the light, turn to God the Father, the Son, and the Holy Spirit. Get a brighter light, read God's Word, and listen to God's voice in the Bible. I said it before, but it is worth repeating. "I was blind and now I see."

I Can See Clearly Now
Part Two

> Praise be to the God and Father of our Lord Jesus Christ,
> the Father of compassion and the God of all comfort, who
> comforts us in all our troubles, so that we can comfort those
> in any trouble with the comfort we ourselves have received
> from God.
>
> 2 Corinthians 1:3–4

As I said in part one, I don't like the dark. God the Father, Jesus,
and the Holy Spirit are the light. I never have to fear the dark again
as I am in eternal light with God the Father, Son, and Holy Spirit.
I see my life clearly. I see my purpose clearly. That has not always
been true. I have always wondered what God had planned for me.
What he wants is for me to give glory to him in everything and all
that I do.

I have been counseling others and receiving wise counsel from
others my entire adult life. Counseling others is my joy and I
believe one of my spiritual gifts. I also get great joy from bringing
encouragement and God's Word to people through counseling and
conversation. My purpose is to love God, love others, and serve the
world. I stay open to the requests of others and have taken on tasks
that would at one time be out of my comfort zone. Through doing
these things, I have really broadened my abilities and belief in the

abilities God has given me. I have also been able to bring glory to God through his gifts.

Through the light, I have found my purpose. I need not be confused or worried. I have peace. I want to devote my life to sharing my spiritual gift of encouragement with God while bringing glory to God. I want to share God's Word in person, through e-mail, Internet, books, and teaching others. I also want to remain open to wise counsel from others and especially those more spiritually mature than me.

Staying in the light of God keeps me safe and gives me a clear purpose in life. It helps me to see things in the world that I may not ordinarily see. It helps me see God's word in the Bible and see God in his creation.

I Can See Clearly Now

Part Three

I pray also that the eyes of your heart may be enlightened in order that you may know the hope to which he has called you.

Ephesians 1:18

Having God's light in my heart lets me see things I would not ordinarily see. Now that I am in God's light, I see the beauty in people. I also see the hurt in people. A lot of these people's anger has been caused by hurt in the past. Hurt from divorce, adultery, parents, children, deceit, perceived failures, toxic religion with manmade rules, school, and many other causes.

Being in the light of God and being able to see with my heart, I can see the pain. Jesus gave us two further commands, to love God with all our hearts and love one another as we love ourselves. Loving God means we follow his commands, serving and loving each other. While we love others, we look beyond what we can see with our eyes and see with our hearts. You will find people that say, "I don't care" the loudest care the most. Look into people's eyes when you are listening. You will see what they are not saying. Love is patient and kind and an action according to Paul in 1 Corinthians 13:4. Speaking with people both kindly and patiently helps open the door to healing.

Coming into God's light and having his light in my heart now makes my goal to bring others into God's grace and light. Coming out of darkness and into the light makes me feel differently about life and others. As Christians, Jesus wants us to make disciples. We can do that by building relationships and connecting with people and sharing God's Word with love and patience. Some may be difficult because of past experiences, but we need to see through the anger and pain and help them to see that we are in the presence of a loving God. Let's help others see the light and be able to see clearly.

Today, let's look beyond the masks and façades people wear. Let's look over their built-up walls. Let's look with our hearts. Let's bring people to the peace that they so desperately desire—that we may have wanted for ourselves and received through Jesus. God is light. Satan is darkness. We choose our direction. Let's help others find the light from God.

I Can't Hear Him

When I was about twelve or thirteen, my father was in the hospital a lot for cancer treatment. When he would go in, he would be there weeks at a time. I loved him and missed him terribly. One time, he came home for a weekend while I was at a Boy Scout camp. I called home from a pay phone, and the other kids were very noisy. They were all fooling around and making a lot of racket. My father had had extensive surgery around his mouth, and he was hard to understand for a while, and the noise was deafening around me. I wanted to hear and understand what my father had to say. The distraction was terrible; it was hard to focus, hear, and understand. I was so sad and angry because the phone call felt like a disaster.

Have you ever felt that way about conversations and prayers with God? We are distracted by the things in this world, our own desires, music, television, and all the noise this world makes. We can have so many distractions that they tend to drown out God's voice, but he keeps calling to us and his voice keeps getting louder. During sports season, my desires, my wants, and all the things that keep me from hearing the voice of God become so loud that it is difficult to hear him.

I need to find a quiet place to pray, to read my Bible, and to listen to those who are knowledgeable and spiritual that can help me understand God better. Sometimes the noise around me can be deafening to his voice. As David said in Psalm 119:37, "Turn my eyes away from worthless things; preserve my life according to your word." I must turn my eyes and ears only to him and his Word to drown out the noise. Satan wants me to hear those things that keep me from hearing God's Word and his voice.

We must find a quiet place and time that are deliberately set at certain times of the day to give only to God so we can hear his voice. I want more than a casual relationship and superficial conversation with my heavenly Father. I want a deep and meaningful conversation and relationship. I can't stop all the distractions and noise around me, but I can plan a quiet time and place in my day to be alone and to drown out the rest of the world and spend it with God. Imagine me or you and God alone daily, planning our lives and what we can do for him and him for us.

I Look to the Cross

Where do I look when I need forgiveness? I look to the cross.

Where do I look when I can't forgive? I look to the cross.

Where do I look for real love? I look to the cross.

Where do I look to find what submission looks like? I look to the cross.

Where do I look to see what sacrifice looks like? I look to the cross.

Where do I look to see what a real friend has done? I look to the cross.

Where do I look to see how much God loves me? I look to the cross.

Where do I look in times of trouble? I look to the cross.

Where do I look when tempted? I look to the cross.

Where do I look when there is no way out? I look to the cross.

Where do I look when I feel unlovable or unloved? I look to the cross.

Where do I look when I can't trust? I look to the cross.

Where do I look to find God's plan? I look to the cross.

Where do I look for a real hero and a real champion? I look to the cross.

Where do I look for my salvation? I look to the cross.

Where do I look for hope? I look to the cross.

Where do I look to find Jesus? I search my heart.

I'm In

You are all sons of God through faith in Christ Jesus, for all of you who were baptized into Christ have clothed yourselves with Christ. There is neither Jew nor Greek, slave nor free, male nor female, for you are all one in Christ Jesus. If you belong to Christ, then you are Abraham's seed, and heirs according to the promise.

Galatians 3:26–29

For God so loved the world that he gave his one and only Son, that whoever believes in him shall not perish but have eternal life.

John 3:16

What are the questions on an application? Age, gender, race, nationality, religion, job experience, and education. Pretty exclusive, don't you think? All through my life I have been asked these questions. Any number of these could have been cause for exclusion over America's history. You are too old, you are too young, you are black, and you are female. Many reasons have caused exclusion throughout history. Imagine an application with none of these questions. Imagine an application that says: name and belief.

How about entrance into God's kingdom? Should this be an exclusionary club? What would God's application look like? Good news. He doesn't have one. There are none of those questions on his application. God says that whoever believes in Jesus shall have eternal life in his kingdom. Have you read John 3:16? Do you believe? Have you repented? Have you been baptized? Do you want to be? Come on in. All are welcome. Have you sinned? No problem. Do you want to change? Do you believe in Jesus? Do you want to spend eternity in God's magnificent kingdom? I'm in. I believe that God sent his Son, Jesus, to die for my sins.

> There is neither Jew nor Greek, slave nor free, male nor female, for you are all one in Christ Jesus.
>
> Galatians 3:28

All are welcome. The only question God has is: do you believe? I'm in. Once I believed, I began repenting for my sins and was baptized for the remission of my sin. God doesn't care my age, race, gender, nationality, education, job experience, or anything else. He simply wants to know if I believe. He can use all of us to do his will. I have one question for you: are you in?

I've Got It All Right Here

> But the fruit of the Spirit is love, joy, peace, patience, kindness, goodness, faithfulness, gentleness and self-control.
>
> Galatians 5:22–23

Do you remember Felix the cat? Felix was a cartoon cat who always had his bag of tricks. He didn't leave home without it. Anything he needed was right in the bag. How about Mary Poppins? She seemed to have everything she needed in her bag as well. Batman had his utility belt. MacGyver, all he needed was a paperclip and rubber band, and he could build a helicopter. The professor on *Gilligan's Island* could build everything out of coconuts except a boat.

Ladies, you seem to have everything in your purses. Men, have you ever noticed? If you need a stamp, Band-Aid, hairbrush, or aspirin, you name it, it is in there. How about a Swiss army knife? I hear they have installed a coffee maker.

As Christians, do we carry everything we need? God has placed his Spirit right inside us. God dwells in us. Where does he live? I believe he lives in my heart, soul, and mind. We also live in Christ. When I open my mind, heart, and soul to God, amazing changes occur in my life. I am a new person through baptism. I am in Christ. The fruits of the spirit dwell within me. It is up to me whether I use them and am open to them in my life. Fruits come as God continues his work in me.

Some of life's situations can be rough. Difficult people, stress, disappointments, grief, sorrow, worry, anger, hurt, and a list of assorted things affect us emotionally and physically. What do you have in your bag or utility belt for that? Answers to all life's situations are found in God's Word, the Bible. We can apply one of the gifts of the spirit in every situation. That is why I think God gave us his fruits: to use and live by in all situations. God has given us people as well to comfort, listen, help, guide, counsel, and love us. With all the tools and the presence of God, I have everything I need right here to solve any situation I may have today. Remember the bracelets "Jesus is the answer"? What's the question? Doesn't matter. Jesus is the answer. Turn to him.

Today, living one day at a time, I have been assured I have every tool I need to live as a Christian. God has provided me instructions to live by in the Bible, his fruits of his spirit to use daily in all situations, and God is available at all times and in all places to hear and answer the prayers of my heart. Today, I will use these tools to walk as a Christian, knowing that I've got it all right here, because God has provided it to me out of his immeasurable love.

Imagine This

Can you imagine having problems with your computer, and your doorbell ringing? You answer the door, and there is Bill Gates, just stopping by. Wow, problem solved. Sounds good. What if your phone was having problems? Alexander Graham Bell just happens to be over for dinner. Toilet overflows? Sir Thomas Crapper (inventor of toilet) is over for lunch. Car troubles? Henry Ford is in the passenger seat.

You might be asking, "Come on, Ken. What does this have to do with Christianity?"

What about life problems? What about fear, anxiety, anger, insecurity, grief, loss, financial insecurity, divorce, sin, and anything that causes pain? Can any of these inventors help? What about the Creator of life? Do you realize that God is just a prayer away? In Hebrews 13:5–6 God has said, "Never will I leave you; never will I forsake you." So we say with confidence, "The Lord is my helper; I will not be afraid." What can man do to me? God is always with us, no matter the situation.

Think about this when you feel alone.

Is Seeing Believing?

Just then a woman who had been subject to bleeding for twelve years came up behind him and touched the edge of his cloak. She said to herself, "If only I touch his cloak, I will be healed."

Matthew 9:20

And when the men of that place recognized Jesus, they sent word to all the surrounding country. People brought all their sick to him and begged him to let the sick touch the edge of his cloak, and all who touched him were healed.

Matthew 14:35–36

Imagine reaching out and touching the edge of Jesus' cloak and being healed. It takes great faith to believe this. The people in the verses I have shared had this faith. The sick, infirm, and diseased reached out and touched the edge of the cloak Jesus was wearing and were healed. The faith shown by these people was amazing. They believed before they touched his cloak they would be healed. They had not seen this happen; they just believed in the healing power of Jesus.

Do we need to reach out and touch and see with our own eyes to believe? Is our faith about seeing? How does Jesus say we should believe? Here is what Jesus said to the woman who touched his cloak, "Your faith has healed you."

How is your faith today?

Is There a Light at the End of the Tunnel?

When Jesus spoke again to the people, he said, "I am the light of the world. Whoever follows me will never walk in darkness, but will have the light of life."

John 8:12

Do you feel as though you're maybe halfway down the tunnel and the light you see is an oncoming train? Nothing you do seems to ever turn out right? I have had these feelings. I have traveled in darkness searching for a light. The light at the end of the tunnel is Jesus. Jesus is the light of the world, and whoever follows him will never walk in darkness.

Things at night sometimes seem worse than they really are. Even the noises are exaggerated and may seem scary. I lie in bed, feverishly trying to solve my own problems in the dark, and at all times, the outcome seems bleak. I turn on the light. But more importantly, I go to the light, Jesus. Jesus is the light and brings illumination in his answers to all my self-made problems. I get the right answers and solutions when I go to the light.

The Bible is also a very bright light and removes all darkness. Every answer to any situation is in this book. It is not any book; it is the Word of God. God talks to me through his Holy Spirit and his word in the Bible. Prayer to my Father through his Son Jesus brings light to all my problems, sometimes right away, sometimes it takes a while, but the light comes on. I no longer have to live in darkness. I walk with the light of the world, Jesus. Is it dark today? Turn on the light. Go to the light. He has said, "Come to me."

Is Your Sky Falling?

God has said, "Never will I leave you; never will I forsake you."

Hebrews 13:5

Even though I walk through the valley of the shadow of death, I will fear no evil, for you are with me; your rod and your staff, they comfort me.

Psalm 23:4

In the fable about Chicken Little, he is eating lunch one day, and an acorn falls from a tree onto his head. Chicken Little's misperception leads him to run around telling everyone the sky is falling. Misperception and feeling alone has led me to feel this way many times in my life. I have never run around yelling, "The sky is falling!" But I have thought, *This is the end. I can't take any more.*

When I was younger and a girl broke up with me, my world was shattered. I felt like that was it and I couldn't go on. One day, I lost some schoolbooks. I was about twenty-four, I couldn't find them, and I could see the handwriting on the wall and the path to destruction. I would fail the classes, never get a good job, never have a family because I couldn't support them, and I would live in the streets. Acorn on the head, lost books, and living on the streets, a bit dramatic, don't you think? Later that day, someone found and returned the books.

In times of pain and struggle, we are not alone, God is with us. God promised he would never leave us or forsake us. He is there with his arms stretched out, saying, "Come to me," and he takes our burdens, our pain, and our suffering. Let God wrap his arms around you. The Holy Spirit of God lives within us. Jesus lives in our heart. God the Father answers our prayers. There is no deserted island, and there are no acorns falling on our heads either.

Trust in God's promises. He will answer our prayers; he will never leave us nor forsake us, and whatever valleys we walk through, he is right beside us. Draw strength from God, let him help you through whatever the pain and whatever the loss. I have learned like Job that with faith, whatever the situation, I will come out the other end a stronger person with faith in God. I will be victorious.

It's Time for a Christian Revival

> Then Jesus came to them and said, "All authority in heaven and on earth has been given to me. Therefore go and make disciples of all nations, baptizing them in the name of the Father and of the Son and of the Holy Spirit, and teaching them to obey everything I have commanded you. And surely I am with you always, to the very end of the age."
>
> Matthew 28:18–20

You want me to do what? I feel a call, a tug to spread the good news of Jesus Christ. My friend Jimmy said, "Ken, you have something to say. You need to start writing." I said, "But I am not a writer." My friend Pat asked when I was beginning to look for a job, "Have you thought about the ministry?" I said, "I don't think I am ready." Well, now I am doing both. I share e-mail and Internet devotionals filled with what I hope is encouragement, God's grace, and my experience with both. I counsel people from my church, surrounding churches, and the community. I guess when God says it is time, it is time. God has equipped me to do the work he has put before me.

But I am just an ordinary guy. Should I be writing such things? Who will listen? I guess that is not a good question. Just write, and there will be some people who read and find a message. By no means am I comparing myself with Bible heroes, but when I look through the Bible, many questioned God when commissioned to ministry. Moses, Paul, Peter, the apostles, the prophets; none thought they were qualified. They weren't. God brought them to it, and God equipped them. He has given me the Bible; all the words I need are right there.

There are a lot of people in the world trying to get Christians away from Christ. Some ex-Christians have found new age religions, mushroom churches that just pop up with a "what's happening now" message. Some of these people are very influential, and people flock to them, abandoning God for what is new and supposedly exciting. They are on the wrong path, they are leading people away, and our shepherd wants them back.

It is time for a Christian revival. It is time to get excited about Christianity. It is time to follow Jesus' great commission, to go out and make disciples. We need to talk to people, share the good news, share our testimonies, share our experience as Christians, and share the saving word of the Bible. We don't need to scare them; we need to share with them.

We need to bring our friends, family, and neighbors to church and Jesus. We need to arm ourselves with the love of Jesus. This is a battle for souls that we need to win. Jesus didn't use military weapons; he used the truth and love. Those are the tools we need to use. Jesus called us all to this commission and not just a few of us.

The battle cry is for each and every one to gather the tools necessary to win souls. It is time for a revival. Put on the full armor of God. Satan isn't going to like this. What is your call? What are you being tugged to do? We all have a role in our church and in the kingdom. We are the body of Christ. Are we ready? If not, God will equip each and every one of us with the tools we need. Why? Because he loves each and every one of us and would love to be able to welcome everyone home. Let's go get them.

It's Like an Ice Cream–Eating Contest

> For the Son of Man is going to come in his Father's glory
> with his angels, and then he will reward each person accord-
> ing to what he has done.
>
> Matthew 16:27

Can you imagine Jesus is going to come with angels in our Father's
glory to reward each of us for what we have done? It seems like a
double reward. We have been saved by Jesus, and now he is going
to reward us again for being obedient to his commands. It is almost
like an ice cream eating contest. I was thinking, *What if I were in
an ice cream eating contest?* What if it were sponsored by Ben and
Jerry's or Häagen Dazs? The sponsor gives you gallons of ice cream
to eat, your favorites. Whoever eats the most in a set amount of
time wins a reward. You know what I am thinking? Isn't the ice
cream reward enough? Well I haven't had this offer yet, but you can
be sure my spoon is ready just in case.

Jesus is coming to reward those people who have followed
God's commands and followed the amazing example of Jesus. We
will be rewarded according to our service to man and God. God
will carry my burdens if I bring them to him. I can bring everything
to God, and he will lighten my load. God listens and answers all of
my prayers. God tells us to serve others and make disciples. Feed
the hungry, shelter the homeless, help those in need, and many

other acts of service. God tells us to be his hands, feet, mouth, and heart here on Earth. After all he has done for me, I am so grateful that this is what I want to do. This passage says he will reward us according to what we have done. Isn't that kind of like winning an ice cream–eating contest?

Just in my own church, I know people that have been serving God and his people for decades, and they are looking at some pretty big rewards for their work. I couldn't list them all without forgetting someone important. Their hearts are bigger than Texas; they just keep doing, without looking for accolades, trophies, pats on the back, or any sort of reward. They serve because it needs to be done. They love God with all their hearts and souls. They love others more than they love themselves, and because God has laid this work on their hearts, they answer the call with joy and service in their hearts. They are not looking for a reward, but God is going to give them one. I watch them and do my best to do more; not for rewards, but because they make it look like an ice cream–eating contest. So grab your spoon and dig in. The fields are plenty, and the ice cream is flowing. Oh yeah, there are rewards at the end, and they are from God. I can't imagine how much better it can get. It just seems like serving my loving father after all he has done for me would be reward enough.

Jesus Did It for Me

He was arrested for me.
He was found guilty for me.
He had a friend betray him for me.
He had a friend deny him for me.
He had eleven friends run from him for me.
He took severe punishment and torture for me.
He was blindfolded and punched in the face for me.
He was spit at for me.
He was mocked for me.
He was laughed at for me.
He wore a crown of thorns for me.
He had nails driven through his hands and feet for me.
He wore my sin.
He died for me.

What am I willing to do for him today?

Jesus Is Alive and Well

Do not let your hearts be troubled. Trust in God; trust also in me. In my Father's house are many rooms; if it were not so, I would have told you. I am going there to prepare a place for you. And if I go and prepare a place for you, I will come back and take you to be with me that you also may be where I am.

John 14: 1–3

Jesus said, "I am going there to prepare a place for you." Imagine, the King of kings is preparing a place for you and me. In the love story we know as the Bible, Jesus suffered great pain and torture, mocking, betrayal, denial, disloyalty, and his ultimate death. To the world, some believe Jesus may have been a great man but one who is dead. They think him a martyr, prophet, kook, good guy, or even nonexistent.

The good news is Jesus is not dead. Jesus was resurrected from death by God through the Holy Spirit to bring us out of our sins and into eternal life. The carpenter is in heaven preparing our place. Heaven is a place of no pain, no suffering, and no worry. Jesus is alive and well in heaven preparing our place. Jesus is active, and when all believers' rooms are ready, Jesus will come back for us.

To him who loves us and has freed us from our sins by his blood, and has made us to be a kingdom and priests to serve his God and Father—to him be glory and power for ever and ever! Amen. Look, he is coming with the clouds, and every eye will see him, even those who pierced him; and all the peoples of the earth will mourn because of him. So shall it be! Amen.

Revelation 7:5–7

Be confident, don't give up. Jesus is alive and well. Jesus is preparing a glorious eternal home for us. Jesus will be coming back. Keep your eyes on the clouds. Today, we need to keep doing our Father's will, not just sitting around and waiting. Jesus isn't sitting around waiting. He is active, he is preparing our place, and he has already prepared our way. Now we must be making disciples and doing the Lord's will in all we do today. We know the way. Let everyone know that Jesus beat death and is alive and well.

Jesus' To Do List

When he had received the drink, Jesus said, "It is finished."
With that, he bowed his head and gave up his spirit.

John 19:30

Leave heaven as a king and come into the world as a needy infant.
Check.
Give the blind sight. Check.
Make the lame walk. Check.
Turn water to wine. Check.
Turn a few fish and loaves into a feast for five thousand. Check.
Tell Satan no to all temptations. Check.
Calm a major storm at sea. Check.
Walk on water. Check.
Teach and preach the word of God. Check.
Give two new commands: love God and love one another. Check.
Defy the Pharisees and spread the good news. Check.
Wash feet and serve common people. Check.
Get arrested as an innocent man. Check.
Heal and replace a persecutor's ears. Check.
Be mocked by captors. Check.
Survive a severe beating by the Roman soldiers. Check.
Carry my cross to be crucified. Check.
Ask his Father to forgive those who put him to death. Check.

Freely submit to death to pay the full price of sin. Check.

Die. Check.

Be resurrected. Check.

Continue to teach after being brought back. Check.

Give the great commission and make disciples. Check.

Ascend into heaven and prepare a mansion for all sinners who believe and love me. Check.

What's on your to do list today?

Jesus Who?

"You are not one of his disciples, are you?" the girl at the door asked Peter. He replied, "I am not. As Simon Peter stood warming himself, he was asked, "You are not one of his disciples, are you?" He denied it, saying, "I am not."

John 18:17

One of the high priest's servants, a relative of the man whose ear Peter had cut off, challenged him, "Didn't I see you with him in the olive grove?" Again Peter denied it, and at that moment a rooster began to crow.

John 25–27

Peter witnessed Jesus heal people, bring people back to life, turn morsels into meals for thousands, pull nets full of fish in, calm a storm, walk on water, and perform all sorts of miracles. Peter knew Jesus was the Son of God. When Jesus was arrested, Peter went into battle mode; he cut the ear off one of the soldiers. Jesus put the ear back and told Peter to put away his sword. He told Peter this was what his Father sent him for. Poor Peter, he had a rough night. He had even been scolded by Jesus once or twice at dinner. Jesus even said to Peter, "Get behind me, Satan," because Peter was seeing things only from a human point of view and not God's.

When Jesus was taken into the temple for his brutal interrogation, Peter was right outside. Peter had been told at dinner by

Jesus that he would deny him three times. Peter was probably quite confused by Jesus' statement. But there he was in the temple court. When asked if he was one of Jesus' disciples, he said, "Jesus who?" That is not quite what he said. What he said was, *no*. He said it three times. All eyes were on him. Peter probably thought the people would just snatch him up too. Then the rooster crowed, just as Jesus told him it would after his third denial of knowing Jesus.

I am not Peter's defense attorney, but what I see is a friend filled with fear, not only losing a dear friend, but afraid for his own life. Again, Peter had acted human, not viewing the situation as God did. Peter was human. He still did not have a full comprehension of who Jesus really is; he knew the words but not the whole truth, not what was still to occur. Jesus looked into Peter's eyes, and Peter broke down and wept bitterly. Peter knew what he had done.

Later Peter was reconciled by Jesus. Jesus asked Peter three times if he loved him. Three times, Peter said *yes*. Three times, Peter was given a new mission to care for Jesus' people. You and I have also been reconciled to God, our Father, through the awesome sacrifice that Jesus made for us. We have been forgiven. Now God has a call for us, just as he had for Peter. Jesus gave us the great commission: see Matthew 28:16–20. Not only did he forgive Peter and us, but he also said, "Okay, move on. Go to work. You get it, now make more disciples" (paraphrase).

Today, I want to shout from the rooftops, "Yes, I am a disciple of Jesus. Jesus is my Savior. I believe. I know. I have faith. Can you hear me? I am a disciple of Jesus!" I don't know what I would have done in the time of Jesus' arrest. I wasn't there, but Peter was. Peter was also a disciple of Jesus, who, like me, had a period of doubt and fear. God restores us from doubt and fear to assurance in him. Go to him in study, prayer, and meditation. You will see. He will let you know who he really is.

Kenta, I Love You

And whoever welcomes a little child like this in my name welcomes me.

Matthew 18:5

When I was working at Maryhaven, I began there as a counselor, and became senior counselor in the residential setting. When I graduated from college, I became the behavior management specialist. When I first went to work there, I couldn't get past the smell and sights; later I got used to it. While there, I learned the love these children have.

There was a boy I'll call Huffy who was fifteen years old. When I started, he was assigned to me. He was none of the counselor's favorite. Huffy drooled, perseverated, and was always disheveled, but Huffy became my favorite. He was always happy to see me and would tell me he loved the Mets at least twenty times with his Huffy smile. Then he would tell me with a nervous laugh that the Red Sox stink. One day, while on a field trip, I was driving the van. I was having a rough day; I had just had an argument with my girlfriend at the time, and I was quiet, which is unusual for me. The whole van was quiet. I must have been giving off a vibe. Finally, from the back of the bus, Huffy yelled, "Kenta, I love you." Huffy always called me Kenta. The other kids in the van started laughing and calling Huffy names. Huffy yelled again, "Kenta is upset. I love him." The whole tone of the bus changed. Kids started asking what was wrong. The genuine concern I felt almost made me cry.

I can find love anywhere if I open my eyes. That was a great job, and I loved those kids. I know they also loved me. It was more than a job, it was a ministry. The kids were the ministers. I was ministered to.

Unconditional love is hard to find. I found it there. God was there. God was and is with those kids, who are now adults.

I know God loves those children. I know they are his kids. I am privileged to have met them. When I look back, I can see that God is in them. I know that God loves them. His love shines in them if you have the eyes to see.

Today, I will find the love in all God's people. I will look for the lessons God wants to teach me. I may be amazed who will be the ones to teach me.

Learning to Love Ourselves

Part One

Jesus replied: "Love the Lord your God with all your heart and with all your soul and with all your mind. This is the first and greatest commandment. And the second is like it: 'Love your neighbor as yourself.' All the Law and the Prophets hang on these two commandments."

Matthew 22:37–40

Dear friends, I am not writing you a new command but an old one, which you have had since the beginning. This old command is the message you have heard.

1 John 2:7

Do not seek revenge or bear a grudge against one of your people, but love your neighbor as yourself. I am the LORD.

Leviticus 19:18

Love your neighbor as yourself; that can be a tough one. There are times some people can be pretty hard on themselves. There were and still are times when I am not happy with my own thoughts or behaviors. I am pretty judgmental, and it is not at my brothers, sisters, or even enemies; it is at me. Have you ever had those times? There are times when I wish I didn't even have to hang around with me because no one judges me as harshly as I can. Loving others as I love myself at times would be doing no one any favors.

Not only do we have to love God and love others, you and I have to learn to really love ourselves. Now this isn't an everyday thing, don't get me wrong. Most of the time, I can be my own best friend and really enjoy my own company. I know others that are downright miserable. They feel guilt for things they have done, they feel sadness and pain because of things others have done to them, and they even take guilt on for that. There are others who really believe they are not worthy to come before God and ask forgiveness and ask for his love. We need to learn to love ourselves and others as God loves us. Wow, that's a tough one.

God gave his only Son up to death and torture so that we could spend eternity with him and his risen Son, Jesus. God has sealed us as we believe, repent, and become baptized with his own Holy Spirit. Our sins are forgiven by God when we ask and bring them before him in his Son Jesus' name. Sometimes, people wonder how God can love them after all they have done against him. God really loves us, and we need to love him, each other, and ourselves

Learning to Love Ourselves

Part Two

> Jesus replied: "Love the Lord your God with all your heart and with all your soul and with all your mind. This is the first and greatest commandment. And the second is like it: 'Love your neighbor as yourself.' All the Law and the Prophets hang on these two commandments."
>
> Matt 22:37–40

When I first wrote part one, it was in a blog. I promised in my blog that I was going to have a surprise treat. In this writing, I was going to discuss ways to learn to love ourselves, and reasons that some people struggle with this. Well, the surprise was I was going to say very little and use the comments I received from others on how they have learned this. I received about twenty comments in my blog and one comment in the e-mail. Do you know that each of the comments said it was easier to love God and love others than to love themselves? Each comment said they struggled with loving themselves.

So I have very little to put in from others except if you struggle with this, you are not alone. It seems to be an all too common theme. It seems that some are reaching out and lacking self-love in our own body, the body of Christ. Some of this seems to come from the guilt of sin or from past abuse. Others have lost jobs and feel unfulfilled. Some have faith issues and are concerned; others seem to spend time by themselves because they are ashamed, afraid, and just don't want to burden others with their problems or even their presence.

Some have said we have to love ourselves before we can love others. But at the same time, many who struggle with loving themselves love God and love others with all they have. I believe we all know how to love God and others. A common phrase in the elections seems to be reaching across the aisles to the other party for unity. It seems we have many of our own body crying out on the inside to be loved. We have to reach across the aisles of our churches to love and encourage one another. We have to show each other it is neither narcissistic nor far-reaching to find the love within ourselves that God has for us.

Learning to Love Ourselves

Part Three

> So God created man in his own image, in the image of God
> he created him; male and female he created them.
>
> Genesis 1:27

The past two writings are about loving ourselves. This is not a call
to become narcissistic, prideful, or self-absorbed. It is simply adding us into the equation of loving God with all our hearts and souls
as well as loving others as ourselves, which seems to imply we love
ourselves and look at that in order to identify how we should love
one another.

Forgiving yourself seems to be a key to loving yourself. We
need to believe in our hearts and minds that God has forgiven us.
The Creator of the universe has forgiven us and loves us. God had
made it possible for us to spend eternity with him because of this
forgiveness. We have been forgiven because God has come down
from heaven as Jesus, taking on our sins and being crucified and
punished, paying once and for all the sin debt of man. This is tre-
mendous love; God loves us and forgives us. I have asked myself if
God loves me and forgives me warts and all. Who am I not to love
myself? Do I know better than God?

There are times we look at others created by the media and
Hollywood to be the "beautiful people." Some believe we should

look just like them; they become a benchmark of what we should become. There are many manmade expectations we try to live up to; if we can't or don't, we feel we have fallen short and are no good. That's not what the Bible says. God is not looking at these characteristics; he is looking at our hearts. That is where our true beauty is judged.

Have you seen waterfalls, mountains, lakes, trees, oceans, flowers, fields of green grass, and all the wonders and beauty around us? Well that is God's creation. Have you seen the wildlife, animals, fish, and birds? All have many colors shapes and sizes. Aren't they amazing? They are God's creation. Isn't God's creation beautiful, amazing, flawless, and awesome? Do you sit in awe at the beauty and just love what God has created? But all of that beauty is not created in God's image. "So God created man in his own image, in the image of God he created him; male and female he created them." Do you love all of God's creation? We are his creation and he created us in his own image. Do you love the image of God?

Let Me Spoil the Ending for You

Have people ever told you the ending to a movie you want to see? I won't do that. Have you ever recorded a sporting event and haven't watched it yet? I won't give you the score. So what ending will I spoil for you today? There are many out there that do not believe in God the Father, Son, or the Holy Spirit. There are many out there who are not sure what to believe. There are many who are still on the fence.

Daily, we are subject to satanic attacks. These attacks come in the form of discouragement, depression, lost beliefs, lost values, doubt, sin, temptations, and pride. There are so many distractions that take our thoughts from God. The narrow path may seem long, rocky, and just too difficult. We worry at times about being saved. It says in Romans 10:10, "For it is with your heart that you believe and are justified, and it is with your mouth that you confess and are saved." Believe and confess and you are saved. Hmm, that's one ending that is spoiled.

The other ending I want to spoil for you is that God wins. In the end, God wins. He has already won. He has declared victory from the beginning. Let's take a look at Romans 14:11–12. "As surely as I live, says the Lord, every knee will bow before me; every tongue will confess to God. So then, each of us will give an account of himself to God."

Well then, I have spoiled the ending. Or should I say new beginning? God wins, and for those who don't believe and have mocked God, as Ricky Ricardo used to say to Lucy, "You have a lot of explaining to do." I am glad Jesus will be at my side, claiming me. I also win because of Jesus' great victory.

Let's Celebrate Our Differences

> Just as each of us has one body with many members, and these
> members do not all have the same function, so in Christ we
> who are many form one body, and each member belongs to
> all the others. We have different gifts, according to the grace
> given us.
>
> Romans 12:4–6

When I was a kid, I loved playing baseball in my neighborhood.
One problem though. We had to go door to door to collect the
other kids. Each kid would have to bring different parts of the
game with him or her because no one had all the equipment we
needed. One had a ball, others had mitts, and others had bats.
Some actually would have to bring their doormats so we had bases.
Without one another, we couldn't play. If someone got mad during
the game, he might take his ball and go home; game over.

I belong to a wonderful church with many different people.
They bring many different and unique gifts to our church body and
to our service on Sundays. Some come with great silence and reverence, some bring great joy, and some great service to our assembly.
In our church, we don't use instrumental music, but we bring a
beautiful melody: altos, sopranos, basses, and the rest. Some people
clap while they sing. Some don't. Some are filled with reverence,

some are filled with joy, and some are filled with both. We demonstrate our praise differently.

As Christians, we are all separate parts of one body. We all bring different talents, gifts, and experiences to the church body. We have several ministries within our church; everyone brings their unique abilities. We should be celebrating our differences in, not only our service and ministries, but also in our daily lives. Without each other, we are not really a body. Together, we can do what I cannot do alone. We think and perform differently. I learn about Christ by observing everyone, watching and enjoying the unique gifts each brings with them. I emulate a bit from everyone, each separate and unique person. There is enough division, enough denominations, we don't need more. Let's shoot for unity and fellowship. Let's celebrate one another's uniqueness.

Today, I want to remember my way isn't the only way. Today, I will celebrate the differences. I want to celebrate the unique gifts, talents, and experiences each brings to the body. I don't want to judge people's actions or unique form of giving thanks to our Father. I want to remember Jesus is the head. We need all the parts of Christ's body to function. We need unity and fellowship. Together, let's love God, love one another, and minister to the world as one body. If we start losing these parts of the body, it is game over.

Let's Go for a Walk

As they talked and discussed these things, Jesus himself suddenly came and began walking with them.

Luke 24:15

When I moved from New York to Florida, I began working at Devereux, a residential and school setting for emotionally disturbed children. Today, I want to share with you a story about a boy I'll call Ollie. He was a seventeen-year-old at the time, with a criminal record and disturbed emotions.

Ollie would get in trouble in class daily. The teachers would call me to get him. When I would get him, we would discuss his behavior; he was quite insightful about his feelings. He would tell me what he did. Then we could figure out the origin of the problem. He enjoyed his talks with me. He would regain his self-control and would then go back to class.

I realized that Ollie just needed someone to talk to. So I sat down with him and his teacher and wrote a behavior plan. The plan consisted of a twenty-minute visit with me daily when we would walk around the building and discuss his day, his fears, his accomplishments, and his family. This would get him through a whole day without getting in trouble or becoming belligerent or violent. Just a few minutes of listening time changed an entire person.

Don't we all just need someone to talk to? Do we usually ask for some time? How do we get the attention? Is it in a positive or sometimes negative way? Are there some people around you who thrive on the negative attention just to get attention? What do we do?

How about going for a walk? Sitting down and talking to those who are screaming on the inside for conversation, someone to listen, someone they can tell their, fears, concerns, or accomplishments. Today, I want to listen. I want to talk to those around me so they know I am there to listen. They don't have to do anything special, just talk.

God is also listening. He is the best listener. He doesn't only hear what we say or see what we do. He listens to and sees our hearts. He is always there. God never puts us on hold. He is also there to assure us he will take care of us.

How about taking a walk with someone today and bringing God along? How about a walk with God today? Talk with him twenty to thirty minutes daily, and you will both enjoy the walk. Read his Word daily and listen. He is walking with us and talking to us.

Look Both Ways

Be very careful, then, how you live—not as unwise but as wise.

Ephesians 5:15

When I was a very little boy, my mother always told me to look both ways before I cross the street. At the time, it just sounded like another rule I could break. But one day, I ran across the street, and a car screeched, swerved, and stopped. I then understood that danger may come from any direction. I could be severely injured if I did not look both ways. Look before you leap. What is down there? Weigh the options, think before you act, be aware of your surroundings, and many other slogans get me to think before I enter into dangerous activities. It is a shame that I have had to learn many things the hard way. Hmm, if only I had looked both ways.

As the commercial says, life comes at you fast. Are you ready? Satan is out there with a lot of tempting activities. They all look enticing until we engage in them. Then the price comes, and sometimes it is a very costly consequence. Of course, we then go to God; ask and receive his mercy, grace, forgiveness; and we repent. No matter how spiritual, wise, smart, or ready we are, we need to be vigilant when it comes to the temptations in this world. Rationalization, manipulation, semantics, and Satan's influence can make dangerous sin look harmless until we actually give in.

Vigilance is the key to life—a day at a time, a situation at a time. Satan is like a prowling lion, waiting for our backs to be turned to him before he will pounce. Paul's advice in his letter to the Ephesians was to be very careful how you live—not as unwise but wise. When temptations come—and believe me they will come— we need to heed the advice of my mother, "Look both ways." Oh yeah, and always look up.

Mama Tried

The proverbs of Solomon: A wise son brings joy to his father, but a foolish son grief to his mother.

Proverbs 10:1

Dear old Daddy, rest his soul, Left my mom a heavy load; she tried so very hard to fill his shoes. Working hours without rest, wanted me to have the best. She tried to raise me right but I refused.

Merle Haggard, Song "Mama Tried"

When I was growing up, my mother was very strict about church. Ever since I can remember, she had us in church and Sunday school every week. She taught us about God and Jesus. I remember watching the *Ten Commandments* with Charleston Heston on TV. My mother had the Bible open and had us following along. I was a little kid and was so excited that I could read ahead to see what was going to happen in the movie. My mother always told us about her Catholic upbringing and how she went to Catholic school and was impressed with the education it provided her. My mother taught a Sunday school class for children for many years at the church we attended. My mother always tried to lead me in the right direction toward God. When my father died, she continued to take us to church and to Sunday school. She had to be both mother and father.

Somewhere around that time, I decided I wanted to do my own thing. I decided drinking alcohol was the way to go. It promised courage, friends, and a better way of life, but it never delivered. During this time, I broke my mother's heart. Not only did I get away from church, I decided I no longer even liked God. I blamed him for the horrible death of my father and grandmother and wanted no part of a God who would do this type of thing. My active alcoholism lasted for a five-year period. My mother worried, prayed for, and harped on me the entire time. All she wanted was for me to be happy and healthy, but I wouldn't give her that.

In 1978, the prayers paid off. I got sober. When my mother passed away, I had been sober twenty years. I had two children and had met my current wife. My mother knew I was both happy and healthy. She knew I had God in my life and loved him very much. She knew that at one time I even attended a seminary, considering the priesthood. Since that time, I have come back to Jesus in the Church of Christ. Don't think my mother's resting easy didn't come to mind when I went underwater during my baptism. Thanks, Mom, for all your prayers. They have paid off.

Message from the Crow's Nest

So this is what the Lord says: "If you change your heart and return to me, I will take you back.

Jeremiah 15:19

He will listen to the prayers of the destitute. He will not reject their pleas.

Psalm 102:17

Do you remember this scene in *Forrest Gump?* The seas were raging during a storm, and a very intoxicated, one-legged, angry Major Dan stood up in the crow's nest of Forrest Gump's shrimp boat. Dan was yelling, cursing, and challenging God, "Come and get me, give me your best shot." Major Dan had it, he was finished with life, he couldn't take it anymore, and all he knew of God in his drunken rage was to channel all his anger at him. He had lost his leg in the war. He had lost his money, home, self-respect, and his last friend was Forrest Gump. Like Jeremiah, he felt all were out to get him. For Jeremiah, that was true. He cursed the day he was born.

That scene caught my attention. There was a time in my life I was in that crow's nest, saying about the same thing. I had the desperation that an alcoholic learns to get by with. I have met other people in these situations. These people give the same speech as

Major Dan. They are lost and hopeless, angry at God, finding fault with him. The famous complaint is, "If there was a loving God, how could he let this happen?" Then they curse God. Apparently, they know there is a God but are looking at him through distorted eyes.

God doesn't cause the problems we blame him for. People do, weather does, disease does, weakness does, pride does, and Satan does. When I was doing my Major Dan impression, it was because I really didn't know God. I didn't understand salvation through Jesus and the sacrifice he made. All I knew were my tragic and selfish woes.

Have you ever been there with nowhere to turn, angry at God? God said, "I will never leave you or forsake you. I loved you before you were born." God so loved the world he gave his only Son, Jesus, to die for our sins. Through Jesus, we have eternal life. The Bible is chock full of God's love and encouragement. I had to stop thinking with my own angry thoughts and start reading what God actually said. I needed God to remove the calluses from my heart, and I needed eyes and ears to see and hear his Word.

God has totally transformed my life for the better. Why? He transformed me because he loves me. God told Jeremiah to tell the people, "If you change your heart and return to me, I will take you back." I have accepted his love and grace through the sacrificial death and resurrection of his Son, Jesus.

I don't need to stand in the crow's nest and imitate Major Dan; all I need to do when things begin to fall down around me is turn to God. He is with me. He loves me. He will lead me in the right direction. God gave us others to share our burden and encourage us. Don't let pride get in the way. Just talk with God and meditate on his Word. David also taught us to pray in Psalms. He was quite emotional. I didn't say it was a quiet prayer, but it wasn't a Major

Dan tirade. Today, I will go to God in complete faith that with him I can handle anything with the knowledge that he loves me enough to care and that he didn't create the awful situations I may truly be in at times.

My Father Got Lost

I was about four or five years old when my father and I were walking through a department store. My father was looking at something, and I was looking down the aisle, captivated by everything I saw, down one aisle then the next. Then terror struck. My father was lost. I went up to the front of the store. There was a security guard, and I told him that my name was Kenny Jones and my father was lost. The security guy laughed, got on the microphone, and said, "Mr. Ken Jones, please come to the front of the store. Your son is worried because you are lost."

Distractions have been a big part of my life. When I was a child, I attended Catholic Church and was always in awe of the priests. I wanted to be a priest. Well, until I discovered bright lights, money, girls, and beer. This took me way off track. I always wanted to please God. But again, as I wandered through life, God got lost. I sobered up at age twenty. At twenty-four, I wanted to be a priest again. I went into the Catholic seminary for three years. Again, I got distracted a few years after I left the seminary. I got married, had two sons, and things didn't work out. We divorced. Again, I hadn't put God first.

I got divorced; I couldn't go to church because I couldn't really face God. I thought maybe there was a different God. We all know there is not. Can you believe God got lost again? You know where I found him? He was on my car radio, five years ago on my way to work. I heard Charles Stanley tell me where God had been. He was right where I left him, next to me. Charles Stanley told me God loved me and would take me back again. Charles told me over the radio to find a Bible-based church.

I then decided to attend the Church of Christ. Hey, God is there too. He is everywhere. He was never really lost. I was. Since attending church, I have kept my eyes squarely on God and his Son, Jesus. I have been reading his Word and listening to his voice. I have invited God's Spirit to dwell in me. I was lost, and now I am found.

> So he got up and went to his father. But while he was still a long way off, his father saw him and was filled with compassion for him; he ran to his son, threw his arms around him and kissed him.
>
> Luke 15:20

My Shepherd

I am the good shepherd. The good shepherd lays down his
life for the sheep.

John 10:11

The LORD is my shepherd; I shall not be in want.

Psalm 23:1

In the Church of Christ, we have elders that are assigned to us.
They help us in our spiritual development and maturity as a church
and as individuals. They are also biblically referred to as shepherds.
I think I may have assigned my own elder, or God did. My elder
first taught me about the amazing grace of Jesus, and he baptized
me. He points out my strengths and weaknesses in Christian living
when I ask and sometimes even when I don't ask. Some of the other
shepherds also help me with my spiritual development. Because
my shepherd encouraged me, I am now in full-time ministry. The
other day, while having lunch together, he said, "I will help you
with anything. You know that, don't you?" He is an amazing man
of God.

I also have another shepherd, the good shepherd. His name is
Jesus. Do you know that shepherds count their sheep often and
know each one by name? Sheep only follow the voice of the shepherd, because that is the voice they recognize. At night, sheep are

kept safe in a sheep pen, and there is only one gate in and out; the only way in is through the shepherd. Along the paths, the shepherd keeps track of the sheep and has a staff and crook to keep the sheep together and to keep them from getting off the path. Shepherds protect the sheep from wolves, other wild animals, and all kinds of danger. A shepherd loves and protects his sheep, and even carries them when needed.

Jesus is my shepherd. In Psalm 23, David says, "the Lord is my Shepherd." David called the Lord his very own shepherd. So I call the Lord my very own shepherd. God keeps watch over me at all times. He keeps me safe from all dangers. He keeps me on the path, even if he has to pull me back in, nudge me, or scold me. He watches me night and day. In Luke 15:4, Jesus asks, "Suppose one of you has a hundred sheep and loses one of them. Does he not leave the ninety-nine in the open country and go after the lost sheep until he finds it?" My Shepherd, Jesus, knows my name and has come looking for me when I was lost and carried me back into the fold wrapped around his shoulders. Knowing I have Jesus as my shepherd gives me great confidence, assurance, and a sense of calm.

My Sin Cried Out

Father, if you are willing, take this cup from me; yet not my will, but yours be done.

Luke 22:42

But they kept shouting, "Crucify him! Crucify him!"

Luke 23:21

Jesus stood alone surrounded by armed guards and Pilate. Jesus stood battered, beaten, bloody and bruised waiting for his fate. Pilate called out to the crowd asking, what shall I do with this man? The crowd shouted out, "Crucify him!" Pilate even asked the crowd, "Hasn't this man suffered enough? They shouted out, "Crucify him!" Pilate said I will save one man, Jesus or a murderer named Barabbas. The crowd shouted, "Free Barabbas. Crucify him!" The words crucify him must have rang through every aching pore of Jesus' battered body. Hours earlier Jesus knew what was to come and asked his father to take this cup from him. The crowd answered the question; "Crucify him!"

What if I were in that crowd? What would I have yelled? My heart would be crying out to free Jesus. My sin would have shouted and cried out, "Crucify him! Crucify him!" What has my sin led me to say? Why is it crying out for this man's death? My sin debt had to be paid. Jesus was now paying it. Ten thousand legions of angels chomped at the bit waiting for Jesus call. The angels had to be held back. No call was to come. Why would Jesus submissively go through this torture? Why would Jesus allow this? Why didn't he call down those angels? Jesus came to pay my sin debt. He came to pay yours. Jesus let this happen because he loves us. What will you do with the amazing grace and amazing submission Jesus gave for us? Jesus suffered brutal torture and death. How will this affect you in your thoughts, words and actions?

Need a Hug?

This is what the Lord says: "I will give her peace that will flow to her like a river. The wealth of the nations will come to her like a river overflowing its banks. Like babies you will be nursed and held in my arms and bounced on my knees. I will comfort you as a mother comforts her child. You will be comforted in Jerusalem."

Isaiah 66:12–13

I was thinking back to when I was a child and I would get hurt. I went running to Mom or Dad, whoever was closest for comfort. They would examine the wound, wash it off, clean it up, get a Band-Aid, and kiss it to make the pain go away. But when the pain was great and I was crying, I would get a long hug. I was safe and secure. Nothing could happen to me in the arms of my parents. I was safe in the arms of love.

Even as an adult, don't things get a bit overwhelming at times? Don't we face hardships? When someone wraps their arms around us and gives us a hug, doesn't some of the pain go away? Not all of the pain, but some just seems to fall away. Maybe the hug transfers some of the pain, and the hugger takes it from us. I don't know where it goes, but nothing beats a good hug. Giving and receiving hugs, holding one another, sharing love, comfort, safety, security, and at times a little reassurance makes things better.

Isaiah shared God's message and talked about God's judgment with those who strayed. God was angry at those who turned away from him, those who would not listen to him, those who went against his will, and those who hated him. God said the punishment would be bad, really bad. He even said people would have to live with their worst fears. But do you know what else he said?

> I will give her peace that will flow to her like a river. The wealth of the nations will come to her like a river overflowing its banks. Like babies you will be nursed and held in my arms and bounced on my knees. I will comfort you as a mother comforts her child. You will be comforted in Jerusalem.
>
> Isaiah 66:12–13 (NVC)

For those who are his, this will be the reward. Imagine his hug, imagine his love, and imagine his nurturing assurance. Imagine being held in the arms of God. Wow. Time to practice and share your hugs with others. Let's get ready for the arms of God to be wrapped around us.

No Rest in Sight?

Drop the Rock

Come to me, all you who are weary and burdened, and I will give you rest. Take my yoke upon you and learn from me, for I am gentle and humble in heart, and you will find rest for your souls.

Matthew 11:28–29

As I read the headlines, the Internet, and e-mails, it appears there is no hope in sight with all the murders, rapes, war, illness, famine, rising gas prices, lowering home prices, and wages. Some folks don't even have to read the headlines; they can make their own list: troubled and sick children, aging parents, increasing bills, divorce, death, workload, unappreciated, an unfaithful spouse, and this list goes on and on. I am sure you and I have one or even a few of these. There are so many other stressors and responsibilities we have that weigh us down. It feels as though we have the weight of the world on our shoulders. It is like carrying a heavy boulder around all day while others are adding their rocks on top of ours.

Well, drop the rock. There is hope for those who believe in our Savior Jesus. Our brother, friend, Savior, Redeemer, and Son of God has a plan. What is the plan? What is his answer? He says, "Come to me." He says if you are "weary and burdened, I will give you rest." Jesus says he is gentle and humble in heart; we can yoke with, join with, and learn from him. He will help us carry our load. Jesus will help us find rest for our souls. Not only has he paid our price to heaven, he is with us today and gives us rest. How do we get that rest? Come to him.

How do I know this? Not only have I read this in the Bible, but I have experienced it. I have brought my problems of the death of my parents, divorce, alcoholism, financial ruin, and all kinds of weighty issues to him, and he has given me rest. You may ask how it works. Come to him, let him work out the details, and you will get rest. No matter what your boulder or boulders are today, drop the rock and come to him. He will give you rest. Ahh, sweet rest is in sight.

No Way Out

I have been counseling others for well over twenty-five years in one way or another. People don't seek counsel on a winning streak; they usually come when they don't know what else to do when they are distraught, depressed, lonely, and afraid. Of course, there are things we can do, but the main thing is to give these problems to God. Go to God in prayer and have faith that he really is there to help. People have lost jobs, loved ones, driver's licenses, homes, and marriages. I have all the answers, right? I am the counselor after all. Wait, I am laughing. Yes, I have some answers and a lot of questions. God has all the answers.

Many as well as myself on occasion ask the question and make the statement, "There is no way out of this one. What is God going to do? How is he going to get me out of this one? There is no hope. I lost my job, can't pay my bills, and can't afford gas."

David took on the giant with a slingshot and a shiny, flat rock and nailed him right in the between the eyes. He was all alone? Yeah, right. God was with him all the way. It was God's plan, and this story gives God the glory. Moses was bringing the Israelites out of slavery in Egypt when Pharaoh started chasing them down. They came to the Red Sea; no way out, death was assured or back to slavery. Moses raised his staff, and the sea split in two. The Israelites walked through, and when the Pharaoh and his army came through the sea, it came back together and drowned the bad guys. God did it again. All through the Bible, God had performed miracles of all kinds and solved problems. Leprosy was healed, the blind could see, sinners about to be stoned to death were stopped by a question from Jesus, an ark was built, huge armies were destroyed, prison walls were knocked down, Jericho's walls were knocked down and Nehemiah built walls back up, the dead came back to life, and the accounts of God's miracles are endless.

Close the self-help books. Get off the ledge. Turn off the television, because there is help for every problem, and there is a book with a solution. It is not a self-help book either. It is a book that says, "I love you. Let me help." It says, "I can and will do anything." It gives proof—the proof is a cross on Calvary. This book has all the answers to any problem, no matter how big or small. The examples above I gave are but a few. Open the Bible. Read, listen, and drink it in. Your help is there. It is not advice, but love and strong hands to help and carry us if necessary, a shoulder to lean on, a plan for action. What do we need to do for God's help? Beg, grovel, pay, or plead? Nope we ask, seek, or knock. As it says in Revelation 3:20, "Jesus is knocking on our door," our hearts. Will we let him in?

The fear we have will be overcome by the love of our Father, the love of Jesus, and the love of the Holy Spirit. I am not trying to chase the folks that come to counseling away. Come on, let's talk. I may not have all the answers, but I sure know where they are. No problem is too big or small; there is a solution. If he has to kill a giant, wipe out an army, or part a sea, God will answer our prayer. Why? God will do this because he is nuts about us.

No Wonder We Get Frustrated

> Rejoice evermore. Pray without ceasing. In every thing give thanks: for this is the will of God in Christ Jesus concerning you.
>
> 1 Thessalonians 5:16–18 (KJV)

I don't know about you, but sometimes I feel as though I am spinning my wheels. Sometimes I get frustrated and don't even know why. Have you ever felt like that? Have you ever felt as though your life is full and you are busy but something is still missing? Have you ever sat down and thought about it? Take out a blank sheet of paper. Make two columns. In the first column, write down in order the things that are most important to you, and the places you want to be spending most of your time. In the other column, honestly write down what you spend most of your time doing.

In my first column, I have God, family, friends, church, and fellowship. Where do I spend the most amount of time? Work and other activities take me away from the things that mean the most. Maybe your list is different. If the columns don't match up and you have the feelings I discussed earlier of frustration and feel something is missing, you may see why. Imagine the things we do sometimes keep us from what we enjoy doing and the things God would have us do.

Are the things of the world keeping us from the things God wants and even we want to be doing? Are we praying without ceasing? Are we rejoicing and giving thanks for all God has given us? Are we spending time in God's Word? Are we going to church when the doors are open? Are we getting involved in church and community activities? Are we sharing the good news? Are we making disciples? Are we spending time with family and friends? Are we finding ways to love God and love one another? I know when I am busy in the world with a full life and not spending time with my friends, family, and God, I am missing something. If our lists and columns don't match up, no wonder we are frustrated.

Not Me

So now, go. I am sending you to Pharaoh to bring my people
the Israelites out of Egypt. But Moses said to God, "Who am
I, that I should go to Pharaoh and bring the Israelites out of
Egypt?" And God said, "I will be with you."

Exodus 3:11

Moses had a few excuses for God in this passage why he could not
do what God was asking him to do. For each excuse, God advised
Moses how he would equip him. God not only told him he would
equip him; he told Moses, "I will be with you." Jeremiah told God
he was just a boy and that he couldn't do what God was asking him
to do. God told Jeremiah,

> The word of the LORD came to me, saying, "Before I formed
> you in the womb I knew you, before you were born I set you
> apart; I appointed you as a prophet to the nations." God also
> told him in this passage; do not be afraid of them, for I am
> with you and will rescue you," declares the LORD.
>
> Jeremiah 1:4–8

God told Jeremiah and Moses he would be with them and
Jeremiah that he would rescue him.

When I first came to the Church of Christ, I met with one
of the elders. He led me through the Bible to see I could be saved

and that I needed to be baptized. We talked also about ministry. Hmm, now I didn't know a whole lot about the Church of Christ or exact ministries, but I have seen some things I didn't think I was going to do. I have seen things in the past that looked weird to me. That doesn't make them weird; it was just weird to me. I have seen people dancing in airports, passing out tracts, and going door to door.

I told the elder, Pat that I would never give out tracts. He told me that the church did not pass out tracts. He then added something that stuck in my heart. He said now that I was a Christian and open to God's will, if God wanted me passing out tracts, I would be. Now I am writing daily thoughts, encouragements, blogs, devotionals, and even a book. I send them out every day and post them as a blog. All of my messages revolve around God's love and grace. Hmm, electronic tracts and now a book, not only do I send and read them, I also write them. Am I embarrassed, or do I think it is weird? Not in the least.

Since coming to Christ and giving my life to him, I have discovered I am doing all kinds of things I always said I would or could never do. I think to myself, *Me, a Christian counselor a minister? Me, writing daily Christian thoughts, attending three Bible studies a week, reading the Bible daily, sharing the Bible with others, and just being open to whatever God has for me next?* These things seemed inconceivable to me at one time.

I have said in the past that I wouldn't do this or that. I am not this way or that way. This is just the way I am. This is the way I was made, and I have a myriad of all kinds of excuses. I have found I can do anything God puts in front of me. He will and has equipped me. He told Moses, Jeremiah, and now even little old me, "I will be with you, and I will rescue you."

Don't be afraid to be open to God's call, as strange as it may seem to you. What God brings us to he will bring us through. God will never leave us nor forsake us. God will equip and be with us. Here I am Lord. Yes, me. I will do that.

Now It's Our Turn

During the high priesthood of Annas and Caiaphas, the word of God came to John son of Zechariah in the desert. He went into all the country around the Jordan, preaching a baptism of repentance for the forgiveness of sins. As is written in the book of the words of Isaiah the prophet: "A voice of one calling in the desert, 'Prepare the way for the Lord, make straight paths for him. Every valley shall be filled in, every mountain and hill made low. The crooked roads shall become straight, the rough ways smooth. And all mankind will see God's salvation.'"

Luke 3:2–6

Then Jesus came to them and said, "All authority in heaven and on earth has been given to me. Therefore go and make disciples of all nations, baptizing them in the name of the Father and of the Son and of the Holy Spirit, and teaching them to obey everything I have commanded you. And surely I am with you always, to the very end of the age."

Matthew 28:18–20

When I was between the ages of four and six I guess, my little, black, longhaired mutt, Spooky, would hear my father's car door close in the driveway. My father was home from work. Spooky announced his homecoming, and we bolted out the door, racing to greet our returning hero in his white station wagon. I thought I had a head start since I had control of the door, but that dog was fast. He got there first, but I was taller and could leap into my father's arms and get a hug and kiss. In my mind my dad was a giant at five foot eight and as strong as an ox. Inside my mother and younger brother and sister were anxiously waiting their turn to greet Dad.

Both the Old and New Testament discussed the coming of Jesus. Isaiah foretold of John's calling out in the wilderness, preparing the way for Jesus, the Lord, and baptizing for repentance and the forgiveness of sins. Sure enough, John was readying people for Jesus' coming. Preparation for the coming of the Lord was essential; the Messiah was on his way. John's job was to get people ready and announce his coming. Upon his arrival, he was to baptize Jesus and then let Jesus lead. Isaiah, in the Old Testament, was told by God to proclaim the coming of the Lord.

Now it is our turn. Jesus is coming back to claim those sealed with the Holy Spirit. He is coming back to take those who believe home. Jesus commissioned his disciples, which are now us, to go and make disciples in the world. We must go and proclaim the good news and share the salvation message. We must help the converts grow in spirituality and wisdom of God's Word. We must share the Bible and help move them along to spiritual maturity. Why do we do this? We do this because Jesus has told us to. We do it also because we love God and we love others. By loving God and others, we prepare the way for Jesus' return. Isaiah and John have done their part, Jesus is still doing his, and now it is our turn.

Obedience Pays Big

Jesus said, "Let the little children come to me, and do not hinder them, for the kingdom of heaven belongs to such as these."

Matthew 19:14

And this is love: that we walk in obedience to his commands. As you have heard from the beginning, his command is that you walk in love.

2 John 1:6

As a child, I remember being given many directions and rules from my parents. In school and church, I was also given many directions and rules. Even at the swimming pools there were signs for kids like me that said, "No running. Shower before entering the pool." As a child, it seems my biggest job was obedience to rules and directions. Punishment of some sort followed a breach of the rules. Obedience, on the other hand, was always rewarded. The rewards may be some sort of prize, an "Atta boy," and of course, nothing bad would happen.

Looking back, I can see obedience and following the directions given to me were to keep me safe, help me fit into a family unit, keep order in a class or church setting, or to help me not hurt anyone else. If I needed to know why something had a certain rule, I would hear, "I am the parent, and I said so." Sometimes there was an explanation and a good reason.

Jesus said, "Let the children come to me, and do not hinder them, for the kingdom of heaven belongs to such as these" (Mark 10:14). Of course, I used to think it was because children are so pure, and that may be one of the reasons. Hmm, pure children? You didn't know me very well. God calls us to obedience, to follow his commands, laws, directions, and Word. His guidelines are laid out clearly in the Bible. Belief in Jesus Christ is the way to eternal salvation; belief is a command and not a suggestion. Obedience does not have to be a bad thing. Obedience keeps me safe. As a child, I was called to obedience; as a Christian, I am called to obedience.

Can you imagine that final day when God calls his obedient children home? Can you imagine the voice of Jesus saying, "Let the little children come to me, and do not hinder them, for the kingdom of heaven belongs to such as these." Imagine you and I are the children he is calling. On that day, we will truly see how obedience pays big.

Off the Flannel Board

They said his body was missing, and they had seen angels
who told them Jesus is alive!

Luke 24:23 (NLT)

In January 2008, I wrote a reflection on Peter and received a very
kind response. My friend Jimmy told me I had taken Peter off the
flannel board and out of the first century. Do you know that comment has been on my mind since then? So it is about time I take
that thought out of my head and put it on paper.

When I was a child, I remember going to Sunday school and
having flannel boards or bulletin boards with cutouts of Bible characters. They were all just pictures at that time, people in history,
and just that—characters on a flannel board. I guess I really missed
the point as the Bible was read, movies were shown, and cutouts
were stuck to a flannel board. These cutouts and people in history
were more than a story to keep us kids busy.

Today, these heroes of the Bible have jumped out of the Bible
and off the flannel board and have leapt into my heart and mind.
Today, each and every one I read about is alive to me. They are
people I can learn from. There are early Christians who died in
the movement, whose names never made it into the Bible, but
their stories and their testimonies have made it into my heart. Our
brothers, sisters, and forefathers of the church have shown us how

to live and have left so much more than a legacy; they have shown us how to live, think, pray, and behave. They have cleared the way and shown us what it is like to be one of God's children.

The more we read, the more we pray and meditate, and the more we share with one another, the more our brothers and sisters who have come before us come alive. Peter, Paul, David, Moses, Jesus, and all those written about in the Bible need to jump out of the Bible, off the flannel boards, and into our hearts. Bible history needs to be shared not as old and ancient texts, but as fond memories of our relatives who are no longer with us in body. Although they may not be with us in body, they are still alive in our memory, thoughts, minds, and hearts. We remember relatives and friends who have passed on fondly and with admiration. Shouldn't that be the way we think about our spiritual relatives, our forefathers of the faith, and Jesus himself? Share these accounts fondly and with gusto, because they are people we love, admire, and have learned from. Let's take all of our loved ones out of the Bible and off the flannel board and bring them to life. We need them.

Oh, Really?

Praise be to the Lord, to God our Savior, who daily bears our burdens.

Psalm 68:19

Can anyone hide in secret places so that I cannot see him?" declares the LORD. "Do not I fill heaven and earth?" declares the LORD.

Jeremiah 23:24

When I was about twelve years old, I lived in Patchogue, New York, which is on Long Island; we lived surrounded by water, thus the name *Long Island*. The daily newspaper there was *Newsday*. I delivered this paper for about two years. One day, my friend George helped me deliver the papers. We finished early, and he said, "Hey let's take my brother Henry's boat out for a ride." I said that I might get in trouble, but he insisted that no one would know. Halfway out, we ran out of gas. Luckily, another boat nearby offered to tow us in. We used their anchor and put it up against the bow. Well it started slipping and almost flew off the boat. I caught it, but it pinned my thumb against the bow. I screamed and yelled, "*Stop!*" They did, and I got my finger out. There was blood and innards coming out of my thumb. Uh oh.

When I got home, I wrapped a bandage around it; you could still see the blood. My mother asked what had happened. I told her that I fell on some glass. She didn't ask to see it, but my father did. He asked what happened. I again said, "I fell on some glass." He said to take off the bandage so he could take a look at it. By this time, my finger began to look inside out. Again, he asked what happened and again, I said I fell on some glass. He said, "Oh really?" I had to fess up. He said we would deal with that later. He took me to the emergency room for stitches. A few stitches and the world's longest lecture later, and I knew my mother and father were mad at me but glad I was okay. They were just afraid something worse could have happened. They loved me. They knew I wasn't telling the truth and just wanted to help me. I couldn't hide.

Sound familiar? "Where can I hide?" David asked. Didn't Adam and Eve also try to hide? How can God bear my burdens if I am trying to hide from him? Like he really doesn't know where I am. It is like a small child covering his eyes and saying, "You can't see me." God says he will bear our burdens when I go to him. He also says I can't hide. He knows where I am at all times. He knows what I am thinking and knows my heart at all times. He knows exactly what I need but wants me to come to him. I have a choice. I say it's all good to God. He says, "Oh really." Well, maybe he doesn't, but that's what I hear.

I don't have to hide anything from my loving, heavenly Father. He can see my hurts, anger, sin, wants, needs, and desires. He can see when I want to grow. He can see what I can handle. He gives me all I need not what I think I need but what he knows I need. I don't have to hide anything from God. There may be a time of discipline, but what loving parent doesn't discipline a disobedient child? He continues to shape and mold me when I am open to him.

When my heart is tender, my mind is open, and my eyes are fixed on him.

Today, I won't lie or hide from God. I will bring him all my burdens. I will ask him for guidance and my daily assignment. All wounds will be brought to God without manufacturing manipulations and lies. He already knows me. God loves me. He doesn't want to hurt me; he knows I can do that all by myself. No need to be afraid, God is waiting to help me with all my burdens, and I will bring them to him.

Oh the Pain

And about the ninth hour Jesus cried with a loud voice, saying, "Eli, Eli, lama sabachthani?" that is to say, My God, my
God, why hast thou forsaken me?

Matthew 27:46 (KJV)

What does it feel like after we sin? For me it is very painful, and I am
wracked with guilt. Being wracked with guilt is very emotionally
and physically painful. Jesus had been beaten, tortured, mocked,
spit at, and now his own Father turned from him. Why? He turned
from him because he was filled with sin. Jesus was filled with sin.
God hates sin and cannot look at it. He detests sin. Although Jesus
was filled with sin, it was not his own. It was my sin. It was your
sin, and the sin belonged to the entire world. What great pain Jesus
must have felt to wear all that sin and then have the one he loved
turn his back. Jesus was paying the price for all mankind and now
feeling the pain of physical torture, sin, and the turning away of
our heavenly Father.

When I sin, am I turning away from Jesus and ignoring the
pain he suffered once more? When I sin, am I hammering the nail
again? Am I spitting in the face of my Savior? Today, I need to be
more aware of my thoughts, words, and actions. I want to be able
to look squarely in the face of Jesus. I want to look into his eyes and
say, "Jesus, I am sorry I did this to you." I want to say, "Jesus, for-

give me for what I have put you through. Please help me to sin no more." Today, I don't want to turn my back on the one who loves me so much. Father God loves his Son Jesus so much but could not look at the sin he bore. Today, I want Jesus to know how much I love him. Today, I will be ever vigilant in all my actions, words, and thoughts to sin no more. I will pray to my Father to help me bring him glory and not bring further pain to the Son he loves. I want God to be able to look at me and at his Son Jesus. He bore it all.

One Is the Loneliest Number

In the 1970s a band named Three Dog Night came out with a number-one hit song "One Is the Loneliest Number." At that time, I always felt like one. I was lonely. My father had just died, I had begun drinking, and I was feeling all alone. I had family and friends, but inside, I was one. Another song that came out before that was "I Am a Rock" by Simon and Garfunkel. How many songs can you play on the jukebox and feel lonely?

No matter how much I drank, how many jokes I told, and how many people I surrounded myself with, I felt like one. Have you ever felt like one? Have you ever been in a room full of people and have just been one, or a rock and an island? You know what I have learned since I turned to God? I have learned that I am never one. God promised in Hebrews 13:5, "Never will I leave you; never will I forsake you." In Genesis 28:15, God promised, "I am with you and will watch over you wherever you go, and I will bring you back to this land. I will not leave you until I have done what I have promised you."

Since I have asked Jesus into my heart and the Holy Spirit into my heart and soul, God has been with me every step of the way. I am never alone, even when I think I am by myself. For me these days, I am never one. When I am around people, my spirit is in touch with God's Spirit and the spirits of those around me. God has awoken my spirit, and I have never had to be one again. If I feel alone, I just say, "Hey, God. I feel alone," and marvelous things begin to happen.

Our Testimony Is a Strong Witness

He replied, "The man they call Jesus made some mud and
put it on my eyes. He told me to go to Siloam and wash. So
I went and washed, and then I could see."

John 9:11

While I was in the depths of alcoholism, a man told me he had been
an alcoholic. He told me he had not had a drink in ten months and
that through the love of a fellowship, the members, and the grace
of God, he not only had not picked up a drink but had no desire to.
He said he had asked God to remove the compulsion to drink and
it was. I have another friend who told me through belief, repentance, and baptism he was saved from eternal separation from God.
He told me through the beautiful words of the Bible that I could
find freedom from my sin and forgiveness from God. He told me
about a beautiful man named Jesus; he shared his experience and
how I could have my own. Our stories are our testimonies; testimony is a strong witness to one who is lost and seeking.

I try to share my experience with others freely. In the book
Alcoholics Anonymous, it says, "We will not regret the past nor wish
to shut the door on it; we will see how our experience can benefit
others." Who better to witness to an alcoholic than one who has
overcome alcohol through God's amazing love, grace, and healing?
Who better to witness to the lost than one who was lost, or to a

sinner than a sinner who has been saved through the grace of God through the sacrificial death of Jesus on the cross? Our testimonies are a strong witness for God's amazing grace.

So if you are not sure what to tell someone who is lost or seeking God and seeking salvation through Jesus, how about telling the truth? Tell them what happened to you. Share the good news of Jesus. Our own testimony is a very strong witness. Another quote from the book *Alcoholics Anonymous is* "We will see how our experience can benefit others."

Paid in Full

I Have It Covered

Blessed is he whose transgressions are forgiven, whose sins are covered.

Psalm 32:1

God presented him as a sacrifice of atonement, through faith in his blood. He did this to demonstrate his justice.

Romans 3:25

I was so excited when I graduated from college; years of study and hard work were over. I had had to reschedule my running, work, meetings, dates, and time with friends because all my time had to be centered on school. At the end of school came another wonderful adventure: paying off my school loan. Yikes. Well, years passed, and college was finally paid by me, the taxpayers through the GI Bill, and my beautiful wife, Janie. I received a note in the mail: it had an amount and was stamped "Paid in Full." My wife and I also paid off the car I struggled with before we were married. Again, another note: "Paid in full." Don't you love those notes, "Paid in full"? No more debt to those folks.

Isn't it also nice when you go out to dinner, the check comes, and the other person says, "Let me get that"? I was going through a tollbooth a couple of times and paid for the guy or gal behind me.

I looked in the rearview mirror and watched their dumbfounded faces when the toll taker tried to wave them through.

As a sinner, a recovered alcoholic, and all-around selfish guy, I have repented. God and I have been turning my life around. I am a work in progress. How was I ever going to atone for the sins I committed though? Sins I was truly sorry for and I wanted to change. I asked him, "Please forgive me, God. I love you and am grateful for everything you have done in my life." I still had a debt; no notes "Paid in full" had arrived.

In the Old Testament, blood sacrifices were required. Hmm, should I get my dog out on a makeshift altar and find a squirrel? Where could I find a goat or sheep in Melbourne, Florida? Man, I was in trouble. I thought for sure no matter what I did it was the lake of fire for me. After many years of being away from church, I started to attend the Church of Christ. One of the elders came over and helped me read Scripture. I haven't stopped.

You know what I read? It said, "Paid in full." God has found a way for me to atone for my sins, it is to believe and obey. God gave a blood sacrifice of his own Son Jesus so I could be forgiven and my sins could be forgiven. He made a way to atone for my sins of the past, present, and future. Jesus' last words on the cross were "It is finished." I heard, "Paid in full." His next words to his apostles were "Peace be with you." Peace is right; all sin had been atoned for once and for all. Jesus said, "Let me get that."

By belief in Jesus as my Savior, following and obeying the Word of God, my sin debt is paid in full. I can't be grateful enough. Why would Jesus do that? Jesus did that because he loves me. Why would God love any of us? God loves me more then I can comprehend. What I do know is that because Jesus paid my debt I get to go to heaven and one day I will get the chance to ask him. Jesus paid the way in full.

Paul's Letter to Kenjonesians

Paul, an apostle of Christ Jesus by the will of God, To the saints in Ephesus, the faithful in Christ Jesus: Grace and peace to you from God our Father and the Lord Jesus Christ.

Ephesians 1:1–2

I have received many letters in my life, but none as important as the ones Paul sent to the believers around the world. In a sermon one day a few years ago, our preacher, Steve, asked us, "What if Paul wrote to our church? What would he say?" I was thinking, *What would Paul say if he wrote a letter directly to me?*

Paul always started his letters by identifying himself as an apostle by the grace of God. Then he called the recipients of the letters saints. I would have to wonder if he sent this to the right Ken. He would send me blessings and grace from God the Father and the Lord Jesus Christ.

Paul would then discuss how he was praying for me and for the marvelous works I was doing in God's name. He would list them off and tell me how everyone is proud and talking about my accomplishments and my faith. After I am feeling all warm and fuzzy, Paul would then blast me with what I am doing wrong and how I have sinned and not followed God's Word. Then he would share insight on how I could change. He then might share if it weren't for Jesus, I would be on the down escalator to my lake of fire view. Then he would give me some more insight into what I could be doing for the Lord and then say, "Peace and blessings, your brother, Paul."

After reading this letter, I may need an aspirin; I feel as though I have been through a meat grinder. I thought he said he was the worst kind of sinner. Man, you would think he might show some love. Well, he did show love. Then *bam,* he rocked my world. He gave me some real, honest love. He held me accountable. He wants me to be better; he wants me to obey God's commands. He wants me to discipline myself and mature spiritually, to have a faith that is not just saying, "Yeah yeah, I believe in Christ. Jesus died on the cross. He came back from the dead. I'm saved, let's party. No problem, my faith will cover it." That is not the faith Paul is talking about. Paul is talking about faith with action. Paul is talking about obeying God's commands, serving God, serving others, loving God, loving others, and treating others as I would Jesus. Paul's letters were like a report card with suggestions and teachings.

In Paul's letter to Kenjonesians, he told me to spend more time in conversation with God and more time reading my Bible, serving others, taming my tongue. But on top, he listed the good stuff, my work for God, the stuff that is between me and God. Paul told me how he knows I love God, how he knows I pray, how he knows I obey God, etc.

So enough of my letter from Paul. What does yours say? Come on, you can tell me. Try this: take out a sheet of paper and take an inventory of ministry and obedience to God and then your sins. Where have you been disobedient? What would Paul blast you on? What would he lift you up on? What work are you doing for God? What are you doing to bring God glory? And what are you doing to make God look bad by your own actions? How can you improve?

I am going to take a sheet of paper and do this inventory, take it to someone I trust, discuss it, and get with that person on a weekly basis to help me be accountable. So when Paul writes his next letter to the Kenjonesians, there will be more to be pleased with. Discipline and maturity will be praised at the top of the letter, by God, our Father, and our Lord Jesus Christ and of course, the author, Paul.

Pay Attention

Ask and it will be given to you; seek and you will find; knock and the door will be opened to you. For everyone who asks receives; he who seeks finds; and to him who knocks, the door will be opened.

Matthew 7:7–8

There is an old joke about a man who was on top of a roof during a flood. A man in a rowboat came by and said, "Jump in, and I will save you." The man said, "No, thanks. I asked God to save me." As the water rose, another rowboat went by, and the man inside said, "Jump in, pal, and I will save you." The man again said, "No thanks, I asked God to save me, and he will." Then, as the water was up to his neck, a helicopter rose overhead dropped a ladder down, and a voice yelled, "Climb on. We will save you." The man said, "No thanks, God is coming to save me soon." Finally, the water went over his head, and he drowned. Upon entering heaven, the man looked at God and asked, "Why didn't you save me? I trusted you, and you let me drown." God said, "I sent you two rowboats and a helicopter. What were you waiting for?"

We pray for so many things without being open to his answers. We are not paying attention, or we forget the wonderful responses we have received in the past. God answers prayers, maybe not in the way we think he should, but he will answer prayers. King Saul needed a great warrior to take on the Philistine giant, and God sent a young boy and a slingshot. Moses led the Israelites out of Egypt and straight to the sea. The Egyptian army was hot on their heels. God parted the sea. When they became thirsty, God brought water from a rock. Thousands of hungry people, two fish, and a few loaves of bread, no problem for Jesus. That became a feast.

The world waited for God's promise of a Messiah, a King of kings, and a Savior. The people waited for a great warrior. God sent a baby. The baby grew up to be a peaceful and loving young man. God gave us a man who would give up his life for all and then ask his Father to forgive those who took his life. God answers prayer with unexpected answers at times. As you pray, pay attention for the unexpected. Your prayer will be answered.

Peter and I Couldn't Wait

He called out to them, "Friends haven't you any fish?" "No," they answered. He said, "Throw your net on the right side of the boat and you will find some." When they did, they were unable to haul the net in because of the large number of fish. Then the disciple whom Jesus loved said to Peter, "It is the Lord!" As soon as Simon Peter heard him say, "It is the Lord," he wrapped his outer garment around him (for he had taken it off) and jumped into the water.

John 21:5–7

Before my father died, he was in a hospital about sixty miles from home. We could only visit him on the weekends. We had to take a train to get there. It seemed like the longest ride on record. My father had been in the hospital for months, and we knew he would never be coming home. We never knew when it would be the last time we saw him. When we got to my father's floor, I would leave my mother's side and literally run to my father's room so I could get there first to hug, kiss, and talk to him before my mother got there. I couldn't wait. I couldn't get to him fast enough. I loved him, and I hadn't seen him in a while and didn't know how much longer he would be with us.

I can almost feel Peter's excitement when John told him that the man shouting from the shore is Jesus. He threw off his cloak, jumped out of the boat, and swam to shore as fast as he could to beat the others. I bet he didn't even dry himself off before he ran to Jesus, whom he had denied three times just days earlier. He couldn't wait; he didn't know how much longer Jesus was going to be with them. Jesus had already been put to death and been resurrected. Jesus had visited the apostles one time before. Peter still filled with guilt, remorse, and a contrite heart for what he had done, wanted to be as close to his Savior and friend for as long as he could. I bet the hug made Jesus as wet as Peter. How did Peter know Jesus was still his friend? Because Jesus shouted, "Friends, haven't you any fish?" And Jesus had prepared breakfast for them. It probably felt like the longest swim Peter had ever taken. He couldn't get to Jesus fast enough. Love will do that.

Peter had denied knowing his friend. Me, I have sinned against Jesus, even after he gave his life for me. I also feel the forgiveness Peter received. I am in awe of the amazing grace of God, the forgiveness, and the love. When Jesus first appeared, he said, "Peace be with you." This time, his first word was *friends*. Mercy, forgiveness, and grace were shown to those who had deserted and denied him. Through belief and obedience to God's commands, he calls me a friend. Shouldn't everyone know this great love of Jesus? How can I get the word out? I want to tell everyone about Jesus' great love, mercy, forgiveness, and grace. I have an opportunity to talk to God and listen in prayer and meditation, which improves my personal relationship with God. I should be in a hurry to get to prayer, and I should pray often. I should be making as much time as possible to be with my Creator. I want to pray without ceasing and always be with him. I can't get enough of him. He isn't going anywhere; he always was and he always will be.

Today, I want to be with my heavenly Father, growing in our relationship and sharing with as many people as possible the great love, mercy, forgiveness, and grace shown me. I want to share the keys to friendship, faith, and obedience to his commands. The joy, peace, and assurance are immeasurable. Today, I will jump out of the boat and swim to him as fast as I can to share in our loving friendship and spend as much time as I can with the Creator of the universe, God.

Peter Is at It Again

Love and Determination

"Lord, if it's you," Peter replied, "tell me to come to you on the water."

"Come," he said. Then Peter got down out of the boat, walked on the water and came toward Jesus. But when he saw the wind, he was afraid and, beginning to sink, cried out, "Lord, save me!" Immediately Jesus reached out his hand and caught him. "You of little faith," he said, "why did you doubt?"

Matthew 14:28–31

You've got to love Peter. He never gave up. Pre-Pentecost, it seems Peter had a hard time getting things right. He seemed to always be trying to do the right thing and say the right thing but couldn't quite master it. At Jesus' last supper, Jesus told Peter, "Get behind me, Satan." In this passage, as he walks out on to the water, Jesus says to Peter, "You of little faith, why did you doubt?" (Matthew 14:31). Peter had seen Jesus walking on the water and wanted to walk out to him. Peter asked Jesus to call him out to him. He had taken a few steps, saw the wind, and became afraid and started sinking. Jesus rescued him and then scolded him for his lack of faith.

Jesus was right there in front of him, like a parent waiting for a child learning to walk—ready to catch him if he fell, or sink in this case. It says Peter sank because he saw the wind and became afraid. What if Peter had focused on Jesus? I bet you can see where I am going already. If he had, maybe we wouldn't be having this conversation. Peter became afraid and took his eyes off Jesus, a recipe for disaster. You know, I am like Peter in some instances. Peter seemed to never stop or give up though. Even though he got corrected and scolded quite a bit, he never stopped trying. Peter always wanted to please Jesus. He took the scolding and correction in stride; he took it as a learning experience as it was intended. He always moved on to the next thing and stayed next to Jesus. Even when denying Jesus he was only a look away.

I have taken my eyes off Jesus, I have had fear, and I have experienced moments when Jesus may have said to me, "Ken, where is your faith?" I have faced the wind Peter was talking about, doubt, hesitation, looking the wrong way and of course fear and insecurity. These are termites to faith, eating it away. They corrode my faith. They say I can't do something. I become afraid. I say, "Oh no, look, there is wind." Next thing I know, I am gulping water, yelling for Jesus. "Oh Ken," he says, "Why do you doubt?"

So should I quit trying because I keep failing? Have I really failed, or can I learn from my mistakes? Mistakes are okay. It means I tried; it means I can try again. Fear, insecurity, and turning my eyes from Jesus can cause me to flounder. By fixing my eyes directly on Jesus, putting one foot in front of the other, having faith in Jesus that all will be okay because he is right in my line of sight, I can't help but succeed.

Today, I will focus on Jesus. I will ignore my personal wind, whatever the wind may be for me today. I will try to please Jesus just as Peter tried. I will not listen to the voice telling me, "No way, buddy. You can't do that. This is impossible." I will step out in faith and say, "Jesus, here I come." Like Peter, I will keep trying until I get my eyes fixed directly on Jesus. Peter went from being asked where his faith was to being called "the rock" by Jesus. This pebble named Ken needs to focus, trust, obey, and mature.

Please Allow Two to Four Weeks for Delivery

You did not choose me, but I chose you and appointed you to go and bear fruit—fruit that will last. Then the Father will give you whatever you ask in my name.

John 15:16

So I say to you: Ask and it will be given to you; seek and you will find; knock and the door will be opened to you. For everyone who asks receives; he who seeks finds; and to him who knocks, the door will be opened.

Luke 11:9–10

I love ordering music from my CD and book clubs. I also love ordering my Red Sox attire from Redsox.com. It always says please allow two to four weeks for delivery. So far, so good. It always comes early. I love my music. I play no musical instrument, but I play a mean car stereo. I have Red Sox hats galore. After I order these things, I begin waiting with great anticipation, and when my order comes and I open the box, it is with the glee of a child at Christmas. I knew it would come. That's how it works. You order it, and they send it. It works every time.

Do you order stuff by mail and over the Internet? You know it is coming and will be there when promised. What a great system.

I wonder why I am not always that confident about my prayers. I pray to God in Jesus' name just as Jesus said to do. I ask, seek, knock, and sometimes then I wonder. Why would I, a Christian, have more faith in a CD club and the U.S. Postal Service than God? That doesn't even sound right. Did you ever do that? C'mon, be honest.

You know, I just seem to forget that God has answered all my prayers. My prayers have always been answered. God has always answered every prayer, but since the answer is not exactly the way I would do it, sometimes I don't recognize it. I have asked God to keep me away from a drink, and for over thirty straight years now, it has worked. I have asked God for a life where I might be healthy, happy, and wholesome and I have gotten it. I asked God what I could do for him a few years ago. The next thing I knew, I was very involved in my church, now working there full time as a minister and counselor. I am writing these hopefully encouraging reflections, which are Christian in nature, and some people are actually reading them. God answers all my prayers. My job is to wait with anticipation for the answer.

Some of my prayers sometimes seem selfish and financial in nature at times, not to win the lottery or anything like that, but just ratio of income to debt. I have made some very bad decisions on my own in the past when it comes to money. I have asked God to help me become a better steward with his money. Well, it seems there is still a whole lot more going out than coming in. Everything else I have put in his hands has worked out better than I could have imagined. I know God has it under control. I really do believe that. This is no longer a worry, well 99 percent of the time. There are still those weak moments.

God will give me all I need in life to bring him glory. All I need do is wait with anticipation, and when it comes, pop it in my car stereo—I mean my heart—and turn up the volume. Today, I will go to God with every prayer in Jesus' holy name. I will ask, seek, and knock, then move forward and know it is all in God's awesome hands and will be dealt with in a manner in which it will bring him glory. God answers prayers better and with what I really need in mind. If my music and book club and Redsox.com did that, they would say, "Sorry, we are not sending these things. You need the money more than these items. Play the radio, wear your old hats, and go to the library." See that? God has me thinking already. Seriously, he answers all my prayers in his time and in his way, which bring him glory. He knows best.

Quality Assurance

Who is wise and understanding among you? Let him show it by his good life, by deeds done in the humility that comes from wisdom. But if you harbor bitter envy and selfish ambition in your hearts, do not boast about it or deny the truth. Such "wisdom" does not come down from heaven but is earthly, unspiritual, of the devil. For where you have envy and selfish ambition, there you find disorder and every evil practice. But the wisdom that comes from heaven is first of all pure; then peace-loving, considerate, submissive, full of mercy and good fruit, impartial and sincere.

James 3:13–17

Would you buy a bulletproof vest with a hole near top center marked half price—only used once? This is one of the items that need testing and good quality assurance. We hear the expression "let's put it to the litmus test" about many things. Merriam-Webster Dictionary defines *litmus test* as "a test in which a single factor (as an attitude, event, or fact) is decisive." Testing seems very important and necessary before we use many items or take any advice, and we use it in school to determine that information was learned.

James asks, "Who is wise and understanding among you?" (James 3:13). In my Bible study and meditation class, my teacher said, "God is hoping we all are." All I could think of with this verse was testing. I understood this to mean that what I consider wisdom must be put to the litmus test. The litmus test I could use would be, am I bitterly envious? Or is there selfish ambition in my motives? This would not be godly wisdom. This wisdom is considered earthly, unspiritual, and of Satan.

God's wisdom would include the following: first of all, it would be pure. The other qualities of godly wisdom would be peace-loving, considerate, submissive, full of mercy and good fruit, impartial, and sincere. Do these qualities remind you of anyone? They remind me of Jesus. Jesus is the epitome of wisdom.

Throughout the Bible, wisdom is called for. So if I want the definition for wisdom, I need only see James 3:17 for that definition. Whenever true wisdom is called for, I need only submit the wisdom I am using to the litmus test given me here in James 3: 13–17. What will be the result? The result will be a verse our teacher said would be a great bumper sticker, James 3:18: "Peacemakers who sow in peace raise a harvest of righteousness." True, godly wisdom will bring this crop, so let's put our wisdom to the litmus test. Good quality assurance is required.

Satan's To Do List

Jesus said to them, "If God were your Father, you would love me, for I came from God and now am here. I have not come on my own; but he sent me. Why is my language not clear to you? Because you are unable to hear what I say. You belong to your father, the devil, and you want to carry out your father's desire. He was a murderer from the beginning, not holding to the truth, for there is no truth in him. When he lies, he speaks his native language, for he is a liar and the father of lies.

John 8:42–44

The Bible has many names for Satan; most include names like deceiver, father of lies, snake, and many other names that are derogatory and away from God. Satan manipulates people into not finding God or getting them to leave God. We must all keep our eyes fixed on Jesus, the cross, and God our father. Be aware, Satan has a "to do" list today.

I found a portion of Satan's list (not really, but play along) I want to share it with you, you may know more on his list:

Tell people that a little sin is okay. God will forgive us anyway.

Tell people "Go ahead, you can judge this person. God doesn't like them anyway."

Tell people "God won't forgive me this time."

Tell people God the Father, Jesus, and the Holy Spirit are just a lie to make them feel better.

Tell people God is just a crutch for the weak.

Tell people go ahead, because some controversy and division in their church need to be shaken up a bit anyway.

Tell people "Hey, she/he looks good. You are consenting adults. No one will get hurt."

Tell people foul language, dirty jokes, and gossip are okay. No one will get hurt.

Tell people it is okay to check out pornography. No one will get hurt.

Tell people "Come on, God really didn't mean it that way."

Manipulate people's hearts and minds.

Cause distractions; baffle people's minds with meaningless details.

Help people believe things like: I am tired. I don't need church. I am too busy. I have no time for church events, fellowships, and studying God's Word. God is too busy for me. He isn't listening anyway.

I know you can add to this list. Satan is alive and working in this world to keep us away from God. I am not talking about Flip Wilson's Satan "The Devil Made Me Do It." I am talking about a very real Satan, a very real force in the world. I can be very vulnerable if I am not praying, studying God's Word, or open to correction from God and other mature disciples.

Scars Can Be Beautiful

Then he said to Thomas, "Put your finger here; see my hands. Reach out your hand and put it into my side. Stop doubting and believe."

Thomas said to him, "My Lord and my God!"

John 20:27–28

I have written about getting a fresh start in life. I received a comment from a friend about the scars that are left from our old life. It was just a short statement, but the word pictures it created could make a full-length movie. There is a line in the book *Alcoholics Anonymous* that says, "We will not regret the past nor shut the door on it, we will see how experience can benefit others." So I was thinking of the scars, mostly emotional, and then I began to think of occasions when my scars have helped others. When my past and my scars have helped others, these ugly memories have become beautiful scars.

There has been pain in my life, similar to many of you. I know I am not alone. I lost my grandmother at twelve, my father at age sixteen, my grandfather, at eighteen, and my mother at forty. I have divorced, and my two boys live with their mother. I have had biweekly visits and almost daily telephone visits. I have had more pain I will not bore you with. You can finish this sentence with your list of emotional scars. I have made mistakes in life, no question about that. These mistakes have hurt those around me, and they have also hurt me. They have left memories I would rather forget. Some of the emotional scars are deep. I have prayed, and God has cleaned them out and made them usable assets to help others.

Although I have been saved through Jesus Christ, there are still the occasional bumps and bruises that go along with being human. Life goes on. You know the bumps and bruises in your life; you know the emotional scars they have left.

How in the world can my experience or scars benefit others? How can all this pain and suffering I have felt give anyone comfort? Thomas did not believe Jesus had come back to life, so Jesus came to him and said, "Put your finger in my wounds, see that I have risen." By Jesus showing Thomas his wounds and letting him feel the wounds from his crucifixion, Thomas believed.

Paul was a sinner. I am also a sinner; I have been saved by Jesus' death and resurrection. I have been given a fresh start. This is where my scars led me. Of myself, I have made terrible mistakes and experienced pain beyond belief. The scars are deep wounds only God could heal. He says, "Now go out and bring me others. All need to be saved by the death and resurrection of Jesus" (paraphrase).

How can my scars help save others? Many people are afraid they have gone too far. They feel Jesus will not save them after what they have done. They feel there is no way they can join us in church. They are not worthy; they are too banged and bruised up from life. They think no way those holy rollers are going to let them join us for our church social. Well, let me roll up my sleeves and pant legs. Then, I say put your finger in those scars. They are real. They aren't pretty, but they have been cleansed by Jesus' death and resurrection. His death paid my sin debt. Welcome, let him pay yours. I know your pain. I have been there. Let Jesus' death save you. Don't let his death be in vain. He loves you. They might ask, "How do you know?" I can then say, "Okay, look at these scars again."

Our past and scars can benefit others. We are saved. Don't be afraid of your past or your scars. See how others can benefit from our sharing this with them. Scars can be beautiful. Don't hide them and don't gloat over them either. Jesus' scars show the world his love. How can we use ours?

Searching

Why were you searching for me? He asked. "Didn't you know
I had to be in my Father's house?"

Luke 2:49

I have searched for all kinds of things. Just ask my friend Don. He
says the most memorable part of our camping trip was me trying
to find the things I put in a safe place. These places were so safe
even I had to search a long time for them. Have you ever looked
for something that was lost? Searching is never fun for me because
I never know where to look next.

About six years ago, my life was going fine. I had a great wife.
I had two great sons, two great little dogs, a job, a car, a home, and
even some money in the bank. At that time, I had a relationship
with a God I felt was satisfactory, and my life was good because of
him. So what's the problem? Something was missing. What was
it? When I grew up, I heard about Jesus and following God's commands, but was I following them? Hmm, did I really need to ask?
Voila! I knew what I was missing and began to search. Where to
begin? Should I turn the light on or continue to fumble around in
the dark?

I was listening to a preacher on the radio, and he said, "Go to
a Bible-believing church." So I did. That seemed like a good place
to start. After church, I e-mailed one of the church's elders, Pat.

He called me, and during the conversation, he said something that really got my attention. He said, "Let's meet and see why God has brought us together." So we met. I had many questions, and then he said something again that was profound, but this time it was life changing. He said, "Let's see what the Bible has to say." Did you hear that? "Let's see what the Bible has to say?" Wow. The lights went on. So was my search over? Nope, it had just begun, but now I knew where to search. I knew how to search with purpose and where the answers were. The answers to all of my searching come directly from the mouth of God in the pages of the Bible.

When Pat said, "Let's see what the Bible has to say," he turned on a bright light that illuminated every answer to every question I could possibly be searching for. His biblical statement has given me the tools with which to search. So if you are searching, I have a suggestion. Let's see what the Bible has to say.

Seek Wise Counsel

Plans fail for lack of counsel, but with many advisers they succeed.

Proverbs 15:22

When I was a child, I had the wise counsel of my mother and father. They told me to look both ways, not take candy from a stranger, and say my prayers before going to sleep. Their advice was given to me out of their concern, experience, and love.

I have been in a recovery program now for over thirty years, always having a mentor. A mentor is someone with more experience in the program and life than me. They have lived the steps of recovery and learned to live life without a drink and have been successful at it. If I have a question or concern, to whom would I take it? I take these issues to my mentor. He taught me how to live without a drink. He taught me that only with God's help can I change. I had to take a survey of my life to find out my wrongs and why I did these things. He taught me how to make changes in my behaviors and attitudes toward my family, friends, and employers and those I had hurt. Repent, in other words; change my heart. He advised me to go to these people and let them know what I am doing and that I want to share my contrition and change my behavior toward them. He also advised me to continue to do this daily, seek constant guidance from God, and help others as well as living a godly life every day. This mentor shares his experience with me and teaches me how to use this in my life.

I have found counsel on the Internet from a man laced with grace, a fellow tilted-halo member. He inspires me with his writing and his encouragement. I share these writings because he encourages me to do so. He has recommended a few books I may learn from. He has taken his time and shared his vast experience with me.

These are just a few examples of the sage counsel I have sought and received. These men have God in common. They believe Jesus to be their Savior, they care for others, they give their time freely, and they share their concern, encouragement, experience, and love with me.

The Bible has all the answers. I go to it for ultimate counsel. God's Word is there. Jesus speaks and acts. The Old and New Testaments are a treasure trove of wisdom and sound advice. The Bible is a love story used to bring me to my Savior, Jesus, and follow his lead. The Holy Spirit has come to me as Jesus promised. Before doing anything, I seek wise, biblical, and experiential advice.

And I will ask the Father, and he will give you another Counselor to be with you forever.

John 14:16

Share, Don't Scare

Therefore, as God's chosen people, holy and dearly loved, clothe yourselves with compassion, kindness, humility, gentleness and patience. Bear with each other and forgive whatever grievances you may have against one another. Forgive as the Lord forgave you. And over all these virtues put on love, which binds them all together in perfect unity.

Colossians 3:12–14

Be wise in the way you act toward outsiders; make the most of every opportunity. Let your conversation be always full of grace, seasoned with salt, so that you may know how to answer everyone.

Colossians 4:5–6

When I was in the navy, there were a couple of guys I met who said that they were Christians. These men would always tell me what I was doing wrong. If I had been out the night before dancing, they told me I was going to hell. Anytime I said a foul word or told a dirty joke, I was going to hell. When I was drunk the night before, off I was carted to hell again. These guys were scary. I was afraid of their God. Of course, they were right about a few things at the time, but they sure didn't sound as though they were sharing good news. They would break out their Bibles and show me I was doomed to the eternal fire. I had no way out; they just told me all my faults. Not only was I afraid of their God. I thought those guys were weird.

The media likes to point out all the religious nuts they can find, all the ones who have had affairs, stole money, and said something foolish and anything else they can find to make Christians seem like haters, hypocrites, and just plain religious nuts. Are Christians supposed to look like nuts and know nothing about what is going on in the world? Are we supposed to be going around condemning all nonbelievers to hell? No wonder they don't want any part of us.

Paul said we are supposed to show our love to all people, yep, even nonbelievers. I need to speak of love with those who do not know Jesus. Some of them say they know Jesus, but all they know are the people they have seen that have tried to scare them into heaven. I am called to show mercy, kindness, humbleness, the truth, gentleness, and patience. I am to share my own testimony with others to show them I am just like them and was lost without Jesus. I should exude gratitude and joy for his sacrificial death so that we can be saved. I am sharing good news. Wouldn't it be great if it sounded like good news? I need to show forgiveness toward others as Jesus forgave me. I won't use the wrong for wrong principle. I need to show the mercy of God.

When I have an opportunity to share the good news with others, I should take it. I have been given grace. I have been commissioned by Jesus to share that message and make disciples. Paul says I should be kind and pleasant. So when do I need to be kind and pleasant? When the grocery clerk isn't, when someone is knocking my beliefs, when someone says church is all about money and hypocrites. I should always be treating others with a pleasant and kind demeanor.

I need to learn to share not scare. I don't want to scare through sounding like a religious nut, bore, Pharisee, judge, juror, or executioner. I am trying to help someone find their way to heaven. So if they are not ready, I don't want to ruin a future opportunity with frustration. I will tell you I have been told many times and blew people off. I know it is my soul, but I am glad later in life people were patient with me. When I said, "I know I am going to hell," my friend said, "I don't know where you are going, but let's see what God's Word has to say."

Today, I want to share the good news every chance I get. I want it to sound like good news, a new chance at life—an eternal life with our loving Father and his Son who gave his life for me, Jesus. I want to use the attitude Paul has suggested in Colossians 3:12–14 and 4:5–6. So today, I will share the good news and not scare needy folks away. Share, don't scare.

Sick as Our Lies and Secrets

> When I kept things to myself, I felt weak deep inside me. I moaned all day long.
>
> Psalm 32:3 (NVC)

From age sixteen through twenty-one, I operated in a survival mode. I was an active alcoholic and felt I had to lie and keep secrets, because the things I did brought me great shame and I didn't want anyone to know some of the things I did. Guilt ate away at my heart and soul like a cancer, but that didn't stop the drinking or the lifestyle of keeping secrets to survive. I was as sick as my secrets and lies.

In August 1978, I had my last drink and came into fellowship with other recovering alcoholics. In this fellowship, along with not drinking, there are steps to live by. A new way of life must be established. In one of the steps I was suggested to take, I had to confess to God, to myself, and another person exactly what I did and why I did these things. Psalms 32:5 says, "Then I confessed my sins to you and didn't hide my guilt. I said, 'I will confess my sins to the Lord,' and you forgave my guilt" (NVC). In confession of my secrets and lies to God, myself, and another person, I was freed from the disease of lies and secrets. I felt clean and free inside. The guilt I felt was gone; my sins had been forgiven. Through Jesus, my Savior, I was saved.

Over the years, I have reverted to secrets at times, but I have quickly gone to God, myself, and a person who helps hold me accountable with confession and the truth. I could not bear the guilt and pain I felt. Psalm 32:1–2 says, "Happy is the person whose sins are forgiven, whose wrongs are pardoned. Happy is the person whom the Lord does not consider guilty and in whom there is nothing false" (NVC). Bring your secrets and sins to God, and be forgiven. Don't let the cancer of secrets and guilt eat away at you. Bring all of this to God, and be forgiven. Enjoy God's guarantee of happiness through confession. Free yourself from guilt and secrets today.

Sitting at the Feet of Jesus

> As Jesus and his disciples were on their way, he came to a village where a woman named Martha opened her home to him. She had a sister called Mary, who sat at the Lord's feet listening to what he said. But Martha was distracted by all the preparations that had to be made. She came to him and asked, "Lord, don't you care that my sister has left me to do the work by myself? Tell her to help me!" "Martha, Martha," the Lord answered, "you are worried and upset about many things, but only one thing is needed Mary has chosen what is better, and it will not be taken away from her."
>
> Luke 10:38–42

In 1979 I had the opportunity to have a conversation with a man who had walked on the moon. There were five of us, including this celebrity. He was a friend of a friend who had brought us all there. I was mesmerized just looking at him straight across from me, talking about walking on the moon. This man is known around the world, has been on TV, shaken hands with presidents, and now he has shaken mine. He asked me what I did in the navy and where I was from; he was interested in hearing about me. This man spoke my name and talked to me. I never left the table. I didn't want to miss one second of this man's stories about anything. As long as he spoke, I listened. There was nothing more important in the entire world for those two hours to me then this astronaut. I was star struck. I have never seen or heard from this man again. But what an awesome experience and what a memory!

Imagine having Jesus come to your door with the apostles. They may be hungry and need to be fed, preparations to be made, and there would be Martha, scurrying around taking care of everything. Mary, her sister, would have planted herself right in front of Jesus himself, our Lord and Savior, riveted to his every word. Mary was being spoken to by Jesus. There he sat right in their living room. If there were a TV, it would have been turned off. All noise stopped, time stood still, and there he was talking to her. There was Martha running around, too busy to listen, too busy to learn. What was Jesus talking about? What was he telling Mary? We don't know. Martha doesn't know either; she was too busy making preparations for the meal. She wanted things perfect for Jesus in all fairness to Martha, but she never stopped to hear what he had to say.

Do I read my Bible daily? Do I stop to listen to God daily? Or do I just talk and move on? Do I listen intently all the time when God's Word is being spoken? Well, not always. Why not? Well, you see, sometimes I am just too busy. How busy could I be to not sit at the feet of Jesus? How busy could I be to open up the greatest love story ever written, the greatest book of life ever written from God to us? How busy could I be to not spend time listening for the voice of the Creator of the universe and heaven, the best friend ever?

Imagine having Jesus come to your door, my door, come in, and sit in my living room. He sits down and begins to speak. The same Jesus who once stood with Father God and the Holy Spirit before God put the Earth here or a moon for anyone to walk on. Jesus, who brought the dead back to life, made the blind see, the deaf hear, the lame walk, and brought people back to life. He sits with you, and he begins to speak. What would he say? What great secrets would he share? What pieces of history and the future might he talk about? What will our homes be like in heaven? What questions might you ask him? What would you tell him? We won't know if we scurry, run around, or are too busy to spend time with him.

Today, my Bible will be open; my prayer will be like that of David. In my meditation, I will be still, and my ears and heart will be wide open. I will read what Jesus has to say. I will talk and then listen. I will listen to others who know Jesus and to their experiences. Today, I will sit at the feet of Jesus and listen. No distractions, no movement, and no TV. I want to experience and savor every word and movement of Jesus. Will you join me?

Six Guys, Six Spoons, and a Cheesecake

While camping in Canada, I ate well. Aside from the pancakes my friend Don made two mornings, the cheesecake was the most memorable. The Jell-O no-bake cheesecake was not only really good; it was the most fun. Don would make cherry cheesecake and Oreo cheesecake. He mixed the ingredients in a pan and let it chill in the cold lake, and then we would eat a dinner of fresh fish and wait in anticipation of the cheesecake. We had the cheesecakes three out of the six nights in the woods, and the other three nights we had s'mores.

There we were, men in our early fifties, late forties, and early twenties. We readied ourselves with our plastic soup spoons, and Don would hold the pan of cheesecake. We stood around the pan, waiting our turns to dig in. We had to guess a number between one and six, and the winner went first. We loaded as much of the cheesecake as we could on our spoon.

What I want to share about this is not just the cheesecake itself, but the fun and laughs we had while six grown men took turns with our spoons, waiting to plunge into the pan. Between laughs and anticipation, we ate. We had very busy days canoeing, paddling, portaging, and fishing. We were all tired and just enjoyed the end of the day sharing in cheesecake and fellowship.

Imagine six grown men and the highlight of the day was sharing cheesecake. We had clean, wholesome fun, men who love Jesus, our Father God, our salvation, one another, and cheesecake. Standing in the majesty of God's creation, the great outdoors, our biggest concern at that moment was getting the biggest spoonful of cheesecake and laughing with each other. Now that's what I call living. Today, let's just keep it simple and enjoy the people we are with and praise God for them.

S'mores

When I was a little kid, I went to a day camp at Shorefront Park in Patchogue, New York. The two things I remember most were a girl named Katie and eating s'mores. But since I won the grand prize with my wife Janie, let me just tell you about the s'mores. If you come from a different planet and don't know, a s'more is a graham cracker with a chocolate bar in it, with toasted marshmallows that were held over a fire. The name s'more means you will definitely want some more.

While in Canada on my fishing trip with five other men, I remember sitting around the campfire each night talking and laughing. We had a great time. Three of the nights, we ate s'mores. Those chocolate and marshmallow slices of heaven were a treat and the source of a lot of fun and dining pleasure. The name *s'more* is so appropriate. They couldn't have been made to taste any better, except one thing.

Do you know what did make them taste even better? It was the fellowship that went along with them. The fun we had when it was time to make the s'mores. Don't get me wrong. The three nights we had cheesecake couldn't be beat, but those s'mores make me know why I want s'more. Not just s'more s'mores and cheesecake, but s'more of that fellowship. That fellowship made the chocolate and cheesecake delicacies taste even better. There is nothing better than biting into one of those tasty treats like having them with the five guys you have spent the day with fishing, laughing, and them having to wait for me to catch up.

You can't beat friends. God didn't put us on Earth to be alone. We were made for relationships. In Genesis 2:18 it says, "The LORD God said, 'It is not good for the man to be alone. I will make a helper suitable for him.'" God created a helper and a friend. The bonds that I made and the laughs I shared around that campfire can't be beat. The treats were great, but the fellowship; I really want s'more.

Squandered Treasure

But store up for yourselves treasures in heaven, where moth and rust do not destroy, and where thieves do not break in and steal.

Matthew 6:20

Jesus continued: "There was a man who had two sons. The younger one said to his father, 'Father, give me my share of the estate.' So he divided his property between them. Not long after that, the younger son got together all he had, set off for a distant country and there squandered his wealth in wild living."

Matthew 15:11–13

In one of my writings, I talked about treasures here and in heaven. Which should we really be aiming toward? Of course, an eternal treasure from God stored in heaven is the correct answer. As usual, my head began swimming with thoughts and ideas about this treasure in heaven, God's treasure. I began to think I am and have been this lost (prodigal) son. I have wanted my heavenly treasure right now. I never asked for it, but my loving Father, God, has already given me a portion of the treasure. My Father, God, my loving Abba has given me his greatest treasure. He has given me himself; he has given me his only Son, Jesus. Jesus gave me his treasure: his life on a cross so that I may share in the eternal inheritance. The love of Jesus and my heavenly Father, what greater treasure could there possibly be?

This treasure is beyond compare, but I took this treasure and went out into the world a selfish, self-centered, and self-absorbed person. That is how I said thank you for this beautiful treasure God has shared with me. Living a life with no gratitude or fear of the Lord, I was consumed only in what would please me next. Like the lost son, what I found was ruin, left with nowhere to turn.

I was ashamed when I too came to my senses and realized what I had done. The life I was living was like spitting in Jesus' face yet again. Hadn't there been enough spittle on our loving God's face? How does one come back after total disregard after being given the ultimate gift and treasure, Jesus' life? Well, the lost son came back when he realized what I had realized, and this is the story Jesus told:

> So he got up and went to his father. But while he was still a long way off, his father saw him and was filled with compassion for him; he ran to his son, threw his arms around him and kissed him. The son said to him, "Father, I have sinned against heaven and against you. I am no longer worthy to be called your son." But the father said to his servants, "Quick! Bring the best robe and put it on him. Put a ring on his finger and sandals on his feet. Bring the fattened calf and kill it. Let's have a feast and celebrate. For this son of mine was dead and is alive again; he was lost and is found." So they began to celebrate.
>
> Luke 15: 20–24

I have also learned there is more treasure I have been given, another chance, love, grace, mercy, and forgiveness. I want to grab a towel and say. "Please Jesus; let me wipe your face. Please forgive me." He already has, enough said.

Starting Your Day Off Right

Very early in the morning, while it was still dark, Jesus got up, left the house and went off to a solitary place, where he prayed.

Mark 1:35

Then he opened their minds so they could understand the Scriptures.

Luke 24:45

Starting my day off right sets the tone for my whole day. There are all sorts of suggestions for a good start. I went to a computer search engine and found ten different pages of ways you can start your day off right, from yoga to yogurt, a good breakfast, staying at a five-star hotel, reading, writing, and exercise. Setting the tone for the day should include what I want in my day, to do the will of God. We shouldn't start our day hollering and screaming, ranting and raving. Imagine how this day will go.

Jesus made a suggestion: "Very early in the morning, while it was still dark, Jesus got up, left the house, and went to a solitary place, where he prayed" (Mark 1:35). That is how Jesus started his day. Why should I do anything different? I like to go out on my screen porch with my Bible, read a few verses, and talk with God, thank him for another day, pray for a few people, and ask him for an assignment for the day. There is no better way to start my day than quiet time with my heavenly Father.

So before I face the rat race of the world, I like to get my marching orders. I find them within the pages of the Bible. This is where I find a good, hearty breakfast of God's Word. This breakfast can carry me through any day. Meditating on his Word and talking to him about it helps the digestion of some of my tougher assignments. Sometimes, if there is no time, I have to schedule myself to get up earlier, because the tone of my day will be set at this time. I want to be an example of Jesus throughout the day, I may as well start out the way he did and maybe still does. Do you want a peaceful day? Just because there is panic all around doesn't mean we have to join in. Give Jesus' morning routine a try.

Strength

While they were in high spirits, they shouted, "Bring out
Samson to entertain us." So they called Samson out of the
prison, and he performed for them. When they stood him
among the pillars, Samson said to the servant who held his
hand, "Put me where I can feel the pillars that support the
temple, so that I may lean against them." Now the temple
was crowded with men and women; all the rulers of the
Philistines were there, and on the roof were about three
thousand men and women watching Samson perform. Then
Samson prayed to the LORD, "O Sovereign LORD, remember
me. O God, please strengthen me just once more, and let
me with one blow get revenge on the Philistines for my two
eyes." Then Samson reached toward the two central pillars
on which the temple stood. Bracing himself against them, his
right hand on the one and his left hand on the other, Samson
said, "Let me die with the Philistines!" Then he pushed with
all his might, and down came the temple on the rulers and
all the people in it. Thus he killed many more when he died
than while he lived.

Judges 16:25–30

There stood Samson. He had his eyes plucked out, and his hair,
which was the source of his mighty strength, had been cut off.
Samson had been brought out of his prison cell so he could be

mocked. The Philistines were praising their god and mocking God and Samson. Samson went to God in prayer and asked for the strength just one more time to complete his mission. God granted him the strength he needed to bring down the coliseum by pushing the pillars apart and out from under the structure. Many were destroyed that day. Samson had returned to his faith and found the true source of his strength. Samson was given great strength in his death and in pursuing the will of God that he had been set apart for.

What are we blinded by? Have we also gotten off the path? Have we struggled with faith? Have we given into temptations? Are we letting the power of the world come down on us? There are many forces out there vying for our attention. Yes, temptation, distractions, doubt, illness, and hardships cause great weakness. But just like Samson, we have a loving Father waiting for us to cry out to him with faith for the strength we need to bring him glory in all we do. No matter the situation, we need to look to our Father who loves us. The strength is there for us when we ask.

Tell Me about Your Pulpit

He said to them, "Go into all the world and preach the good news to all creation."

Mark 16:15

At our church, we just had a beautiful new pulpit built by hand by a member of our church, named Tom. Tom did a beautiful job. It is natural wood with a glass front and has a cross etched in it. It is a labor of love. It is varnished and shiny. It is beautiful and adds beauty to the wonderful sermons of our preacher.

I am not a preacher, but I am called to go to all creation and preach the good news of Jesus. I don't think they will let me take the pulpit out of the church, nor do I think the grocery store or the mall will let me in with it. One of my particular pulpits was made by Gateway; it is my computer. I send out daily devotionals to the members of my church, other good friends, and to all who will read them on the Internet. I preach the good news of Jesus Christ. I talk about his love, grace, forgiveness, mercy, and commands. I talk about his sacrificial death and resurrection. I talk about the Bible, the voice of God, and his amazing grace in our lives.

Sometimes my heart, mind, and voice are another pulpit. When I am around people, I demonstrate the love of God. Someone told me once to live a sermon, not just speak one. Someone else told me, "Preach a sermon, and when necessary use words." My actions should demonstrate my Christianity. My words should also demonstrate Christianity. I am a Christian counselor and help others come closer to God. We also resolve problems and issues according to God's Word. I discuss the good news with those who will listen. I try to be kind, friendly, and patient. I heard a song once that said, "They will know we are Christians by our love."

The good news is really awesome news, and I want people to see what it looks like in action before I speak about Jesus. I want people to know of his love and the sacrifice he made for us so we can live eternally and free from sin. Preaching the good news daily all around, on the computer, phone, and in person is how I share the good news and use the pulpits I have. What is your pulpit?

The Background Is the Forefront

> These are the names of the twelve apostles: first, Simon (who
> is called Peter) and his brother Andrew; James son of Zebedee,
> and his brother John; Philip and Bartholomew; Thomas
> and Matthew the tax collector; James son of Alphaeus,
> and Thaddaeus; Simon the Zealot and Judas Iscariot, who
> betrayed him.
>
> Matthew 10:2–4

So, how many of the twelve apostles do you know? Okay, so you
may have memorized their names, but what do you know about
all twelve of them? Peter was the most notable and outspoken.
Thomas was a doubter. John was loved by Jesus and wrote a gospel, plus four other books in the New Testament. Matthew wrote
a gospel and another book. Who can forget Judas? I don't think
any of the other eleven wanted his job in the end. James and John
were humiliated when their mother went begging for them to sit
at Jesus' right and left in the kingdom. Phillip worried that they
didn't have enough bread to feed the crowds. Andrew found Peter
and told him they found the Messiah. What did Thaddaeus, James
the son of Alphaeus, and Bartholomew do? I can't find anything
notable. They were kind of in the background.

Well, what they didn't do was yell like James and John, "Hey
Jesus, I want to call your attention to us." Jesus sent all twelve out

two by two to spread the good news. The three I mentioned were included. They get no fanfare but were just named in the twelve. Jesus handpicked all twelve, although they received no other notoriety in the Bible. God loved them; he selected them to be one of the original twelve to spread the good news with Jesus. Although they were in the background, they were really in the forefront. They were always there with Jesus. Jesus washed their feet, performed miracles in front of them, ate with them, gave them powers to heal, and later they received the Holy Spirit. I think we should know their names. God certainly does. Their names are written on God's hand. Every hair on their head is counted. These men are necessary. Are some of these men taken for granted?

At church, do you know the names of the people that clean the bathrooms? Isn't it great that they are clean when we need them? Who fills the plates with bread and grape juice for communion? Who operates the sound? Who watches and teaches the children? Who goes to the nursing homes? Who loads the mission truck? Who helps with home repairs? Who changes the light bulbs? Who sets up and cleans up after all the events? Who drives others to and from church when they need a ride? Who are the people you don't know? Do you know the background people? Do you know who is sitting across the isles? They are loved immeasurably by God.

If you asked in the world, do you currently know any Christians? They would probably say, "Well, yeah. You." Okay, who else? Hmm, well Billy Graham, Charles Stanley, Max Lucado, Rick Warren, Joyce Meyer, and the notable list goes on. Yes, they are important, but so are the background people. I say three cheers for the background people. Of course, they don't want three cheers. That's why they are background people. Their jobs are so important that they are not at all background people to God; they are in the forefront. God knows each and every one of their names, each and every one of their ministries. He knows every hair on their head, and most importantly, he knows they have the joy of a servant's heart.

There is a catchy slogan and a catchy exercise I have heard over the years. "Do something nice for someone today without getting caught." Well yeah, that is a great exercise, but these background people, they do that every day. So we need to get in the habit of doing this catchy exercise. If we do it with love and with the joy of a servant's heart with no fanfare, no accolades, no "hey, look at me," and we make it a daily habit, we may just be elevated to the lofty status of background people.

The Benches Cleared

One night, the Red Sox were playing the Rays when the Rays' pitcher threw the ball and hit the batter Coco Crisp. Yep, that's his name. Coco then feigned a move toward first, but ran out to the pitcher's mound. The pitcher threw a punch, and then Coco threw a punch. The fielders came running in, and then both teams' benches cleared, and the brawl began. Coco didn't stop his team when they came out. He was thinking, *Come on, guys. Let's get these so-and-sos.*

> Then the men stepped forward, seized Jesus and arrested him. With that, one of Jesus' companions reached for his sword, drew it out and struck the servant of the high priest, cutting off his ear. "Put your sword back in its place," Jesus said to him, "for all who draw the sword will die by the sword. Do you think I cannot call on my Father, and he will at once put at my disposal more than twelve legions of angels? But how then would the Scriptures be fulfilled that say it must happen in this way?"
>
> Matthew 26:50–54

When the soldiers came to arrest Jesus because they didn't like what he was teaching, Peter immediately sprung into action to protect his friend. He pulled his sword and cut off the ear of a Roman soldier. Jesus told him, "Put your sword away." He also healed the ear. Jesus told Peter that he could call down twelve legions of angels to help him but there would be no bench-clearing brawl. Well that's not quite what he said, but that's what I heard. Jesus was going with the soldiers willingly to his death an innocent man.

Jesus was going to fulfill prophecy and the will of his father, to pay the ultimate price for sin, his own death. Jesus knew full well that he was going to willingly submit to severe torture, mocking, and death on a cross. The price of sin had to be paid according to God's law, and Jesus was to pay that price for all of us. There would be no retaliation, no twelve legions of angels coming down to help and crush the enemy for Jesus. The angels were probably chomping at the bit, waiting to protect Jesus, but no call would come. There would be no bench-clearing brawl.

Why not? This is Jesus. Because Jesus loves us so much, he willingly and submissively went to his death to pay for the sin of the world for all time. Why did he do this? Because he loves us. His Father told him to. He is nuts about us, and he wants us with him for eternity. Will you submit yourself to God's will today?

The Bond That Can't Be Broken

Therefore, there is now no condemnation for those who are in Christ Jesus.

Romans 8:1

Neither height nor depth, nor anything else in all creation, will be able to separate us from the love of God that is in Christ Jesus our Lord.

Romans 8:39

When I was a child, no matter what I did, nothing could separate me from the love of my father. He would get mad at me when I got into trouble, but Dad would always sit me down and give me the chance to explain myself. I always knew even with punishment and a lecture that he loved me. That bond was never broken. I learned from my father that when I did something wrong he loved me but he didn't love what I did. He would always love me and always be my father. No matter what happened, I would not be disowned or separated from his love. I was his.

I also belong to God, my Father, and through Jesus, I am truly his. I have learned that when I gave myself to him through Jesus, he sealed me with his Holy Spirit. Assurance is an awesome piece of knowledge. Are we really sure of anything? We can be sure of God's love and no condemnation for those in Christ Jesus. Believing, repenting, and being baptized has sealed me to God through Jesus with his Holy Spirit. Nothing can separate me from his love. I do not have to fear anything as I am connected with the Father through the Son.

Psalm 23:4 says, "Even though I walk through the valley of the shadow of death, I will fear no evil, for you are with me." God is always with me, and I have no condemnation in Jesus. Do you have concerns today? Do you have troubles, worries, fears, or nervousness in the pit of your stomach over anything? Are you feeling unsure or lost? Do you need assurance? Let me give you some. I didn't make this up. I read it, and God said it in Romans 8:39: "Neither height nor depth, nor anything in all creation will be able to separate us from the love of God that is in Christ Jesus our Lord." I never tried to get in trouble as a child, but when I did, nothing could separate me from the love of my father. He didn't love what I did, but he sure loved me. How much greater is our heavenly Father's love?

The Bottom Dropped Out

He fell to the ground and heard a voice say to him, "Saul,
Saul, why do you persecute me?"

Acts 9:4

When I was about five years old, I lived very close to the school I
attended. The school was in North Babylon, New York. I would go
down there and climb up on a seven-foot brick wall. You had to
stand on a metal grate that was over the basement entrance to an
electrical room to get on the wall. One day, I got on my bike and
rode over to the school, stepped on to the grate, and the bottom
dropped out, down about eight feet. When I landed, I was standing straight up, but oh boy, my legs hurt. I was a little skinny kid.
I was all alone; there was a straight ladder, which I used to slowly
climb back out. I walked my bike home about a half mile. When
my father got home from work, my mother had him take me to
the emergency room. Nothing was broken; I just had a really bad
sprain in both legs and a lot of pain.

From the time I was sixteen, shortly after my father died, I
began drinking beer. Not a little beer, but massive quantities of
beer. It took away the pain, depression, insecurities, and fear I was
feeling. When I was about twenty, the beer started to take away
my friends, family, self-esteem, and my reason to live. I no longer
wanted to go on. The bottom dropped out again. I was angry with

God after my father died and was not on speaking terms with him, except to ask him to let me die.

I found recovery when I was almost twenty-one. I began a program of living, and I once again began speaking to my loving God, who had never left me. Since my retuning and developing a relationship with God, I have never doubted his love again. When I was about forty-five, I felt a void again. I began praying more and more, but something was still missing. I began feeling great guilt, remorse, and concern that many of the things I did throughout my life were surely going to cause eternal separation from God. I thought I was surely hell bound. I had been there before in my mind and was afraid that I would return, except this time for real. I knew of Jesus but didn't really know him. I didn't really understand the mercy I could be shown for my sins once I accepted Jesus as my Savior and began walking God's narrow path. It felt as if the bottom had dropped out again, down one more level.

So what does one do when the bottom drops out? There are many who choose drugs, alcohol, other addictions, and of course, suicide. However, there is a much better choice: we can turn to God. I made that choice this time. I called on God in prayer and meditation. I even began listening to a preacher on the radio. God used all of this to answer my prayers. I would pray about something at night, and Charles Stanley would talk about that topic the very next morning on the radio. He also said to read the Bible, pray, meditate, find a Bible-believing church, and so I did all four.

This time, when the bottom dropped out, I landed on my knees. That was the best position to be in, humbled and convicted. But I also felt loved beyond words by the almighty God. I have grown to know and form a relationship with Jesus, the Savior of the world. I have learned that his death paid my sin debt; I needed to know this and believe it. I learned to follow God's commands and follow his narrow path. I continue to repent for my sins and have been baptized. I have learned that God will help me bear any burden and that he meets all my needs. I am never alone. I have the assurance of eternal salvation because of God's love. Today, I am sober and saved. What an awesome combination. I have learned if the bottom drops out to land on my knees and look up.

The Clutter Sale

> Therefore, if anyone is in Christ, he is a new creation; the old has gone, the new has come!
>
> 2 Corinthians 5:17

Rummage sales, yard sales, garage sales, tag sales, and you name it; people are trying to get rid of stuff. One day, my neighborhood was having garage sales. My church was having a rummage sale to raise money for mission trips to Honduras. You name it, and it was for sale. People cleaned out garages, storerooms, attics, closets, under the bed, and I may have even seen a kitchen sink for sale somewhere. Everything must go to make room.

As a new creation in Jesus, I too must make room. I have to clean house. I have to clean out my heart to make room for Jesus. I have to make it acceptable and livable for my savior, the King of kings, Jesus. Out with the old. Sin must go: greed, gluttony, sloth, lust, selfishness, envy, debauchery, gossip, foul language, dirty jokes, and anything else that does not bring glory to God. Everything must go. I can't sell this stuff. No one wants it. Either they have enough of their own, or they are also disposing of theirs.

Once I get rid of all the old junk, I can move in all the new good things. I am making room for an entire makeover and have already started moving things in. My heart now has room for Galatians 5:22–23: "The fruit of the Spirit is love, joy, peace, patience, kindness, goodness, faithfulness, gentleness and self-control." Getting rid of all the old junk makes room for my occupants in my heart: Jesus, the Holy Spirit, and the fruits of the spirit. This remodeling and redecorating is just what has been called for. So, in the theme of those rummage and garage sales, all the junk must go. Out with the old, and in with the new.

The Gift

I mean that you have been saved by grace through believing.
You did not save yourselves; it was a gift from God.

Ephesians 2:8 (NVC)

Don't we all like to give and receive gifts? The gift I remember most
as a child was when I was in second grade. I grew up Catholic, and
I was having my first communion. I was too young to truly appreciate baseball, and I was a Yankee fan (I have since recovered from
this malady). Well anyway, before the ceremony, my father told
me to go out to his car and get something for him out of the glove
compartment. When I went out there, I found a box, wrapped,
with my name on it. I brought it in and opened it in front of my
mother and father; it was a watch with Mickey Mantle and Roger
Maris on it. I was so excited. I don't remember any of the ceremony, but I did know what time it was.

It meant so much to me even at that age. I knew my parents had
to pinch pennies; we never had much money. But they bought me
a watch. When my sons were young, they used to make me things
in school. I still have many of them, and the boys are eighteen and
twenty. When I go out to get a gift, it takes me forever because I
want it to be perfect; I want it to be something the receiver will
enjoy and be able to use.

When I receive gifts, I am always grateful and feel that some-one got me something they thought about. They went shopping and had me in mind. I was someone's only thought for even a short time, and they were getting me something. I also love the gifts people give me with their time, inviting me to their homes, sharing meals, taking me places with them, and just talking and listening.

I am not greedy, but I do enjoy gifts and appreciate them very much. Paul says in Ephesians 2:8 that I have been saved by grace, not by my own power or works. He says it is a gift from God. A gift from God, can you imagine? He has already given us the Earth, the oceans, lakes, mountains, trees, flowers, rainbows, and all kinds of beautiful things. He has given us children, parents, extended fami-lies, church families, friends, and these aren't even the gifts Paul is talking about.

God's gift is salvation from our sin, eternal life, a friendship with him and his Son, Jesus. He has given us his word in the Bible, a manual, compass, guidebook, and love story to live by. Can you believe that God who has known us since before the creation of the Earth, who thinks about and loves us, has given us himself? We can go straight to him with anything at any time. God has only us in mind and has given us a gift we would enjoy and that is perfect.

A lot has changed since I was seven. I am certainly not a Yankee fan. God knows exactly what I want and what I need. He has given me everything I need. He knows what I want, and he knows what is necessary and good for me. My needs are met here on Earth and more importantly in my eternal, spiritual life. Faith and obedience have allowed me to accept these gifts with overwhelming gratitude. I will spend eternity with God the Father and with Jesus, my Savior and friend. It is a gift paid for by Jesus.

Maybe a gift we could give today would be to share our knowl-edge and experience of Jesus with someone who doesn't know him.

God's gift to them will become evident as we share. The gift is for everyone. It is an individual gift for all. Today, let's share this awesome gift with others; there is plenty to go around. Jesus paid for it already. We just have to deliver it.

The Human Pretzel

So Jacob was left alone, and a man wrestled with him till daybreak. When the man saw that he could not overpower him, he touched the socket of Jacob's hip so that his hip was wrenched as he wrestled with the man. Then the man said, "Let me go, for it is daybreak." But Jacob replied, "I will not let you go unless you bless me." The man asked him, "What is your name?" "Jacob," he answered. Then the man said, "Your name will no longer be Jacob, but Israel, because you have struggled with God and with men and have overcome." Jacob said, "Please tell me your name." But he replied, "Why do you ask my name?" Then he blessed him there.

Genesis 32:26–29

When I was in ninth grade, we had to wrestle in gym class. I was not a very good wrestler. Okay, I stunk at wrestling. The gym teacher would match us up in our weight class. This day, I was to wrestle Sal, who was number one in the state for his weight class. Sal knew moves that would turn kids into human pretzels. There I was, hands out, bent over, staring into the eyes of Sal, the pretzel maker. He pinned me in twenty-three seconds; it took him twenty seconds to catch me and the other three seconds to pin me. He told me to stop running and he would take it easy on me. I don't know what the move was, but somehow he wrapped my legs around my head and my arms were around my waist. I have never been able to do that particular move again. All I heard was a count: "One, two, three, winner!" as Sal's hand was raised into the air. After I unfolded, he shook my hand and said, "Good match." Yeah, right.

Jacob wrestled with God all night till daybreak, and he won. Of course, Jacob was the one that came away with a limp and a new name. God touched the socket in Jacob's hip, and he came away with a limp for life. Jacob knew he had been wrestling with God until daybreak.

I have wrestled with God until daybreak many times. I have never been pronounced the winner, but I still wrestle. I have wrestled with financial problems, job problems, relationships, resentments, death, illness, what-am-I-gonna-do-now problems, and all kinds of problems. I talk and wrestle with God all night, trying to figure out the best way for God to fix it. Notice I said talk and not listen; now I get it. Well, I finally realized I needed God to figure out how to fix my problems because I am the one who got myself into the pretzel position. At the same time, I am wrestling with myself. (Now there is a picture for you.)

Instead of wrestling, I need to trust God and not wrestle with him. He knows the answers, and he wants to share them with me if I would just be quiet and turn off the noise in my head. In Jeremiah 17:7 God said to Jeremiah, "But blessed is the man who trusts in the LORD, whose confidence is in him."

Trust in the Lord to be blessed; have confidence in him. Give your problems to God without wrestling over them. He knows what to do. God has got it. I need to trust that he will take care of me.

When God touched Jacob's hip socket, he made him limp. I think of limping as needing to lean on something or someone. I am reminded by this encounter that I need to lean on God. He is all-powerful, all knowing, and ever-present. He wants me to talk with him. Well, I don't wrestle as much anymore. I am still God's work in progress.

Today, I will go to God in prayer, thank him in advance for all he has done and will do for me. I will realize God does not really need my help, nor do I need to wrestle with him. I need to trust and have confidence in God, and I will be blessed. By having faith, leaning on God, giving my problems to him and not wrestling, and trying to help him figure them out, I won't be turned into an emotional pretzel.

The News Isn't All Bad

Have you been following the news lately? How can you not? The economic system is in turmoil. Lending is at an all-time low. Gas prices are at an all-time high. War, famine, natural disasters, and disease are all around the world, and there is more.

Depressing people is not my intent, and the news isn't all bad. You may be saying, "So what's the good news, Ken?" One name and two numbers: John 3:16 "For God so loved the world that he gave his one and only Son, that whoever believes in him shall not perish but have eternal life." How about Paul's letter in Romans 8:1–2? "Therefore, there is now no condemnation for those who are in Christ Jesus, because through Christ Jesus the law of the Spirit of life set me free from the law of sin and death." How about Romans 8:39? "Neither height nor depth, nor anything else in all creation, will be able to separate us from the love of God that is in Christ Jesus our Lord."

We have eternal assurance for those in Christ Jesus. Nothing or no one in this world can take away what Jesus has provided. Now it is up to us to believe what is important. It is up to us to choose the security we want and what we will put our confidence in. Should we put our faith in the things of the world or in the good news of Jesus? Spiritual confidence can be attained by belief in Jesus who paid our sin debt on the cross. The news here is really good.

The One Who Counts
Knows My Name

Fear not, for I have redeemed you; I have summoned you by
name; you are mine.

Isaiah 43

Several years ago, I was at a conference for state employees. I was
a child abuse investigations supervisor. The district administrator
came over to me and introduced himself as John Smith (not his real
name) the district administrator. I answered with a hello, telling
him my name and that I was a P.I. supervisor. He said he had heard
very good things about me. Isn't that cool? Later that evening, I
was standing with my boss, and Mr. Smith said hello to her, called
her by name, then looked at me, shook my hand, and said, "Hello,
my name is John Smith, the district administrator." Again, I said
hello and told him my name, Ken Jones, P.I. supervisor. Again,
he said he had heard very good things about me. Hmm, déjà vu
all over again. Even later, I was talking to my boss's boss and was
telling him about the experience, and we were laughing. Wouldn't
you know it? Mr. Smith came over to my boss's boss and said hello
to him by name, turned to me, and said, "Hello, my name is John
Smith. I am the district administrator." I smiled, and my boss's
boss poked me and said, "Behave." You know, I don't know if that
man ever did know who I was.

There have been times in my life I have felt alone, afraid, and defeated. I have been made fun of, scorned, persecuted, lied about, and insulted. The New Century Version of the Bible says in Isaiah 43:1, "Don't be afraid, because I have saved you. I have called you by name, and you are mine." God knows my name; he created me. He knew me before I was in my mother's womb. Jeremiah 1:5: "Before I formed you in the womb I knew you, before you were born I set you apart; I appointed you as a prophet to the nations."

God has my name written on his hand. God knows me personally. I am his; he sees everything I do and knows everything I think, good or bad. God knows my heart. Whenever I need him, I can cry out to him in prayer. James 5:13: "Is any one of you in trouble? He should pray. Is anyone happy? Let him sing songs of praise." Whenever I am troubled or whenever I am happy, I can go to my Father with prayer and praise. He is always here. He said, "Don't be afraid, because I have saved you. I called you by name." Today, I have the assurance from my heavenly Father. I am under his care and protection, and nothing anyone says or does will have the eternal effects my Father has. He is my protector, and he will always know my name. I pray one day when I say, "I am Ken Jones," he will say, "I know. I have heard very good things about you." And he will really mean it.

The Real GPS

Because of the tender mercy of our God, by which the rising sun will come to us from heaven to shine on those living in darkness and in the shadow of death, to guide our feet into the path of peace.

Luke 1:78–79

For my birthday, my wife got me a GPS for my car. Do you know what GPS stands for? It stands for the global positioning system. It works from satellites. When I type in an address a computer voice gives me directions right to where I want to go. If I am lost, I can push a button that says "take me home," and that same voice takes me home.

When I was a little kid, my father did all the driving. He could drive anywhere. It didn't matter where we were going; he seemed to know where everything was. I always wondered how we could go so far away from home and get back. I just sat back and didn't have to even think about it. Dad had it under control and knew he would get us from point A to point B, and he could go to all the points of interests we wanted to go. My father was a human GPS.

The other day, I was questioning where I might be going spiritually in life. That same day, my wife bought me the GPS, not knowing of that thought. This GPS needs some updates, and I bought the card that will do that. I want to be up to date and know exactly where I am going and when I will get there. I had to ask myself, "Is this realistic in my spiritual life and in my Christian walk?" What happened to trusting my dad, just sitting back, and trusting that he would get me where I needed to go? Okay, guess what I figured out. My heavenly Father is always with me and is bringing me through life. Wherever he brings me to, he will bring me through. Where God wants me, he will bring me.

The word *trust* comes to mind. Trust is a big word. Other words include *faith, belief,* and *assurance.* If I continue to put one foot in front of the other, following the direction from the Bible, the real GPS, and trusting in God, I will get exactly where I need to be. I don't need to worry about it. If I follow Jesus, follow the guidance of the Holy Spirit and the words of God in the Bible, I will never get lost. I have clear precise direction. I also know God will take me on the beautiful scenic route.

The Three Pigs and Christians

He is like a man building a house, who dug down deep and laid the foundation on rock. When a flood came, the torrent struck that house but could not shake it, because it was well built. But the one who hears my words and does not put them into practice is like a man who built a house on the ground without a foundation. The moment the torrent struck that house, it collapsed and its destruction was complete.

Luke 6:48–49

Remember the fairy tale of the three little pigs? Momma pig sent the three out to seek their fortunes. Well, each needed a place to live. One built his house of straw, the other out of sticks, and the last out of brick. The first two pigs were lazy and put no real time or effort into their shelter. Then, when push came to shove and the big bad wolf came, he huffed and puffed and blew their houses down. The third pig built his house with brick on solid foundation, and the wolf couldn't huff and puff and blow it down. It was solid.

Our faith is like that. Some like to take faith for granted, use God only when they are in trouble. Some are like foxhole Christians, when the going gets tough they sweat and wish they could just hide. They use straw and sticks to build their faith. Between temptation, distractions, and the things of the world, they have no time to build a solid foundation of faith through Bible study and a relationship with God. There is no time to follow God's commands we may be too busy with the self-imposed hustle and bustle of everyday life. We can also get caught up in chasing the almighty dollar and things that glitter. It says in Matthew 6:24, "No one can serve two masters. Either he will hate the one and love the other, or he will be devoted to the one and despise the other." We cannot serve both God and money.

Satan is out there, starring in today's role as the big bad wolf. His job is to cause distraction, temptation, and add to the turmoil of hustle and bustle. Is your foundation strong? Have you used a solid foundation? Is Jesus your cornerstone? Satan is prowling. He is coming to attempt to shake and rock your world and foundation. He is coming to huff and puff and blow your faith down. Can Satan, the big bad wolf, knock down your faith? Can the storms of life shake your foundation and wash you away? Have you built a deep foundation in God?

Do you continue daily to build up your relationship and study his Word? Deep and solid foundations are required, bricks are needed, and a cornerstone of Jesus is essential.

The Vote Heard Round the Universe

We have just come out of an election year. We have elected our next president. We were given a choice, and each of us voted. Every four years, we get to make this choice. It is a big decision in this country, but none as big as the votes I am talking about here. You may ask, "What could be a bigger vote than the president of the United States?"

> Now it was the governor's custom at the Feast to release a prisoner chosen by the crowd. At that time they had a notorious prisoner, called Barabbas. So when the crowd had gathered, Pilate asked them, "Which one do you want me to release to you: Barabbas, or Jesus who is called Christ?"
>
> Matthew 27:15–17

There Jesus stood, after being beaten and battered, an innocent man. The crowd, filled with hate and envy and not knowing who Jesus really was, was asked to vote. Pilate, the governor, asked, "Who should I release: Jesus, or the notorious criminal, Barabbas? Reading this account over two thousand years later seems like a no-brainer; Jesus was the innocent one. He should go free. Barabbas, a notorious murderer, criminal, and sinner should be punished and put to death. That's not how the crowd saw it. They voted to let Barabbas go free. Now Pilate had a second vote. What should I do with Jesus? Again, they voted. They all yelled, "Crucify him!"

Jesus took the place on the cross for Barabbas. I too am Barabbas. We are Barabbas. He took our place on death row and the cross for our sins as well as Barabbas. God sent Jesus to pay our sin debt. Are you starting to feel like Barabbas? Who is really guilty? Was it Jesus, or is it us? Jesus has been elected and served his term on the cross for each and every one of us.

The Wanderer

Suppose one of you has a hundred sheep and loses one of them. Does he not leave the ninety-nine in the open country and go after the lost sheep until he finds it?

Luke 15:4

Between the ages of four and five, I was quite a wanderer. I used to just leave my yard and go for walks without my parents' knowledge. I wasn't running away. I was just investigating and wandering. One time, I wandered over to the bowling alley about a mile from my house, across a very busy intersection. Someone there knew me and called my mother. Once, I wandered to a local school, and one of my older neighbors recognized me. Imagine the surprise when the school called my mother about me. Two times, I ended up at the bottom of a hole. We had a large fence I wasn't supposed to get out of, but I could climb it. My mother even tried a harness with a runner on it. But I could talk my sister into unhooking me. I am glad my mother always came to get me.

Those are but a few of my wandering stories as a child. As I got older, I wandered into more trouble. I am grateful I never wandered into jail. I wandered into alcoholism, sin, and many dangerous situations. I was found by my friend Henry in 1978, and he showed me my way home from alcoholism. You would think I might stop wandering. Oh no, more wandering: in and out of church. Mostly out. Somewhere else always seemed to be where I wanted to be. I was never quite pleased with where I was.

So I would wander. I wandered to places I thought angels feared to go. I am glad they were not. The further away I thought I was getting, the closer the good shepherd was. I have been given a new life in Jesus, and my heavenly Father has never given up or lost sight of me. I am more than grateful to have been found. I have found my place right next to Jesus, my heavenly Father, and his Holy Spirit. Now what I hear is from Psalm 46:10: "Be still, and know that I am God," and then I hear, "No more wandering."

There Is a Hole inside Me

That good thing which was committed to you, keep by the
Holy Spirit who dwells in us.

2 Timothy 1:14

Have you ever tried to put a square peg in a round hole? How
about a round peg in a triangular hole? I could go on, but you get
the picture. They just don't fit, do they? Well let's make sure. Let's
try it again. Does it fit this time? Okay, let's go for three out of
five. So, we have been shut out. How about seven out of ten? Am I
beginning to sound ridiculous? Maybe I am. This may just be the
definition of insanity, trying the same thing over and over hoping
for different results. It just doesn't fit.

There is a hole inside me that I have tried to fill for years. Do
you know the hole inside, where you need something and can't
figure out what to fill it with? Years ago, I used alcohol to try to
fill the hole that just wouldn't be filled. I could feel the hole and
wanted it patched. Since then, I have tried all kinds of other things
to fill that hole. I have tried relationships, overworking, achieve-
ments, money, search for security, etc. Others have tried drugs,
alcohol, sex, pornography, adultery, divorce, cars, jewelry, and all
kinds of other extravagances. The hole doesn't want to be filled.
It is like a thirst that won't be quenched or a hunger that can't be

satisfied. I just couldn't get that square peg in a round hole, but I kept trying.

That hole is crying out to be filled. Only God can truly meet our needs and fill that hole. Alone, I am powerless. God is the power. My sins can't be forgiven without God, and the payment couldn't be paid for sin without Jesus. This is a hole that can only be filled by God. God gives us his Holy Spirit to dwell in us, and Jesus lives in our hearts. God fits perfectly. The desire is filled, the thirst is quenched, and hunger subsides. God is running my life, he is within me, and I am fulfilled. All is as it should be. As problems and issues come up, they can be dealt with in a spiritual manner as God is within. Peace, joy, and assurance are abundant as God is in his place as the piece that was missing in my life.

Jesus is knocking. Let him dwell within. Accept him as your personal Savior. Since I have let him in, that hole is full, and I am grateful.

Things Change,

Part One

How do I know things change? Have you looked in the mirror lately? Go back to where you grew up and look around. I have, and a lot has changed. The boy I used to call my little brother is four inches taller than me and getting a bit grayer.

The world has also changed. Prices have skyrocketed and continue to climb. Crime and terrorism are at an all-time high, and there are concerns about more. Moral values are at an all-time low. There is an upside—technology has amazed us, but many have even found a way to abuse that.

Do you know what hasn't changed? The Word of God hasn't changed. God still loves us, and he is still in charge. Nothing about that is changing. Jesus has still saved us. Hebrews 13:8 says, "Jesus Christ is the same yesterday and today and forever." God is still our Father, Jesus is still our Savior, and the Bible is still the same. God's Word is better than an old friend you can count on. Your eternal life has only changed if you have given your life to Jesus, and that is for the better.

Curl up with the Bible today. Sit with an old friend, God, and listen to his Word. The Bible is the voice of God. He will talk and listen with us. See and hear his assurances, promises, and words of love as you read. Spend some quiet time, relax, and enjoy our loving father God. He waits patiently and lovingly for the visit.

Listen to the same voice that Adam, Eve, Moses, Noah, Isaiah, Jeremiah, and even Jesus heard. Relax to the voice of wisdom, love, and mercy from our old and unchanging friend. Relax and know God will be the same friend we have always known.

> Praise the LORD. Give thanks to the LORD, for he is good; his love endures forever.
>
> Psalm 106:1

Things Change,
Part Two

Because God wanted to make the unchanging nature of his purpose very clear to the heirs of what was promised, he confirmed it with an oath.

Hebrews 6:17

When I was a child and looked in the mirror at the kid who looked back making funny faces at me, I didn't even know what sin was. I went to Sunday school. I heard about sin and salvation through Jesus, but I didn't understand how it applied to me. That freckle-faced kid looking back only knew that God loved him, Jesus loved him, and God lived inside him, and that was enough for me.

As the first half century of my life has gone by, there have been many changes: broken fingers from Little League have turned into arthritic fingers. Gray hair, wrinkles under my eyes, and I have views on topics I only heard them talk about on the news in black and white. My own alcoholism really changed my life, and sin was in full swing. I found sobriety but still sinned. At sixteen, I didn't think God was as loving anymore. Waving good-bye to my children after weekend visits was torture. Learning the ills of the world as I have gotten older as a child abuse investigator and a counselor, I have heard and lived my share of hardship.

I look at life with different eyes these days. The guy I used to look at in the mirror still makes occasional faces, but those eyes have seen a lot. I don't see the innocence I once saw. Do you know what else has changed in my life? My understanding of my need for a Savior and my loving God has changed. I know now what my need for being saved means. I also know and rejoice that God would show this less then innocent man mercy, love, and forgiveness.

Thank you, Father, for your unchanging nature. Thank you for the promise of your love. Thank you for never wavering in salvation through your Son Jesus. Thank you for your assurance of eternal life for those who turn to Jesus. Thank you for never changing your mind when I was not consistent in my loyalty to you. Thank you for being my rock. Thank you for allowing me to always come to you. In your Son Jesus' name, amen.

> Praise the LORD. Give thanks to the LORD, for he is good; his love endures forever.
>
> Psalm 106:1

This Is How a Real Hero Enters

Early on the first day of the week, while it was still dark, Mary Magdalene went to the tomb and saw that the stone had been removed from the entrance.

John 20:1

On the evening of that first day of the week, when the disciples were together, with the doors locked for fear of the Jews, Jesus came and stood among them and said, "Peace be with you!" After he said this, he showed them his hands and side.

John 20:19–20

My childhood hero was John Wayne. When there was trouble, John Wayne swaggered in, the room became silent, and there was always some dunderhead who wanted to have a shootout with the Duke. Never a smart move, the Duke always won. Just his presence and voice could silence a room. Another favorite was Chuck Norris, who played Walker Texas Ranger. He told a bad guy one time, "I am going to hit you with so many rights, you will beg for a left." I like the endings where the good guy wins.

Imagine Jesus on the cross, Jesus, Prince of Peace and Lamb of God. Those names didn't really instill fear in his executioners. They even told him, "If you are who you say come down from that cross." Well he didn't, not quite like the John Wayne movies I paid to see. This was no movie; this was real life. Jesus didn't come to fight in the way Duke or Walker would fight. Jesus was armed with love, mercy, grace, and the truth. Jesus could have gotten down, but he was nailed to that cross, not only with nails, but with love. His love for us and the needed payment for our sins kept him nailed to the cross. He had a mission, and he finished it.

On the third day after his death, Mary Magdalene came to the tomb where they had buried Jesus. The boulder was pushed aside, and the tomb was empty. They thought maybe the body was stolen; they didn't know. The apostles checked and were saddened. Where did he go?

Enter the hero, through locked doors, barred windows, a fortress for the apostles in hiding. Jesus walked through the door and said, "Peace be with you" (John 20:20). The crowd went wild, or they should have. That is how our hero enters a room. The Lamb of God, the Prince of Peace, King of kings, and the Savior of the World entered the room. Jesus showed the wounds in his hands and feet. John 20:20 says, "The disciples were overjoyed when they saw the Lord." Maybe they went wild. Someone should. That was one heck of a hero's entrance.

Jesus beat death; Jesus got up from his two-day slumber after a contemptuous mocking, atrocious beating, and horrific death and walked out of the tomb. He walked through the door and said, "Peace be with you." Jesus didn't skip a beat. He wasn't mad. He wasn't out for revenge. He came to continue teaching and serving. He gave the disciples peace, and he gave them the Holy Spirit. Jesus not only died for our sins. He was resurrected, and he woke up. He came back to life. No call to arms, a call for peace was given.

This is my hero, Jesus. He teaches me that all the rights in the world won't call for a left and all the gunfights won't help anyone. Jesus said, "Peace be with you." He told us we would be with him in heaven. All we need to do is believe and follow God's commands. Jesus did the hard part for us; he took on our sin and died with it so we could live. Then he came back from death as we know it and gave us eternal life.

I know most of you know this story, but I just wanted to share that Jesus is my hero now. As John Wayne might have said, there is a new sheriff in town. There are new rules. Jesus laid them out: love God, love one another as you love yourself, love your enemies, make disciples of the world. I am following that to the best of my ability. I want to pick up my cross and follow my hero, Jesus.

Peace be with you.

Three Steps Back, or Was It Four?

We all stumble in many ways. If anyone is never at fault in what he says, he is a perfect man, able to keep his whole body in check.

James 3:2

Before my voice changed, I was told I had the voice of an angel. I sang solos in all the school and church musicals. My favorite was walking a cute girl around the stage in third grade, holding her hand with an umbrella, singing "April Showers."

One year, around the third grade, I got a lot of laughs in one musical, and it wasn't even a comedy. We had lined up to sing our parts for the song "The Nights of Hanukkah." We were to sing our part and gently tap the candle, and it would turn on. When we all sang, we were to take four steps back, and the curtain would close. Well it was all done, and I took my three steps back, or did they say four? The curtain was closed, and there I was alone on stage. I ran back and forth looking for a way in and finally did a headfirst slide under the curtain. The crowd went wild with laughter and applause. The music teacher wasn't laughing. She was serious; she was crying.

That night we had a performance, which was the second and final performance for the parents with Mom and Dad front and center. The music teacher told me five steps this time. She was sure of a great performance. I sang my part, tapped my candle, tapped it again, and again, and swung it. I looked at my dad. He made a twisting motion with his hand. I turned the light by the bulb, and it went on. The place was roaring with laughter. I looked back. My music teacher was crying again. Well the good news is I took five steps back without further incident.

There is a lighted sign on the church next to mine. The letters light up sometimes saying "This is the Perfect Church for Imperfect People." I told one of the elders I should go there; he assures me I am in the right place, that all churches are perfect churches for imperfect people. As a person, I stumble, fumble, and fall. I make mistakes and have temptations. I have not become perfect. I am perfect and righteous before my Father only because of Jesus' sacrifice. God knows me and knows I am not perfect. When I was in the Catholic seminary in the eighties, I had a spiritual director named Father McGovern, who told me the only thing I will do perfectly is be perfectly human with all the mistakes, frailties, and fumbles humans make.

No need to cry, Ms. Whateveryournamewas. Progress is essential. Perfect was crucified. God knows when we are trying. He knows our hearts. Keep putting one foot in front of the other, keep your eyes fixed on Jesus, and obey God's commands. We need to keep living life to the best of our ability, asking God daily for strength, wisdom, and direction. Take an extra step back if you need to and twist the light. God won't cry.

Tilted Halos Revisited

I love to share the Word of God, and I love to share some simple reflections I have on it. I do this through blogging. At the end of each of my blog posts, I sign my name, and under that I write the letters *THS*.

The idea for my signature came from a few sources. Max Lucado alludes to the Tilted Halo Society (THS) when he talks about Matthew's background and choice of acquaintances in his books. Brennan Manning, in his book *The Ragamuffin Gospel*, spends a chapter on it. My friend Jimmy Pruitt discussed it in one of his writings and claims himself a member of THS.

Pompous, stiff-necked people would not be in the Tilted Halo Society. They are more for their own glory than God's. Tilted Halo members don't wear the halo too tight. Ken, are you saying you have a halo? Well, not a literal one but a figurative one. Any of you who have known me any length of time wonder how I could have any kind of halo. That's the point: it is tilted. I am not perfect. I have shortcomings, foibles. I have made mistakes and have said the wrong thing at the wrong time.

I may wear a tilted halo, but I take God and his Word very seriously. I am human with blood running through my veins; I am going to make mistakes. I have done things I am not the least bit proud of. I have gotten some scrapes and scars along the way. It is only because of Jesus I have been forgiven. His death and resurrection are what have atoned for my sins. Now I have to forgive myself. I also have to change and move forward. I have to do my very best to follow God's commands. There are no excuses for sin. I need to change and do what God has commanded. Does this mean I have become perfect? No, I have not. There are times where I fall short and act human. That humanness tilts my halo.

Maybe you are a member of the Tilted Halo Society already and just don't know it. Welcome to the human race and the Tilted Halo Society. When I take myself too serious, puff my chest out, and hold my head way up, my neck gets stiff. When I realize I acted that way, I can laugh at myself and try to straighten the halo again. But since it is loose fitting, it tilts.

Next time you make a mistake, do anything wrong, feel a bit off, or realize you're not perfect, you too can be a member. I hope you can see I am simply having a little fun with this at my own expense. Yes, it is a goofy thing, but THSers can be goofy at times. It's a rule. God is perfect. God's Word is perfect. I have to stop beating myself up for not being perfect and continue to strive and move forward. The only thing perfect about me is that I am perfectly human, with all the flaws that are attached. I am aware of the flaws and continue to strive to be more Christ like.

Enjoy your tilted halo.

Time to Shrink

He must become greater; I must become less.

John 3:30

There are times I am my own favorite topic. I have heard the expression "I am not much, but I am all I think about." I don't know who coined the phrase, but it is sadly true at times. During those times, I have pressing issues on my mind, and I get all wrapped around the axel with them. Pressing? Pressing to whom? Have you ever had those times in your life when you have a decision to make and it encompasses all of your thoughts during your waking hours? Have you had times when you have done something well, or even something wrong, and it just possesses your thoughts? How about thoughts, concerns, and problems with friends, family, work, etc.?

These decisions, problems, and concerns become all consuming. I have to ask myself one question: "Where is God when all this is going on?" Well, I know he is right here, but I mean, where in my thoughts is he? Why am I not making him the biggest part of any of these concerns? Why am I not giving him my burdens? Why am I not reaching out and serving him and others? How did my concerns become greater than the work God has put before me? I have to start thinking of what God has for me to do and not be all consumed with my own thoughts and turn my thoughts over to him and do his will. I must also become less so Jesus can become more.

John the Baptist said he had to step aside for Jesus. He said he had to become less so Jesus could become more. Today and every day, my thoughts of my own wants and desires need to become less so Jesus can become more. Thoughts, prayers, meditation, and service to God need to become the main priority in my life. It is time to get out of my own head and back in the heart of Jesus.

Turning to God

Do not judge and you will not be judged. Do not condemn, and you will not be condemned. Forgive, and you will be forgiven.

Luke 6:37

When things in my life go wrong, I turn to God. He is the source of my strength. I wish I could say everything goes my way all the time, but that would not be true. God is my light in a dark world. Recently, I was deceived by someone. This was not the first time, and I am sure it won't be the last. I find strength and love in my heavenly Father. He has told me to find forgiveness in my heart for this person. Through forgiveness I have always been able to find freedom and joy.

Why do I want revenge when I am cheated and deceived? I go to my Father, and he says in the Bible that he will forgive me as I forgive others. It is tough sometimes to forgive, but I am a disciple of Jesus, who forgave his murderers and torturers. I must find that same forgiveness. While Stephen was being stoned to death, he asked God to forgive his killers. I find examples of forgiveness throughout the Bible. If there is to be vengeance, it is God's vengeance, not mine. I have suggested some ideas for vengeance, and God says, "Be still."

By turning to God, who takes my burdens, tells me to be still, and answers prayer, I have found peace. I simply need to take the steps necessary to remedy the situation and leave all the results in God's hands. I need to understand that I am dealing with people that God loves and I should love. I am also called to love my enemy. Maturing is tough stuff, but by turning to God, I find peace and assurance that all is well in the world and learn to count my blessings. I can't dwell on one situation. My blessings are many. Forgiveness has been granted. God has forgiven me much. I have only a little to forgive in comparison.

Unchanged

I the LORD do not change.

Malachi 3:6

Jesus Christ is the same yesterday and today and forever.

Hebrews 13:8

A lot has changed in my life over the years. Actually, just about everything has changed; I merely have to look in the mirror. A lot has changed in the world over my lifetime as well. I remember when I started driving and gas was thirty-two cents a gallon. When I was a child, we had a thirteen-channel black-and-white TV with an antenna on the roof of the house. My father also had a voice-activated TV remote. All he would have to do was say, "Kenny, turn on channel four, and *poof* he could just sit there, and I would get up and turn the channels. My mother also had an automatic dishwasher and dryer. I would wash, and my sister would dry.

There have been numerous presidents with several different ideas. Technology has changed everything. The changes are endless. Remember the five-cent candy bar and the fifteen-cent hamburger? The sad part though is values and morals have changed and not always for the better. We sure accept a lot of change in the name of political correctness and not wanting to alienate people, even if what they are doing is wrong.

Although I left the church for many years, when I came back to church, do you know what I noticed? Nothing about God or his Word had changed. He still promises salvation to those who believe and accept Jesus as their Savior. The Word of the God has not changed. No amendments. God has not changed, nor has he reneged on any of his promises. Consistency is a tough thing to find in life and the world today. It is awesome to know that God will always be consistent, and his love for me will not change.

God has said in Malachi 3:6: "I, the Lord do not change." Isn't it great to know that Jesus is the same yesterday, today, and forever? Ahh, the blessed assurance we have in the never-changing Word of God. These are the most comforting thoughts and promises I have.

View from the Bridge

And God said, "Let there be light," and there was light. God
saw that the light was good.

Genesis 1:3–4

When I was in my early twenties, I was in a Catholic seminary,
studying to be a priest. I didn't complete the seminary, but I learned
valuable lessons. I had a spiritual director, named Eugene McGovern,
a Catholic priest. I used to spend a great deal of time with him, discussing all sorts of things. I had many questions for him. I also came
to him with problems I was having. I seemed to obsess on my problems. I was like a horse with blinders, looking only at one thing, my
problem. My whole life would become that one problem. Father
McGovern would tell me to take a view from the bridge.

Take a view from the bridge? What did that mean? There was
a bridge nearby, the Throgs Neck Bridge. Did he want me to go to
it and look out at the horizon, finding peace and tranquility? Did
he think my problem was so big I should jump? What in the world
was he talking about?

I learned he was telling me to look at the whole picture of my life.
He was telling me to take a look at the wider view. He was telling me
to turn on the light. My whole life should not be wrapped up in one
thing. There are people who say we should make a gratitude list when
we feel mired in problems. There are also others that say when we

begin prayer we should begin with thank you. If I thank God for my many blessings, I will find that I have a whole lot less gimmes.

I have spoken in a room with one hundred people, and ninety-nine say, "Excellent job." Then one says something negative. I take the negative with me. I may have one or two things going wrong and have a whole lot more going right. When I have a problem, I can harp on that instead of the view from the bridge and the love of God. I have a wife that loves me; two wonderful, healthy sons; a home; two cute dogs; good friends; transportation; sunshine; a God who loves me and has shown me mercy and grace. And this should be the most important thing in my life: God loves me. God will show me his view. I simply need to go to him and read his Word. He is all-powerful, all knowing, and has helped me solve all problems I come up with.

You know what is going on in your life today. I know what is in mine. We can of course help each other carry burdens. God will help us carry all our burdens. God has taken our biggest burden of sin; Jesus has wrapped himself in it on the cross. I have so many blessings. I look at them today when one problem becomes all consuming. I need the widescreen view. I need the view from the bridge. I go to the bridge with my loving Father in prayer and meditation. He turns on the lights and points. He helps me see the whole picture, which is beautiful if I will just look with him.

When I look at the wide view of my life, I look to God for comfort. The things of the world are temporary. When I put things before God, they do not bring lasting comfort. When I put God first, I have everlasting comfort and assurance. So when I look squarely at God, he will show me the view I need to see from the bridge. The road is narrow leading to God, and his view is wide.

Today I will look squarely at God and have him show me his view from the bridge. Would you like to join me?

Waiting

Part One

> We continually remember before our God and Father your work produced by faith, your labor prompted by love, and your endurance inspired by hope in our Lord Jesus Christ.
>
> And to wait for his Son from heaven, whom he raised from the dead—Jesus, who rescues us from the coming wrath.
>
> 1 Thessalonians 1:3, 10

The Thessalonians were waiting for Jesus. When I think of the words *wait* or *waiting,* I think of a waiting room, a red light, a bus stop, and sitting around doing nothing. I think of standing around bored. But that's not how one waits in Thessalonica. Some people in other areas in those times were actually doing that, sitting around waiting. People had quit their jobs and did nothing while waiting for Jesus' return.

Not the Thessalonians. They didn't quit their jobs or stand around. The Thessalonians were praised by Paul for their waiting. Why would anyone get praised for waiting? Well, the Thessalonians have a different definition of waiting than I do. How did they wait? They waited with patience, labor, service, work, endurance, love, hope, and faith. Their hard work was produced by their faith in Jesus, their labor was produced by their love, and their endurance was inspired by hope. Hope, love, and faith are action words. The Thessalonians' idea of waiting was action.

Waiting with love, faith, and hope is not something to just think and feel; it is something to do. Paul praised them for this and told them they were an example to the world in all they did. He told them they were chosen by God. Today, my heroes are the Thessalonians. I want to imitate them as they imitated Paul, Silas, Timothy, and especially Jesus. So today, I will suit up and show up for action and wait. So what kind of waiting can we do today? For one we need to be sharing the good news and making disciples. There are so many ministries in our churches we can be active in. We can be active in our communities. We can show the world how Christians wait. Christians waiting is action seeing a need and meeting it. Today let's look in our churches and fill the needs through ministry, let's look at our communities and see how we can help others and bring glory to God. Today let's be busy meeting the needs of others. Share God's Word with friends, family, and all who will listen. And after all this waiting you may just need a nap. How do you wait?

Waiting

Part Two

And she gave birth to her firstborn, a son. She wrapped him
in cloths and placed him in a manger, because there was no
room for them in the inn.

Luke 2:7

Mary and Joseph knew their new baby was to be born. The proph-
esied Messiah was to be born to the Virgin Mary. The Son of God,
Emmanuel (which means God is with us) was to be born Jesus the
Savior of the entire world. Mary and Joseph knew this. They looked
for a place to stay, but there was nowhere to be found except a manger
for sheep and cows. Joseph prepared a bed out of a feeding trough and
put hay in to keep it warm for the baby. Joseph and Mary had nine
months to prepare and wait. Imagine the joy and impatience they
must have felt. But they had to wait till it was time, God's time.

I know about waiting, especially around Christmas. When I was a
little child living with a brother and sister living in a two-story house,
Christmas Eve was always a sleepless night. We waited with the excitement of knowing that when we got up there would be presents. What
we were getting? My siblings and I would wait upstairs while our parents slept downstairs on a pullout couch so they would be awake when
we decided it was time to get up. Oh, the agonizing waiting. One
year, we had a plan. My siblings sent me downstairs, to sneak past the

guards and check under the tree—some reconnaissance, if you will. I made my move and then went back upstairs and reported the sizes of boxes. We couldn't wait, but there was more waiting. That morning, we got all our gifts and sat down to breakfast. I forgot to mention we had a dog, Spooky, a great little dog and friend. While eating and thinking of all the gifts and smiles on our young faces, Dad said, "The funniest thing happened this morning. I saw Spooky walking around the Christmas tree wearing Kenny's pajamas." Whoops. Dad smiled.

Imagine Saturday, the day after Jesus was crucified. The apostles had scattered in fear but returned to a house to hide. They didn't know what was going to happen. They sat in anticipation, anxiously waiting to learn their fate. Their Savior was dead, their hopes shattered, what was to become of them? The apostles didn't even know what they were waiting for, but their waiting paid off when Jesus walked through the wall, very much alive.

Now this is our Saturday. Jesus promised us he would come back again. But when? We don't know the hour or the day. He will come like a thief in the night. We do know he will come on a cloud with tens of thousands of angels to get us. We will hear a horn. But when will he come? Oh the waiting. As Christians, should we sit and wait like travelers waiting on a bus? No, we are to pass on the message, the good news of Jesus. God has a plan. God's plans are always awesome. God has his own time. We don't need longsuffering and a schedule. We need to be active. We need to grow in our spiritual disciplines and maturity. We need to be preparing for his return, for the day he brings us home where we belong, at his side with our Father. Oh, what a glorious day that will be. We wait, not impatiently, but ministering, being of service to one another, spreading the word of Jesus, and taking as many people home as we can minister to. God has a plan. God has his own time. Believe and have faith that the time will be right and the plan will be awesome.

Watch for Rocks

What comes out of a man is what makes him "unclean." For from within, out of men's hearts, come evil thoughts, sexual immorality, theft, murder, adultery, greed, malice, deceit, lewdness, envy, slander, arrogance and folly. All these evils come from inside and make a man "unclean."

Mark 7:20–23

In 2005 I went on a camping trip to Canada with Pat, one of my best friends. He and I were out for about eight days, no electricity, no plumbing, and no McDonald's. Our transportation was a canoe, which we used daily. The lakes and rivers were beautiful and clear. In the rivers and lakes we traveled, there were large rocks underwater, some coming to the top. I rode in front and Pat in the back. It was his job to steer and my job to paddle and watch for rocks. Sometimes the water would be calm, sometimes choppy. It was hard to see the rocks, and Pat would remind me often, "Watch for rocks." If we were to hit the rocks we could have damaged our Kevlar canoe, tip over (which we did once without the help of rocks), get stuck on the rocks, or any other thing that would be considered dangerous in the middle of a huge lake or river. So watching for rocks was a very important job. So was the voice from behind saying, "Watch for rocks."

In my daily walk, I also have to watch for rocks. I am talking about the rocks of sin and temptation. I need to watch for these rocks and need reminders every day to watch for them. I don't want to crash, stumble, get stuck, or get crushed by the rocks. Jesus has warned me to watch for rocks throughout the Bible. As a matter of fact, the Bible tells me the rocks are coming and the rocks are already here. The rocks are everywhere.

There are so many temptations in the world that we can wander away from the path of God. It is a rocky road out there. Although the Bible says there is a wide road and a narrow road, both are filled with the rocks. We make choices each day. I have to continue to watch where I am going. What am I doing? Am I listening for the voice saying, "Watch for rocks"? There are so many rocks of sin, which are not always easy to see until you hit one. When you do, it is right there in plain sight. Sometimes it is hard to get off of, or it can put a hole in the canoe and sink it. Accountable relationships also help us because there is the voice in the back saying, "Watch for rocks."

Today, I will use the eyes of the Bible, prayer, meditation and turn to a guide who knows the path, knows where the rocks are, and can see the rocks coming up. I don't want to be shipwrecked or canoe wrecked. I also don't want to be living in sin. The only hope after hitting the rocks is Jesus. He can save us. He has saved us. We must believe in and obey him, and he will help you watch for rocks. Keep your eyes open. Those rocks are tricky. They can just pop up anywhere at any time.

Watching the Light Go On

I have three very special friends in my life that were there when the light went on in me, Henry, Eddie, and Pat. Henry told me that I never had to drink again and that I could have a life beyond my wildest dreams. He also told me he would love me until I could love myself. When he told me this, I was a practicing alcoholic who saw no way out of a life of alcoholism, where I was hurting everyone around me and myself. I hated myself and wanted to die. That was August 13, 1978. He told me if I followed the steps of recovery and changed my way of thinking I would learn to live a life I could only dream of. First, I needed to stop drinking and follow him.

Eddie has watched me grow and has been my best friend for almost thirty years through all kinds of trials, tribulations, growth spurts, and accomplishments. Pat met with me and told me I didn't have to dread death and the thought of eternal separation from God. I was certain I was going to hell for the things I had done, and I was terrified. He introduced me to Jesus as I never understood him before. Pat is still helping me in this relationship. Henry, Eddie, and Pat got to see my light turn on. Today, I am sober and saved. The grace of God is in my life like never before.

One night, a friend and I had an experience with a young man who was struggling with staying sober and felt guilt when it came to speaking with God. During our conversation, we got to see the light turn on. We shared the grace of God as it was shared with us. We shared how one can stay sober a day at a time through the help of others and a growing relationship with our loving God. He understood there were two men in front of him that loved him, and our only motive was to help him through his struggle. The light went on.

That light is hope, which comes from faith, which turns to strength and eventually courage. With God in our lives, all things are possible. We should never give up on others or ourselves. God doesn't. God helps us carry our burdens and change our hearts. We need to ask and believe. Jesus has made it possible to have eternal life and come to our Father, God. Some things take time. We need to be patient. Growing in our relationship with God is like any relationship; it needs time to grow.

Love one another; be patient; share; demonstrate the grace, mercy, and forgiveness that has been given us; and let people know they are important and loved by us and God. Enjoy the miracle of watching the light go on. It is an experience beyond your wildest dreams. Thanks, Henry, Pat, Eddie, and everyone else who has watched me light up and has given me the opportunity to watch others find God.

We Are What We Eat

> Brothers, I could not address you as spiritual but as worldly—
> mere infants in Christ. I gave you milk, not solid food, for
> you were not yet ready for it. Indeed, you are still not ready.
> You are still worldly.
>
> 1 Corinthians 3:1–3

We are what we eat. Well, you have to know I am really not a pint of Häagen Dazs or, these days, a chicken Caesar salad. I have always loved to eat, and I have never turned into anything except extremely full, and I have grown and shrunk over the years.

So what does the statement "I am what I eat" mean to me? I believe it means I am what I put into my heart and mind. If I am putting filth in on a continual basis, I become what I ingest. We can do this with anything we are indulging in: television, Internet, video games, violence, and so on. If that is what we are taking in, that may be what we are demonstrating in our lives.

Paul told the Corinthians they were not ready for solid food as they were still living in the world and were still worldly. He was telling them they were not following God's commands and they needed to live God's way and to follow Jesus' example. It was time to follow God's commands. It was time to put spiritual disciplines in their lives.

Let me tell you about a great meal, the word of God in the Bible. What a meal for the mind and heart. The Bible is more than filling, and it has a lifetime of nourishment. Imagine dining on the fruits of the spirit in Galatians 5:22–23. "But the fruit of the Spirit is love, joy, peace, patience, kindness, goodness, faithfulness, gentleness and self-control." This is a feast where I want to be what I eat. I want to take all nine courses. This is a nine-course meal that will let me be a mature Christian with the Holy Spirit dwelling inside me, directing my life. After dining and feeding my heart, mind, and soul on this fare, what I become benefits all I come in contact with and brings glory to God.

How about the next day's menu? How about 1 Corinthians 13:4–7? "Love is patient, love is kind. It does not envy, it does not boast, it is not proud. It is not rude, it is not self-seeking, it is not easily angered, and it keeps no record of wrongs. Love does not delight in evil but rejoices with the truth. It always protects, always trusts, always hopes, and always perseveres." Ahh, I have ingested God's definition of love. Whom should I love this way? According to God, I am to treat everyone this way, even my enemies.

Wow, this stuff is tasty, and it is solid food. There is a whole Bible filled with information to live by. There is a whole manual in the Bible on how I can live. There is a compass and GPS to show me the direction my life should be going. They say there are no good books on how to treat spouses or raise children. Well, take a look in your Bible.

So I am what I eat. Just the words *Bible study* and *small group* sound boring to some. If there was a way to become a million-aire, lots of people would attend that seminar and take notes. How about eternal life, salvation, adventure, drama, romance, poetry, espionage, just to name a few topics in the Bible? The Bible can also be studied on your own. This is a feast waiting to be eaten.

We Can Bring People Back to Life

My brothers, if one of you should wander from the truth and someone should bring him back, remember this: Whoever turns a sinner from the error of his way will save him from death and cover over a multitude of sins.

1 Corinthians 3:1–3

We have the ability to bring people back to life. How exciting is that? Those who are against God or who turn away will not be with him at the end of time as we know it. There will be no eternal life in heaven for them. Why would there be? They have made the choice not to believe or follow God. This is very sad. They will not have the joy of heaven with our heavenly Father or his Son, Jesus Christ. Those who believe Jesus is their Savior will be saved; those who do not will not share in eternity with him in heaven.

So how do we bring people back to life? We share the good news that they can be saved as we were. Jesus has told us to make disciples. He wants us to share the good news. In sharing the good news, we can help people understand that no matter what they have done they can be forgiven.

In twelve-step recovery, I learned to approach a suffering alcoholic by sharing my experience, strength, and hope. As a Christian, when I share the good news, I share my experience, strength, and hope. I tell others how I was going to die. I tell them how I knew my final fate was destruction and hell.

I share that story with others. I share some of my testimony. I share my past fears. I share the love of Jesus and how he gave his life for me. I share my new way of life. I share how God is there for me. I share the assurance of eternal life. I give this away freely.

Do you know someone you want to bring back to life? What an awesome feeling: guiding someone who is dead back to life, eternal life in Christ. How good would you feel? The idea excites me. To God, all the glory is given when another person is saved.

Today, let's share the good news with someone who doesn't know Jesus or understand him. Let's help them come back to life and cover a multitude of sin. I can't imagine anything more exciting than helping someone else find Jesus, forgiveness, peace, and life.

We Need You

So in Christ we who are many form one body, and each
member belongs to all the others. We have different gifts,
according to the grace given us. If a man's gift is prophesying,
let him use it in proportion to his faith. If it is serving, let him
serve; if it is teaching, let him teach; if it is encouraging, let
him encourage; if it is contributing to the needs of others, let
him give generously; if it is leadership, let him govern dili-
gently; if it is showing mercy, let him do it cheerfully.

Romans 12:5–8

At times I have looked at other people I admire and wished I could
be more like them. I have not been happy with who I am, looking at the skills and talents of others. But if I were like them, who
would be me? Who would use the gifts, talents, and skills God has
knitted specifically into me? Psalm 139:13 says, "For you created
my inmost being; you knit me together in my mother's womb."
Knitted together, not mass-produced on an assembly line. God created me and you for specific purposes that would bring him glory.

Imagine if John Wayne or Chuck Norris wanted to be like Fred
Astaire or Gene Kelly? Can you see the Duke or Chuck Norris dancing around stage holding an umbrella? What if Gandhi wanted to
be John Wayne or Chuck Norris? Can you imagine Gandhi looking
at his adversary saying, "I am going to hit you with so many lefts

you are going to beg me for a right"? What if Bill Gates wanted to go into plumbing like his neighbor?

God has created each one of us to be part of Christ's body here on Earth; we each have a specific task and have been given specific gifts, skills, and talents. I believe a gift I have been given is the desire to encourage others, which lets me love God and love others and brings glory to God's kingdom. I don't believe I am sharing this to bring honor to myself but to use the gifts, talents, and skills God has given me to bring glory to him and fulfill my role in the body of Christ. Ask yourself today, "What is my role in the body? How can I best use my talents, gifts, and skills to bring glory to God and perform my part in the functioning of the body of Christ?" I know you have them. I have seen them, and God knitted them into you slowly and on purpose.

We Spoke in Tongues, Sort Of

One afternoon, I sat down with a man who wanted to be saved and wanted to study the Bible. He had questions on baptism and other subjects. I met with this man a few times, and we formed a great friendship. He asked me to perform his wedding ceremony and to baptize him. His friend told me how much he trusts me. Now this may not sound strange for me as I am a counselor, but this man speaks no English, and I speak no Spanish.

This man's friend translates for us. As we sat to study the Bible, I would read, and his friend would interpret. It was going slow, and it was almost boring. I went in the other room and pulled out a Bible in the Spanish language and showed him what I wanted him to read. When the two of us spoke, we looked into each other's eyes, we sat next to each other and spoke to each other. The interpreter simply translated. We formed a bond.

Here was a man who wanted to be saved, and I wanted to help him get there. We both had Bibles in our hands and read the same passages. It was as if we really understood what each other was saying without having any idea of the words coming out of our mouths. We heard the voice of God through the Bible, and we heard the language of love through our hearts.

It turns out this man is quite a storyteller, and so am I. We may have led the interpreter to become hoarse. We have formed a friendship. He has met God and Jesus Christ, and now he is ready to be saved. I have been praying to God to put me with people I can bring to him. Isn't it interesting he sent me one that doesn't speak my language nor I his? With Bibles in hand and God speaking to us both through the Bible, we may not even need an interpreter.

The language of God through love breaks all barriers. In this case, it has broken a language barrier. It made me feel today that we were speaking in tongues. We were speaking the language of God, the language of the heart, and the language of love.

What Are My Needs?

And my God will meet all your needs according to his glorious riches in Christ Jesus.

Philippians 4:19

Grace and peace be yours in abundance through the knowledge of God and of Jesus our Lord. His divine power has given us everything we need for life and godliness through our knowledge of him who called us by his own glory and goodness.

2 Peter 1:2–3

What are my needs today? Do I know the difference between wants and needs? There have been many things in life I thought I needed that turned out to be wants and desires. Some of my desires have been selfish. I have brought many prayers to God for the things I want and need and have waited for the results. In Paul's letters to the Philippians 4:19, he says, "God will meet all my needs with his glorious riches in Jesus Christ." So does that mean I can have whatever I pray for? Is it like going to God with my Christmas list or wish list?

In Peter's letter he says, "His divine power has given us everything we need for life and godliness through our knowledge of him." He also said, "Through our knowledge of God and Christ Jesus." So what are our needs? It appears we may learn what our actual needs are for life as we get to know God better. Reading the Bible lets us know our Father better. As we read, we should take in what is truly important in life. Can my good deeds alone get me to heaven? Well we know the answer is *no.* We need Jesus' sacrificial death and our belief in him to get there. We need the amazing grace of God to get us in. Eternity is a long time. Can chasing my worldly desires and being a good guy get me them and into heaven? Again, the answer is *no.* We need Jesus.

Today, I realize all my needs are met through the sacrificial death of Jesus. Paul said God will meet my needs through the riches in Jesus. Peter said, "His divine power has given us everything we need for life and godliness through our knowledge of him." Who is "him"? Jesus, of course. All our needs have been met through Jesus. Jesus has already met all of our needs. Our job is to believe in him and get to know him and his will for us. We are to follow his commands and those of our Father. As I have gotten to know Jesus better, I am beginning to understand that my needs have actually become my desires. My desire is for more wisdom and understanding of God. I want to bring God glory in all I do. I have a need for eternal life in heaven, and that need has been met. I need a way to go to my Father in prayer. That need has been met. My only real need in this life is Jesus.

What Are You Thinking About?

Be careful what you think, because your thoughts run your life.

Proverbs 4:23 (NVC)

Above all else, guard your heart, for it is the wellspring of life.

Proverbs 4:23

Keep thy heart with all diligence; for out of it are the issues of life.

Proverbs 4:23 (KJV)

When I first stopped drinking, I knew that things in my life had to change. I figured I had to change my friends, my hangouts, my routines, and many things I did. I thought, *Wow, this is a big task.* A man named Fred was speaking about this issue at a meeting one night, and he said all we have to change is our way of thinking. Phew, now that would be much easier than I thought. Then I started to think about that statement.

Becoming a Christian and a disciple of Jesus, I knew things needed to change. I knew I needed to change both my language and my actions. Then the words from Fred returned. Really, all I need to change is my way of thinking. That's easy enough. Yeah, right. Changing the way of thinking that I learned thirty years ago changes everything. It changes what I say, where I go, and any motives I may have. Changing my way of thinking is not as easy as I first thought. Thoughts are filtered through my heart.

I read Proverbs 4 and looked at three different Bible versions. The NVC says, "Be careful what you think, because your thoughts run your life." The KJV and NIV both talk about the heart and guarding it, because it is the wellspring and issues of life. I tried to go two out of three, but man, they all said the same thing. So I am not only responsible for what I say and do but for what I am thinking. Because what I am thinking affects the way I will live. My thoughts are filtered through my heart and affect my actions.

Jesus also tells us to be careful what we are thinking. Jesus tells us that just the thought of lust is actually lust. Do I want more? Is that what I am thinking about constantly? I need only look into my checkbook for the answer. What have I spent my money on? Do I allow jealousy to run my life and make enemies with those whose possessions I covet? When I am angry at someone, do I gossip to the point of murder through character assassination? While I am reading the Bible, do my thoughts of living a godly life call me to action? Does trying to think like Jesus lead me to emulate him? There sure is a lot to think about. What are you thinking about?

What Can I Give God?

David sang to the LORD the words of this song when the LORD delivered him from the hand of all his enemies and from the hand of Saul. He said: "The LORD is my rock, my fortress and my deliverer; my God is my rock, in whom I take refuge, my shield and the horn of my salvation. He is my stronghold, my refuge and my savior—from violent men you save me. I call to the LORD, who is worthy of praise, and I am saved from my enemies."

2 Samuel 22 1–4

One night in our Bible class, we discussed several verses in 2 Samuel. This particular verse is a song sung by David bringing praise to God because he delivered him and made him victorious over his enemies. David also gave us many ideas of what God is to him. God is David's rock, fortress, deliverer, shield, horn, and salvation. He is also David's stronghold, refuge, and Savior. David gave God his praise.

God is all these things to me. Our teacher asked us what else God is to us, and we went around the room and gave one example each. The words other than the ones already mentioned that came to my mind were *Father, encourager, comforter, go-to guy, strength,* and *love*. God is my everything. God is my all in all.

So what can I give God? I see through David I can give him my praise and glory for all my victories, which are really his as he is everything to me. I can bring God my burdens. I bring him my sins through Jesus Christ for forgiveness. I bring him all my problems, addictions, ailments, concerns, worries, and battles. I bring God everything, and he has the solution.

I can also bring him disciples through sharing his words. I bring the talents, skills, and love to others in his name to help bring them closer to him. I can give God all of me. All I give God is already his. It is up to me whether I go to God with anything. Given what God has already done for me, why wouldn't I go to God? God came to us in the shape of man as his Son Jesus and gave his life so we could be with him and forgiven. We can bring God our burdens, but most of all we give him our faith, love, and our undying devotion as we follow his commands. What is God to you? What can you bring to God?

What Do Your Feet Look Like?

And how can they preach unless they are sent? As it is written, "How beautiful are the feet of those who bring good news!"

Romans 10:15

After that, he poured water into a basin and began to wash his disciples' feet, drying them with the towel that was wrapped around him.

John 13:5

Romans 10:15 says, "How beautiful are the feet of those who bring good news!" Well, God thinks all of us who share the good news have beautiful feet. These feet are quite functional and get us around to do his will. He loves these feet. In John 13:5, Jesus washed the feet of his apostles. Although this was something done in those times by servants, the feet were washed by the King of kings to teach service by everyone. Later in chapter John 13:14, it says, "Now that I, your Lord and Teacher, have washed your feet, you also should wash one another's feet." So what's up with all this talk of feet?

Maybe Jesus thought the feet of these men who had been traveling and preaching the good news were pretty special and beautiful feet. Maybe he thought they were feet that should be washed as a thank you and an act of service from the King of kings himself. I don't want to add to the Bible here, but God himself talked about how beautiful the feet are that spread the good news.

I believe God is talking about our actions. I believe he is talking about the commands we are following, making disciples. He is bringing attention to the feet that are moving from one place to the next to help others find Jesus and find salvation. Well, I still look down and see some funny-looking feet, but as long as I am doing the will of God, he thinks they are beautiful. How do your feet look to God?

What Is Your Cornerstone?

Consequently, you are no longer foreigners and aliens, but fellow citizens with God's people and members of God's household, built on the foundation of the apostles and prophets, with Christ Jesus himself as the chief cornerstone. In him the whole building is joined together and rises to become a holy temple in the Lord. And in him you too are being built together to become a dwelling in which God lives by his Spirit.

Ephesians 2:19–22

Jesus is the cornerstone. Jesus is the cornerstone of what? Jesus needs to be the cornerstone of my whole life. Everything I do needs to be built around Jesus. The foundation for my life is built on the discipleship of the apostles. So my question to myself is, "What does my life look like to God and others?" The main cornerstone, the central focus and main objective of my life, needs to be built around Jesus. Everything I do needs to reflect the cornerstone and foundation.

Do all my actions reflect Jesus? Does my ministry and life reflect the foundation set by the apostles? I have a guide, a blueprint, and the directions to build off of the cornerstone; it is the Bible. The cornerstone in this case is Jesus. He is not only the cornerstone of the church; he is the cornerstone of my life. Everything I do in life has to work in concert with what Jesus would do and what his Father commanded.

Take a look at the blueprint, the Holy Bible; it gives the directions to build off the foundation of the apostles and the cornerstone of Jesus. We need to take a look and make sure all the bricks of our lives are in place. Do they go together and work with the cornerstone? The bricks of sin will not go with my cornerstone. I need to inventory my life and actions as I am building off of my cornerstone. And only the right bricks, obedience, humility, submission, repentance, love, forgiveness, mercy, and self-sacrifice, will work well as I build my life. When this type of life is built with the foundation of the apostles and the cornerstone of Jesus, then and only then will I be able to bring glory to God and do his will.

How is your building going today?

What Time Is It?

But they refused to pay attention; stubbornly they turned their backs and stopped up their ears.

Zechariah 7:11

When I worked with developmentally delayed children, there was a boy I'll call Jerry that I knew well. Jerry was a short boy, about sixteen years old. He was always happy to see me. He usually was happy and quick to laugh. Jerry's teachers were quite upset with Jerry because they couldn't teach him to tell time. Jerry's father came in one day to talk with the teacher, and she told him Jerry couldn't tell time. Jerry's father smiled and said, "Jerry, what time is it?" Jerry looked at his watch, which was a gold Seiko, and told his father the time. The teacher, stunned, said, "Jerry, why won't you tell us what time it is?" Jerry looked to the little wooden clock used for instruction, and he said, "That's a baby clock, and you know what time it is."

As Christians, we are called to believe in Jesus, repent, and be baptized. Have we done these three things? Are we holding out on any of these? How about having a church home where we worship God together and fellowship with our brothers and sisters in the body of Christ? People don't go to church for various reasons. Of course, some cannot physically get there. Some say there are hypocrites and judgmental people in the church. Yes, we do have real live people with real live human foibles. Of course, none of us should be hypocritical or judgmental; we should leave the judging to God. We come to church services to worship and praise God, not one another. We come to worship God together.

We can't let stubbornness keep us from doing what God calls us to do. God knows best. Believe, repent, and be baptized. Jesus died so we can live. Jesus died to pay for our sin debt. His love is beyond words. I believe, continue to repent, and have been baptized because he was and that is what he wants of me. Not only are these commands, but I am doing them as an act of love and gratitude. God calls us to do many things. Are we doing them? Are we following Jesus? Is stubbornness keeping you from followings God's commands?

What's Love Got to Do with It?

Part One

Love is an overused word. I have been a perpetrator in the misuse of the word *love*. I have said that I love ice cream, coffee, lasagna, the Red Sox, my car, my cell phone, my house, and all sorts of things. I also love my wife, my two sons, and my brother and sister. I have been also known to say, "I love my two little dogs, Buster and Mugsy." I love God, so what does that mean to someone after they hear all my loves?

Do I love God the same way I love ice cream? Does God love me the way I love ice cream? Can you see the predicament one may have who doesn't understand English very well? There is a commercial on TV where a woman swings her soft, long, and beautiful hair and says, "I love my hair." The marketing industry tells us love is a physical attraction to something beautiful. Jesus went to the cross because he loves us and because our Father loves us. So do we love Jesus' sacrifice the way that woman loves her hair? Would Jesus sacrifice his life for the love of hair? I don't think so.

You can see why one who speaks a different language might misunderstand the word *love*. Even someone who speaks our language may misunderstand us when we say we love something. How about us? Do we understand the word *love*? "God so loved the world that he sent his only begotten son" (John 3:16). "Greater love has no one than this that he lay down his life for his friends" (John 15:13). How about this passage:

> Love is patient, love is kind. It does not envy, it does not boast, it is not proud. It is not rude, it is not self-seeking, it is not easily angered, it keeps no record of wrongs. Love does not delight in evil but rejoices with the truth. It always protects, always trusts, always hopes, and always perseveres. Love never fails.
>
> 1 Corinthians 13:4–8

What's Love Got to Do with It?

Part Two

In one of his songs, Clint Black sings, "Love isn't something we say. It is something that we do." Now, I like that form of love. It implies we demonstrate our love. Jesus demonstrated his love by going to the cross for us. God our Father demonstrated his love in giving his only Son to die on the cross. He gave his son to fulfill his law and condemn sin once and for all for all of us, that we may have eternal life with him. God's spirit lives in us to lead, interpret, testify, and show his love.

> Love is patient, love is kind. It does not envy, it does not boast, it is not proud. It is not rude, it is not self-seeking, it is not easily angered, it keeps no record of wrongs. Love does not delight in evil but rejoices with the truth. It always protects, always trusts, always hopes, always perseveres. Love never fails.
>
> Corinthians 13:4–8

Meditate on this verse and where it says *love,* change that to *God,* because God is love, pure love. Now put your name in there, where it says *love.* Does it fit?

What's That Smell?

But thanks be to God, who always leads us as captives in Christ's victory parade. God uses us to spread his knowledge everywhere like a sweet-smelling perfume. Our offering to God is this: We are the sweet smell of Christ among those who are being saved and among those who are being lost.

2 Corinthians 2:14–15

Have you ever caught the aroma of someone wearing a beautiful perfume or cologne? I always want to ask, "What is that scent?" I want to know what it is and where to get it. Have you ever walked down St. George Street in St. Augustine, Florida? There is an ice cream shop that serves waffle cones, and they make the cones right there. You can smell them way down the road. Like a Bugs Bunny cartoon, the scent hits you, and carries you right to the cone.

Paul says we are the sweet smell of Christ. When we are sharing our love and faith with others, can they smell it? Are we like freshly baked chocolate chip cookies that someone says, "I want some of them. Where do I get some?" Does our faith show that to others? Can they smell the aroma of Christ on us and in us? Do our words and actions draw people to want what we have? Does what we have give off an aroma that makes people ask, "How do I get that, and where do I get some?" Sharing the good news should have an even better aroma than those waffle cones on St. George Street, just calling to passersby, whispering, "Come to me. I am not far.

We are the aroma of Christ for those seeking, struggling, and lost. Do our actions and words bring the scent of Christ? Is the aroma pleasing and calling? Are we kind and gentle in our approach as Jesus was? Does it look and smell like Jesus? Today, I want the scent of Jesus to permeate my every action and word. I want someone to say, "What is that aroma? What is that, and how do I get some?"

When I Grow Up, I Want …

You are our hope, our joy, and the crown we will take pride
in when our Lord Jesus Christ comes. Truly you are our glory
and our joy.

1 Thessalonians 2:19–20 (NVC)

Brothers and sisters, God loves you, and we know he has chosen you … and you became like us and like the Lord. You
suffered much, but still you accepted the teaching with the
joy that comes from the Holy Spirit … And the Lord's teaching spread from you not only into Macedonia and Southern
Greece, but now your faith in God has become known everywhere. So we do not need to say anything about it.

1 Thessalonians 1:4, 6, 8 (NVC)

When I grow up, I want to be a Thessalonian. Can you imagine
getting a letter of encouragement like this? This letter is awesome.
There was so much persecution, suffering, and illness at that time,
but the Thessalonians lived in the joy and assurance of Jesus Christ
and salvation. Paul told them they were the hope, joy, crown, and
glory of the Christian faith. He told them he took pride in them
and could hold them up as an example when Jesus returns. Wow.

Earlier, I wrote about keeping my eyes on the goal to achieve
the prize of salvation spending eternity with God and his Son,
Jesus. Imagine an added bonus prize when we get to heaven and we

hear, "Well done, good and faithful servant! You have been faithful with a few things; I will put you in charge of many things. Come and share your master's happiness!" (Matthew 25:23). Jesus spoke these words in the parable of the talents. This parable speaks to me about evangelism, and it talks to me about multiplying God's kingdom and being fruitful in all I do.

So in this day and age, given the distractions, how am I expected to help God's kingdom multiply? How am I supposed to find time for prayer, meditation, church, ministry, and Bible study? How am I supposed to find time to spend with God and live the way he would have me live? There are so many things that take up my time, so many things that distract me, and so many things I want to do. Paul was applauding the Thessalonians for their faith. He was encouraging them to continue to grow, despite the obstacles. He was there for them.

Do I have an encourager? Am I an encourager? How about you? Do you encourage? Do you need encouragement? It seems Paul, the mature, loving, encouraging, and wise apostle calls us to be an encourager. With all the obstacles we face in the world, maybe what we need is some encouragement from each other. Maybe we need to help each other grow spiritually, to say, "I really appreciate what you do for God, for me, and for others. I really am amazed at the faith you are showing through your ... " Wouldn't this be helpful?

Let others know they are on the right track or not. If not, we can help them back on the right path, the narrow path, through Jesus. The prize is in heaven, but we can give some accolades here to help others along. Love and encouragement is my mission. I am not always there; I need to be encouraged along. I need to go to God in prayer, meditation, and his spoken word in the Bible. I need to use my time wisely. I need you to remind me and encourage me. I want to grow. Support me, and let me support you.

Today, I will make a call, pay a visit, e-mail, mail a letter, or say a kind word to encourage someone. I want to make it a point each day to encourage at least one other person that they are doing well, what their faith means to me, and how it encourages me. Let people know when you see their heart for God and others. Encourage those who serve in the background. Let's be like Paul, and write to the Thessalonians and let them know we are proud of them.

Where Are Your Eyes?

I pray also that the eyes of your heart may be enlightened in order that you may know the hope to which he has called you.

Ephesians 1:18

I love music. I like walking through music sections of stores, looking at the CDs. There is a young man who works in that section who has Down's syndrome. This young man is filled with joy. One day, as I was leaving the parking lot, he was waiting for the bus. He had his headphones on, and he was dancing and singing at the top of his lungs. I witnessed pure joy from this young man. When I walk through his section, he comes over to me and always says, "Hey, big guy, do you need some help?" I do notice some people ignore him. Maybe they are looking at him with the eyes in their head. I see him with the eyes in my heart.

How many people do we know that we listen to and see only the words and actions they are using and only see through the eyes and ears in our heads? Paul says we have eyes in our hearts. What a beautiful way of expressing love to actually use them. We can use the eyes in our hearts to see what people are really saying, what they are really experiencing, and what they are really going through. Do we look for their pain, their joy, and their love?

I have been blessed with so many people in my life who have seen me with the eyes in their hearts. They ask how I am doing. I say, "Fine." These people that see with the eyes of their hearts say, "You don't look fine. Would you like to talk about it?" It is no coincidence that they encourage me or say just the right thing at the right time. They see what I need because they are using the eyes in their hearts.

What do we see when we look at the homeless, alcoholics, drug addicts, and people who brag, gossip, complain, yell, or use foul language? Do we simply get annoyed? Or do we see them through the eyes in our hearts? Do we see them as children of God crying out for love or attention? Do we see them, not the visual, but who they really are? Do we see them with the eyes in our hearts?

Paul prayed for the people of Ephesus, for the eyes of their hearts to be enlightened, to look at things differently, lovingly, spiritually, and the way God sees things. To stop, look, listen, and feel what people are saying and doing. Who are they really? We find this out by looking at them with the eyes in our hearts. We find out what people are going through. If we know, we may even be able to get rid of some old resentment if we look at them through our heart's eyes.

Today, I challenge you to pay closer attention to everyone through the eyes of your heart. Your life will be enriched for it.

Where Is the Joy?

You have made known to me the path of life; you will fill me with joy in your presence, with eternal pleasures at your right hand.

Psalm 16:11

But from now on, the Son of Man will be seated at the right hand of the mighty God.

Luke 22:69

Where do I go when all seems bleak? I have had seasons of sadness in my life. I have looked for pleasure and joy in all kinds of ways. Some have been self-destructive. Some I have sought through people or nature, which are wonderful and bring me great pleasure and joy. All may appear good solutions, but something is missing.

David writes in Psalms 16:11, "He has learned the path of life through the teachings of God which brings him joy." He also writes that he derives eternal pleasure from God at his right hand. That doesn't mean David gets to sit at God's right hand. Who sits at God's right hand? Jesus does. The Savior of the world. David knew that back when he wrote this, but many may not have understood. Joy comes from God the Father and pleasure from Jesus, his right hand. We can be calm, confident, and assured through the saving, loving grace of our Father and at his right hand, Jesus, our Brother, Savior, friend, and the King of kings.

Today, let us find the joy and pleasure we seek in our Father God and our Brother Jesus. No need to look any further.

Who Are Your Friends?

Greater love has no one than this, that he lay down his life for his friends.

John 15:13

You are my friends if you do what I command.

John 15:14

I heard a joke once that a friend would bail you out of jail but a good friend would be sitting in the cell next to you, laughing with you about what you both had just done. When I was a much younger man, I agreed with this. As I have matured, I have added, "A really good friend would help you think through what you are about to do and help you see that doing something you could get arrested for is not in your best interest." These are friends that would hold you accountable for your thoughts and actions and be honest with you. Over the years, I have had friends that hold me accountable. Not that I would do anything I would be arrested for, but I may be about to make a mistake. These friends are really there for me.

I have made some real friendships over the years. Some of them are long distance, but I know if I need to talk or I am down, I can call and they will lift me back up. There have been times in my life my self-image was quite poor. I felt I wasn't good enough. I'd say, "I will never get that job, that girl would never go out with me, I will never be able to accomplish this or that, I am not good enough for this, and I am just not good enough." I have said, "Nobody really likes me. They just feel sorry for me and will tolerate me." When I have failed at something, I say, "See, I knew I couldn't do it." I had very poor self-esteem and felt very alone and very sorry for myself. I was a self-made victim.

I have friends that have helped me mature and have told me I have never truly failed at anything. They would say, "Isn't it great you tried?" Only a real man would even consider giving something like that a shot. They told me courage isn't the absence of fear but that it is facing that fear. My friends would build me up. Over the years, I have learned to not listen to the negative thoughts. I have great friends. Why would they even be my friend? They saw something in me that made them want to be my friend. I have matured through friendships. I want to be there for my friends, and I have actually had the chance to be the mature one at times.

Jesus said he gave up his life for his friends. I am his friend because I trust and believe in him. I also obey his commands. God counted Abraham as his friend because he believed God and obeyed his commands. If I believe and obey his commands, God counts me as a friend. As God's friend, how could I possibly have low self-esteem? God has chosen me as a friend. Imagine: I am the friend of the King of kings, the Creator of heaven and Earth. If I obey his commands, I am his friend. God is always there for me. James said, "Faith without deeds is worthless." So works may not get me into heaven, but faith does. The deeds of faith are an act of obedience and true belief that seals my friendship with God.

Next time you think you might be inferior, remember who your friends are. Through faith and obedience, you are counted as God's friend. How much better can it get? If God loves you, who are you to say you are not good enough? Jesus made you good enough. He made you righteous to his Father by his sacrifice. To be God's friend brings me great joy and builds me up. My friends love me, God loves me, and now it is my turn to love me. If God is for us, who can be against us? Not even me.

Whoops! How Did I Get Here?

A certain man of Zorah, named Manoah, from the clan of the Danites, had a wife who was sterile and remained childless. The angel of the LORD appeared to her and said, "You are sterile and childless, but you are going to conceive and have a son. Now see to it that you drink no wine or other fermented drink and that you do not eat anything unclean, because you will conceive and give birth to a son. No razor may be used on his head, because the boy is to be a Nazirite, set apart to God from birth, and he will begin the deliverance of Israel from the hands of the Philistines."

Judges 13:2–5

One day Samson went to Gaza, where he saw a prostitute. He went in to spend the night with her.

Judges 16:1

Samson was set apart by God from birth and had a mission from God. He was born to a sterile mother, which was a miracle in itself, and then Samson was given unimaginable strength and a mission from God. Samson was set apart by God for his purposes. How and what in the world was Samson doing spending the night with a prostitute? What was Samson thinking? Hadn't he been set apart with boundless strength and a mission from God?

I have a mission, to love God, love others, and serve all. Now this has more to it, but this is my mission. As a young child, I was raised going to church, where I was taught all about God and the right way to live. There were nights as a young adult that I was drunk and in places I was taught not to go. I asked myself the question with all my training and my upbringing: "What I am doing here?" I had gotten off the path. Now as a Christian, do I find myself in situations I should be set apart from: indulging in gossip, not forgiving others, and not showing love and service?

Am I set apart as a Christian? Do I look different from the evil and mundane? Let's see what Paul tells the Philippians:

> Each of you should look not only to your own interests, but also to the interests of others. Your attitude should be the same as that of Christ Jesus: Who, being in very nature God, did not consider equality with God something to be grasped, but made himself nothing, taking the very nature of a servant, being made in human likeness. And being found in appearance as a man, he humbled himself and became obedient to death—even death on a cross!
>
> Philippians 2:4–8

This is also my mission. Does this set me apart? Like Samson, we can stray from where God intends us to be, but like Samson, we must come back and fulfill our mission.

What is your mission? Are you on course? Have you had distractions?

Without a Trace

Then Jesus told him, "Because you have seen me, you have believed; blessed are those who have not seen and yet have believed."

John 20:29

Have you ever watched the TV show *Without a Trace?* It starts out with people doing things, and then all of the sudden, someone just vanishes, *poof.* The rest of the show, the FBI is looking for that person. When I go to the mall, this happens to me with my wife and my son Nick. I will be walking with Janie, and I turn around, and *poof!* She is gone. Where did she go? Ever since Nick was a little guy, five or six years old, I would be walking through the mall with my sons Kenny and Nick, and all of a sudden *poof* Nick vanishes without a trace. When he was younger, I would be frantic. I would say to Kenny, "Where is Nick?" Kenny would laugh and say, "He is right behind you." I would turn around, and there he was, right behind me, smiling.

I have heard many people during tragedy say, "Where is God?" Years ago, I used to say the same thing at times. Does God know what's happening here? Does he care? Where is he? I have heard others ask the same questions. Have you ever asked these questions? I have heard people say, "God is not here. Where is he? Doesn't he know what I am going through? How come he isn't helping me?"

In Hebrews 13:5 God says, "Never will I leave you; never will I forsake you." God has said, "I will never leave you." Do you believe that? No matter the problem, achievement, or situation, God will never leave us. Where is God? He is right here as he smiles. But I don't see him. John 20:29 says, "Blessed are those who have not seen and yet have believed." We don't have to see or even feel his presence. We are called to believe. The Holy Spirit is within us, Jesus is in our heart, and our Father is a call for help away. He is right here.

God is right here, even though we don't see him. He is right here, never leaving us nor forsaking us and meeting all our needs in his time. Have faith and have trust that God is right here. He always has been and always will be. Do you want to blessed? Believe without seeing. Just know that God is right here. He never left. He never vanished. He never went *poof,* without a trace.

Work in Progress

Make sure that nobody pays back wrong for wrong, but always try to be kind to each other and to everyone else.

1 Thessalonians 5:15

My first year in Little League baseball, I was about nine years old. My team played twelve games, and we lost twelve games. I didn't get one hit in twelve games. I got up to bat, each time watching the pitcher, standing at the plate. The ball would come, and I would put my heart and soul into my swing but missed or fouled it off. I have to tell you, I was trying. The next year, I was a pitcher and first baseman. I had good years after that. At age ten, I pitched a no-hitter and hit a grand slam in the same game. My story was in the local paper, the other team bought me an ice cream pop from Bungalow Bar, and everyone cheered. My mother embarrassed me. She was crying and hugging me. What was the difference in a year? I was so embarrassed the year before that I worked out with older kids to learn the game better. I tried very hard to play a game I loved.

Since becoming a Christian, I have gone through a lot of growth. God's commands may not be burdensome, but they sure were a strange language to me. Be kind to each other and everyone else? But what if they are mean to me? What if they hurt me, lie to me, cheat me, or anything else that hurts my feelings? You mean I can't retaliate? I have to repent? Change my heart? Treat others better than I treat myself? Give my life for another? But I want to get even, be right, and let people know when they are wrong.

As I have read the Bible, prayed, meditated, and recognized the voice of the Holy Spirit, I have been quite convicted. My behavior quickly became repulsive to me very early on in my walk with Christ. I began to change quickly. I wanted to serve God and bring him glory. That old behavior wasn't going to be acceptable to God or me in this new life in Christ.

I have become a work in progress. There has been great progress. I have been in arguments, made judgments, and other things. I have asked for forgiveness from those I hurt and God. I have confessed sins to God and to other Christians. There has been great change in my life but not perfection. I am so grateful that I have been saved by Jesus. I want to be more like him, and I try daily.

Trying, as it says in the verse I mentioned, means to attempt and accomplish. I need to be diligent and patient with myself. Growth and maturity are happening in my life. I have spiritually matured, but I still have a distance to go. Most importantly though is that I am trying hard to please God, whom I love with all my heart and soul. Paul says, "But always try." I am attempting and accomplishing as I try the very best I can. You can too. Be patient and keep your eyes on Jesus.

Ya Gotta Believe

Anyone who believes in the Son of God has this testimony in his heart. Anyone who does not believe God has made him out to be a liar, because he has not believed the testimony God has given about his Son.

1 John 5:10

And the scripture was fulfilled that says, "Abraham believed God, and it was credited to him as righteousness," and he was called God's friend.

James 2:23

The New York Mets baseball team was born in 1962 named the Metropolitans. The name was shortened to the Mets. From 1962–1969, the Mets were a horrible team. They were known as the cellar dwellers. In 1969, something amazing happened. They began winning and winning a lot. In 1969, Met fans nicknamed the Mets the Amazing Mets. Those who loved the Mets began calling them "the Amazins." Tug McGraw, a young, brash relief pitcher for the Mets, would throw up his arms after a win and yell, "Ya gotta believe!" Tug didn't feel that the Mets would go all the way; he knew it.

I have spoken to a few people lately who have been saying they don't feel God, they don't feel spiritual, and they are not feeling the joy of the Lord. There is nothing better than feeling the joy of the Lord. But you know what? When I don't feel the joy of the Lord, that doesn't mean the Lord no longer exists or the Lord doesn't love me anymore. Do you know what it means when I don't feel it? It means I don't feel it. Feelings aren't facts. Faith in God is not about feelings. We are not called to feel; we are called to believe. That is faith. There will be times of quiet and seasons of not feeling it. But we believe in God, and he loves us. That doesn't stop just because we don't feel it.

Do you know the NIV Bible uses the words *believe, believes,* and *believing* two hundred and fifty-nine times? If I believe that God so loved the world that he gave his only Son, I will have eternal life. Case closed. John didn't tell us "he who feels that God gave his Son." I believe and know that God gave his Son to fulfill the law and pay my sin debt. I also know God has sealed the deal with his Holy Spirit. Although feelings are nice at times, it is belief and knowing that gets us to heaven. It is believing, not necessarily feeling, that God loves us. If you are feeling alone and as though God isn't paying attention, guess what that is? It is a lie. It is a false feeling, because whether you feel it or not, God is nuts about you. Ya gotta believe.

Yes

So Pilate asked Jesus, "Are you the king of the Jews?" "Yes, it is as you say," Jesus replied.

Luke 23:3

I am grateful and thankful for the people who said *yes*. Ken Jones Sr. asked Rita Kelly to be his wife, and she said, *yes*. If she said *no*, who knows if I ever would have been born. I am thankful my wife Janie said *yes* when I asked her to marry me. When I asked God for children in my life, God said *yes*. Now I have two great kids, Kenny and Nick. When I needed help, I asked people to help me get sober, and they said *yes*. When I asked people to help me get closer to Jesus, many said *yes*.

Mary and Joseph said *yes*. Moses reluctantly said *yes*. Saul got knocked down, and when he got up as Paul, he said *yes*. Twelve other men, fishermen, tax collectors, and all sorts of men said *yes* when Jesus called them. All the prophets said *yes*. All through the Bible, we find examples of people saying yes even if they were reluctant, unsure, or afraid. When Jesus was asked to go and die on a cross for me and you, Jesus said *yes*.

I am grateful for the people who said *yes*. Jesus is the greatest example of *yes*. Today, I want to be like Jesus and say *yes*. When someone asks, "Can you help? Will you listen? Will you pray for me?" I want to say *yes*. That comes only from a thankful heart for all those who have come before me and said *yes*. What will your answer be?

Yes, He Can

The LORD Almighty is with us; the God of Jacob is our fortress. Selah Come and see the works of the LORD, the desolations he has brought on the earth. He makes wars cease to the ends of the earth; he breaks the bow and shatters the spear, he burns the shields with fire. "Be still, and know that I am God; I will be exalted among the nations, I will be exalted in the earth." The LORD Almighty is with us; the God of Jacob is our fortress. Selah.

Psalm 46:7–11

I remember being about twelve or thirteen when my mother and father brought home our first microwave oven. In the early 1970s, this was one of the "new-fangled inventions" that my mother and father had to have. It was a gadget that got things cooked a whole lot quicker. I remember thinking, *Man, we could probably cook a whole turkey in like five seconds.* Well I have to admit, I am one of those folks at times that just can't wait. When I want something, I want it now. When I call the doctor's office for an appointment, I expect them to say, "Can you come in now?" When I get there, I want them to say, "Come right in."

When I get into some type of trouble or turmoil, I want a quick fix and for all parties to forgive and forget by last Thursday. I have no time for a healing process. Mourning also should be a quick process. It hurts way too much, and I want it to end quickly.

Trust in God, patience, persistence, and time are needed in any situation. Rushing into situations headfirst never seems to pan out for me. The quick fix is like putting a bandage on a hole in a dam. It will burst. Whatever I am going through today, I need to put in the hands of God. By being still and trusting in God, I feel peace and assurance during a storm. Will God really help me through anything? Yes, he will. Can he help me with this one? Yes, he can.

You Can't Look Both Ways

> But one thing I do: Forgetting what is behind and strain-
> ing toward what is ahead, I press on toward the goal to win
> the prize for which God has called me heavenward in Christ
> Jesus. All of us who are mature should take such a view of
> things.
>
> Philippians 4:13–15

I was at a house once, talking to my wife behind me. I was walking forward, continued to look back, and when I turned around,
my face slammed right into the sliding glass door. *Ouch.* Can you
imagine driving down the interstate at seventy miles per hour looking in your rearview mirror? *Bam!* You can't look forward if you are
continually looking back.

There have been several incidents in my past that left me with
heavy emotional baggage to carry around. The emotional baggage
comes from incidents, perceived or real, from the past. I am carrying it wherever I go and looking back. Looking back at the pain
and guilt has not let me look forward to anything. It has caused me
not to set goals or achieve. The past has crippled and paralyzed me.
I can't look ahead if I am too busy looking back.

Paul, in his letter to the Philippians, said that the mature person forgets what is behind and moves forward toward the goal.
That means I have to have a goal so I can win the prize. He says as

a Christian, the prize is that God is calling me heavenward in Jesus Christ. But what about all this emotional baggage I have? I need to carry it and worry about it. How can I move forward with all this? I need help. Ahh, there is the answer.

Paul also said in this same letter to the Philippians 4:6–7, "Do not be anxious about anything, but in everything, by prayer and petition, with thanksgiving, present your requests to God. And the peace of God, which transcends all understanding, will guard your hearts and your minds in Christ Jesus." Don't be anxious about anything? We should use prayer, petition, and thanksgiving to God. But doesn't that assume that God will answer my prayer and petition? No, not assumes, it assures. Paul assures that through Christ Jesus these prayers and petitions will be answered and there is no need for fear or anxiety. We can let the past go, we can give the baggage to God, and we can get rid of it.

God has forgiven us for our past, and he has relieved us of that burden. We can move forward. Psalm 68:19 says, "Praise be to the Lord, to God our Savior, who daily bears our burdens." God will carry our burdens. Guess what we have to do? We have to give them to him, release the baggage, let it go, and drop the bag. It is no longer your problem. That is easier said than done. I agree, but it can be done. Paul said mature people do that.

Today, I want to be a mature person. I will give God my baggage, my burdens from the past. Jesus has worn our stripes. He has carried the biggest burden, our sin.

Let go of the past. Look forward to the goal where there is our prize. Keep your eyes upon Jesus. Moving toward our prize, we will win heavenly citizenship with our loving Father and his Son Jesus. Look forward, not behind you.

You Might Be a Christian

> Then he called the crowd to him along with his disciples and said: "If anyone would come after me, he must deny himself and take up his cross and follow me."
>
> Mark 8:34

Jeff Foxworthy is a comedian, and one of his famous jokes is "you might be a redneck if…" Along those lines:

You might be a Christian if you believe that Jesus left heaven and became a man to fulfill the law of God and die for the sins of all mankind.

You might be a Christian if you change your heart and repent of your sin.

You might be a Christian if you are immersed in baptism for the forgiveness of sin. You are immersed in baptism to die and be reborn into Jesus Christ and make a public statement of love.

You might be a Christian if you love God with all your heart and soul and you love others as you love yourself.

You might be a Christian if you love your enemies.

You might be a Christian if you forgive those who have harmed you.

You might be a Christian if you follow and obey the commands and teachings of God our Father and Jesus our Savior.

You might be a Christian if you find yourself hurting because others hurt, mourning when others mourn, and being compassionate.

You might be a Christian if you yearn to serve others.

You might be a Christian if you find yourself sharing the good news of Jesus with family, friends, coworkers, neighbors, and anyone that will listen.

You might be a Christian if you find yourself saying, "Can I help you with that?"

You might be a Christian if you realize mistreatment of anyone is wrong.

You might be a Christian if you look forward to reading the Bible and realize God is speaking to just you.

You might be a Christian if you find yourself praising God more for blessings than whining over desires.

You might be a Christian if you are thanking God for the blessings of others and praying for their needs

You might be a Christian if you know who the Holy Spirit is and what he does.

You might be a Christian if you know the sacrifices you have made are a blessing and you haven't been cheated out of anything.

You might be a Christian if you know that all you do and say should be for the glory of God.

You might be a Christian if you are grateful for the sacrifice Jesus made and you thank him and pray without ceasing.

You'll Never Eat at the Ritz

For just as through the disobedience of the one man the many were made sinners, so also through the obedience of the one man the many will be made righteous.

Romans 5:19

God made him who had no sin to be sin for us, so that in him we might become the righteousness of God.

2 Corinthians 5: 21

When I was a young child, I was a messy eater. My mother told me there was food everywhere. She said I wore more than I ate. She also told me that my grandmother used to tell me that I would never eat at the Ritz. When I was young, we went to Woolworth's for a hotdog, and I asked my grandmother if this was the Ritz.

Well, I guess sloppy eaters can't get into the Ritz. I have still never been to the Ritz and don't even know if there is one. I have heard there are restaurants where you have to wear a tie; I haven't been there either. One time, I went to hit a bucket of golf balls with my friend Bernie, and they wouldn't let us in because we were wearing jeans. I guess I just don't fit the mold for some places.

Sin is worse than a pair of jeans at the golf course. All our sin is unacceptable in God's eyes. God does not like sin. As a matter of fact, he hates sin.

With my past behavior, how do I expect to get to heaven? How do I expect God to even pay attention or take me seriously? Why would God even consider me for heaven? Because of my righteousness. Not righteousness on my own merits, good deeds, or works, but because Jesus, who was sinless, took on my sin and made me righteous and acceptable to our Father. Jesus is like a shepherd who knows his sheep. He will bring them home safely. We follow him, obey him, love him, love others, and serve his children everywhere.

A famous Bible verse, John 3:16, says that everyone who believes in God can have eternal life. When I know this, I can then look to Acts 2:38. "Repent and be baptized, every one of you, in the name of Jesus Christ for the forgiveness of your sins." My sins will be forgiven if I believe in Jesus Christ as my Savior. I will have eternal life in heaven with God.

By Jesus' death on the cross and my belief in him, I have been made righteous to stand before the Father with Jesus at my side, letting God know that I am one of his, that I am one of his sheep.

God's amazing grace is why I am righteous. I may never eat at the Ritz or play at a fancy golf course in jeans, but because of God's grace and Jesus' sacrifice on the cross I have been found righteous to be in heaven with God for eternity. Thank you, Jesus, for your selfless sacrifice and your willingness to take on my sin so that I could be found righteous in front of our Father.

You Packed?

But the day of the Lord will come like a thief.

2 Peter 3:10

The only thing I like more than a vacation is the anticipation of the vacation. I like the excitement of going to a place that Janie, my wife, and I selected, planned, and made the arrangements for. Now it is time to pack. Now the fun starts. We like to go to the mountains in North Carolina and rent a cabin for a week. Let's see. What do we need? We don't want to forget anything: clothes, underwear, socks, shoes, shampoo, soap, toothbrush, etc. We get it all together in advance. Janie loves lists; she has her list ready at least a week in advance. Nothing happens without the list.

I tease about the list, but preparation is the key to having everything we need when we reach mountain destination, which usually includes at least a forty-five-minute drive on mountain roads and fourteen hours on the highway, far from civilization. The preparation and anticipation are well worth it because we have everything we need. My main job is getting the stuff packed in the car and deciding which CDs we can listen to on the trip up. We have had our oil changed, tires checked, and a full tank of gas. We have a cooler of soda and snacks for the ride. Everything is strategically placed in the car, with pillows within arm's reach of Janie. Did I leave anything out? I don't know. Janie has the list.

Today, I spent time studying 1 and 2 Peter. He is all about preparation. He is very concerned about our well-being and wants to encourage us. He has a list; he wants us to know we will be persecuted as Christians. He wants us to know there will be false teachers trying to lead us astray. He is also preparing us for the return of Jesus. He is not just telling us these things are going to happen; he is telling us to be ready. He is telling us how to be ready, and he is telling us how it will happen. Peter is being a very good shepherd.

As I look around in the world, I see the false teachers and the false doctrines that Peter warned us about. Some include wealth and feel-good dime-store psychology. Some people tout these doctrines and are leading others astray. We are to stand strong, be humble and loving, and bring the lost back. We are not to listen to the new church of "what's happening now" doctrine and should listen to the warnings of our shepherd, Peter.

Are your bags packed? Do you have your list? Peter reminds us that Jesus is coming back. We don't know the day or the hour, only that he will come like a thief in the night when we least expect it, and we need to be ready. We need to prepare. We need to be living holy and humble lives. We are to love one another, not following false teachers. We need to be following God's commands out of love and not just because we are supposed to. Jesus is coming back. He said so himself.

I need to be living a godly life out of love and gratitude. I am not afraid that Jesus is coming. I have been given the list. I believe Jesus died for my sins, and I am following God's commands. I am being patient as Peter advised. I am spending time in Christian fellowship. I am sharing the good news of Jesus Christ. I am spending time with God in the Bible. I will not stray; God has been very good to me. My service to God and time spent following God's commands are out of my deep love for him.

We don't know the time or hour, so we need to be ready. The details have been given throughout the New Testament; take a look. Jesus is making preparations in heaven right now, preparing our new homes. Are we ready to go? Let's get packed.

You're Fired

We always thank God for all of you, mentioning you in our prayers. We continually remember before our God and Father your work produced by faith, your labor prompted by love, and your endurance inspired by hope in our Lord Jesus Christ.

1 Thessalonians 1:2–3

Donald Trump is famous for his TV show where week after week, viewers waited to hear, "You're fired." At season's end, Donald would finally hire someone to work for him. Now there's a prize, the opportunity to work for someone who seems to enjoy firing people.

People are fired from jobs every day. I have heard there are some company executives who take people to lunch and fire them. I guess that is to soften the blow, but I know it would spoil my appetite. There are many people out there looking for jobs. Résumés and applications are filled out daily; people are being turned down or rejected. Like being fired before they were even hired. I have been in both positions. Bosses try to soften the blow saying, "We are going to have to let you go. The numbers are not there." But what do we hear? "You're fired." You know what I hear? "We don't want you." That hurts.

But you want to know what I have really learned through all of that? I am not my job. That's not what my friends and families base their love for me on. I am not my job; I am my heart and my love for God. When we get to heaven, we won't hear, "Thanks for being a chemist, fireman, dog catcher, doctor, lawyer, Indian chief," or any other worldly title we may have held or hold. We will be thanked for the service we gave to God in loving him, loving one another, planting his seed, harvesting his field, tending his sheep, spreading his good news, being fishers of men and women, and following his commands. Not only are we saved through Jesus; we are fellow workers with him now, doing his will and his work. We don't only work for God; we work with him. Paul tells us in 1 Corinthians 3:9, "For we are God's fellow workers; you are God's field, God's building." God will never say to one of his own, "You're fired." The two words we will hear are *thank you.* The words I long to hear from my heavenly Father are from Matthew 25:21, "Well done, good and faithful servant!"

Your Personal Invitation

For God so loved the world that he gave his one and only Son, that whoever believes in him shall not perish but have eternal life.

John 3:16

Here I am! I stand at the door and knock. If anyone hears my voice and opens the door, I will come in and eat with him, and he with me.

Revelation 3:20

I love invitations. It means that somebody wants me to attend a party or some sort of function they are having. I just love to know someone is thinking of me and wants me to attend.

Throughout an earlier part of my life, my self-esteem was pretty low. I thought when people invited me they just felt sorry for me. At one time, I was very shy, and the laughter and outgoingness were just a cover to not let people hurt me. For a while drinking took away the pain until it made it worse.

I was invited in 1978 to a twelve-step recovery group, and I have been attending ever since. Since that time, I have been able to make sober and sane decisions. The best decision I have made is to accept Jesus into my life.

When I was baptized into Christ, my sins were washed away by blood and water. I have a new life because of Jesus' death and resurrection. I have been invited into a life where I receive Jesus in my heart, the Holy Spirit to guide me, and God my Father as my all in all. I have been invited to spend eternity in my Father's heavenly kingdom. I have been invited to a heavenly banquet. I am invited to bring all who want to come with me. The invitation is addressed to all who will accept. All you need do is to ask. Then you will spend eternity with God in heaven.

It says in Revelation 3:20, "Jesus is knocking; if I open the door and let him in he will eat with me and me with him." I needed to open the door and invite him in. Now I get to also invite others. Who? I am inviting you today to accept this invitation, paid for by Jesus. It is the best invitation I have ever received and the best invitation I have ever delivered. Join me. Our names will be called by Jesus wherever we are at the time of his choosing, and our transportation will be provided by Jesus. RSVP to God your intentions by accepting Jesus as your Savior, repenting of your sins, being baptized and following his commands. Let the joy begin.

listen|imagine|view|experience

AUDIO BOOK DOWNLOAD INCLUDED WITH THIS BOOK!

In your hands you hold a complete digital entertainment package. Besides purchasing the paper version of this book, this book includes a free download of the audio version of this book. Simply use the code listed below when visiting our website. Once downloaded to your computer, you can listen to the book through your computer's speakers, burn it to an audio CD or save the file to your portable music device (such as Apple's popular iPod) and listen on the go!

How to get your free audio book digital download:

1. Visit www.tatepublishing.com and click on the e|LIVE logo on the home page.
2. Enter the following coupon code:
   5990-44ce-ce37-b353-addd-2c11-1b85-4acd
3. Download the audio book from your e|LIVE digital locker and begin enjoying your new digital entertainment package today!